Readings in
Contemporary Criminology

Readings in Contemporary Criminology

Stephen Schafer
Northeastern University

Reston Publishing Company, Inc.
Reston, Virginia
A Prentice-Hall Company

Library of Congress Cataloging in Publication Data
Main entry under title:

Readings in contemporary criminology.

Includes index.
1. Crime and criminals—Addresses, essays,
lectures. 2. Corrections—Addresses, essays,
lectures. I. Schafer, Stephen.
HV6028.R38   364'.08   76-11769
ISBN 0-87909-702-7

© 1976 by Reston Publishing Company, Inc.
A Prentice-Hall Company.
11480 Sunset Hills Road
Reston, Virginia 22090

10 9 8 7 6 5 4 3 2 1

Printed in the United States of America

To the memory of my parents

Contents

Preface

This *Readings in Contemporary Criminology* is intended to be a supplement to the author's *Introduction to Criminology;* yet, they are independent volumes which can be read and studied separately from each other. Here the editor wanted to present a few of those issues with which contemporary criminology seems to be currently involved. It is not a total coverage of contemporary criminology; it calls attention only to selected problems.

The editor of this volume takes the opportunity of this Preface to acknowledge the priceless assistance of Regina Ryan who has contributed so valuably to the development of this Reader.

STEPHEN SCHAFER

Introduction

Crime is as old as mankind itself, and, maybe, it was in the Garden of Eden where a memorable human act has been first regarded as the violation of prohibitions issued by a power—at that time by the heavenly authority. Since then, societies have been developed, laws have been created, prohibitions have now been declared by earthly powers, and the violations of forbiddances, which began with the Biblical stealing of the apple, have continued. Crime has been with us from the very beginning; it has never ceased to disturb men's living together. Moreover, it has become a common societal phenomenon, viewed by some as a normal symptom, as if it were a functional component of the organization of human groupings. All the time, it has been observed to increase in volume, and it has experienced an expansion in its varieties from year to year, decade to decade, and generation to generation. The more society has become aware of the harms, injuries, and damages caused by the ever increasing and menacing crime, however, the more a growing concern for the solution of the crime problem has developed; and, conformable to the gradually deteriorating societal peace and safety, more-and-more thoughts, examinations, and investigations have emerged to understand the lawbreaking conduct, and mounting efforts have been made to reduce or even to eliminate the criminal violations of prohibitions. The ways of thinking and methods of combatting crime have varied from one era to another, and the modes in which societies have reacted to criminal behaviors may offer insight into the societal systems of values, prevailing concerns, and the degree of striving for and capacity for responding to crimes and criminals.

In the pages that follow, this book attempts to bring into focus the nature of some criminological problems which especially engross the contemporary thoughts and the trends of giving an answer to these issues today. They do not cover everything that would make up the entirety of what may be called "contemporary criminology," they are only selected topics which may characterize the present directions of criminological interest. The problems themselves are not really new, in one form or another they have already absorbed attention in the past; what is "contemporary" is the approach to them. The fear of crime, efforts to redefine the orientation of criminology and to view the crime problem from a radical or critical angle, assassinations and ideologies which give the crime a political flavor, criminals who band together for the purposes of breaking the law more efficiently, swindles and machinations whereby the naïve and powerless are criminally exploited by shrewd finesse and trickery, taking other people's belongings by force, stealing merchandise, highway robberies, the practice of violence, attempts to discipline criminal elements by deterrence, changing the prison system, efforts to alter the convict's behavior, work therapy to better the prisoners, stigmatization of those who violated the law, satisfaction offered to victims of crime, and others are "contemporary" issues, yet, the historical origin of all these can be traced in the past understanding of and fighting the crime problem.

The noticeable failures of comprehending, explaining, treating or repressing crimes and criminals and the protection of victims, however, have given rise to expandingly grave concern. The fact that criminals have never before enjoyed a less risky and a more rewarding business, along with the increase in the great variety of crimes at a phenomenal rate, prompted the shrinking conformist part of the larger society, politicians, public officials, and experts and pseudo experts, together with the channels of the mass media of communication, to concentrate on certain issues which may indicate the major targets of contemporary criminology. This is not to say that society in the past was not concerned about the same problems; it should, however, indicate that in our time, in the contemporary society, these issues are receiving particular attention and that they are approached with a somewhat different way of thinking.

If it is a "contemporary" issue to strive "toward a new criminology"—that is, as it has been explained by some contemporary writers, *to draw on the findings of hidden crime studies, to abandon the search for the causes and a cure for the criminal,* to make a shift of attention from the stigmatized to the stigmatizers, and to decide which crimes cause the greatest social harm along with a commitment to the equal distribution of punishment—then a perpetuation of the "old" criminology is apparent, and a continuation of centuries old efforts and ideas can be clearly seen. If only Romagnosi (1827), Guerry (1833), Lord Brougham (1860), Abegg (1866), Quetelet (1869), Ferri (1881), Krohne (1881), Oettingen (1882), Fuld (1884), Féré (1888), Mischler (1888), and Bonger (1899) are mentioned here, then indeed only a very few of a long list are named who so forcefully struggled against the unreliable nature of crime statistics and demanded the recognition of the numerical distance between, to use Enrico Ferri's term, the "natural and legal" crimes; and all these only from the nineteenth century, not to mention those before them and those others who have followed their path in the twentieth century. To begin hidden crime studies in order to reveal the "dark figures" (committed crimes which do not appear in official statistical tables) might be useful for reaching closer to the real volume of crime, yet without conducting historical studies of crime and without making the numbers comparable figures by mirroring them in the social conditions and societal values of their own time, the quantitative results would represent only an erroneous and misleading conclusion. It may be the case that this is one of the major factors why the "old" criminology failed in registering the true amount of crime. The "new" criminology may use more sophisticated statistical methods in detecting the hidden criminal violations of the law (the "hidden crime" is one of the focal concerns in contemporary criminology), yet the question remains open: what can be done, even with maximal possible numerical revelations, to make the criminal elements law-abiding members of the society if the search for the causes of these newly detected crimes is to be abandoned, and were our criminological ancestors not wiser in trying to think about the understanding and cure of the known criminals, regardless of how many they were?

To shift attention from the stigmatized to the stigmatizers and to decide which crimes cause the greatest social harm implies the question: who has the right to declare what right is and how serious is the declared wrong? If organization in a society is necessary for orderly living together and without social control an undesirable anarchy would develop, the stigmatizer and the stigmatized, however repelling these terms may sound, cannot disappear; lawmakers and lawbreakers do seem to be unextinguishable elements in any

social groupings of humans. The stigmatized are those who are breaking the law, and the stigmatizers—the only ones who have the right
to say what right is and how wrong is the wrong—are primarily those
who are making the laws which are violated by the stigmatized; actually, the lawbreaker is stigmatized for the very reason that he has
broken these laws. Professional and lay writings and also the media of
mass communication, not to mention the loud voices of certain groups,
try to make us understand that there is a contemporary demand for re-
defining the direction of "stigmatization" (whatever it may mean) and
for redeciding the degree of seriousness of crimes. Even if the question
were disregarded whether or not these writings and voices are sufficiently knowledgeable and significant, there would remain an issue,
in fact centuries old, that should belong to the sphere of the philosophy of law. Again, it is a problem that is not new at all, and only the
demands for a certain orientation of redirecting the stigmatizing process and for a reevaluation of human conduct are contemporary. From
the Ten Commandments, the Hindu Manu's Brahma, Yajnavalkja's
Institutes, Narada's Naradasmriti, Mohammed's Koran, the Egyptian
Hermes Trismegistus, or the Babylonian Code of Hammurabi to our
time, the law, actually the official instrument of stigmatization, has
always been the formal expression of the value system of the prevailing
social-political power, and it will be so as long as humans live in an
organized society. Although law disciplines conduct, it is not exclusively a regulative tool. It is, perhaps, first of all a teaching instrument in the service of the existing social-political power structure:
it teaches according to the values of the lawmaking power what
is right and what is wrong, and how wrong the wrong is. As such,
the law is not really concerned with justifications as to why particular types of behavior are required or prohibited, or why certain
actors should be rewarded and others stigmatized. The law attempts
to achieve certain ends established by the reigning "sovereign," regardless of whether this sovereign is a one-man-dictator, or a congress
or parliament. Human rights, as defined by the law (that is, the prescriptions of the given power), can be understood only in the mirror
of this power-established value system. Since, however, powers are
changing, values are also changing along with those changes; thus
the direction of stigmatizations and decisions over the seriousness of
crimes are changing with them. The social history of man offers
abundant evidence for this truth. If writings and voices in our contemporary world now claim changes in stigmatizations and in the
assessment of the seriousness of crimes, this means that they are in
disagreement with the prevailing power's values; they may be "right,"
but even so they can accomplish success only if they are able to get

the right of declaring what right is and the power to rank the wrongs.

A commitment to the equal distribution of punishment is a popular yet not new demand that has been voiced so often from the distant past, mainly whenever it was possible to do so without endangering the protestor himself; therefore it is no wonder that now again contemporary criminology is expressing dissatisfaction over the administration of criminal justice. Abuses of criminal law are not novel phenomena in the history of judging crime. Probably the best known and greatly influential judicial miscarriage which awakened the interest of the general public was the conviction and execution of the French merchant Jean Calas in 1762 by the criminal court of Toulouse, which prompted Voltaire's exposition of this case, in all its injustice, to the world at large. In the same year Beccaria published his first work; this was followed by his famous *Treatise on Crimes and Punishments* that achieved such an inordinate success that the Swiss *Sociète Economique,* even before knowing the name of the author, decided to award the book a gold medal, given to a "citizen who dared to raise his voice in favor of humanity against the most deeply ingrained prejudices." Voltaire's campaign resulted in Calas's *post mortem* rehabilitation and Beccaria's demand for justice in punishment received high and worldwide acclaim; yet, the unequal distributions of penalties and the abuses of criminal law have continued—not only in France and Italy, but everywhere at all times. A "new" criminology already has a formal "commitment" to a bias- or prejudice-free distribution of punishment and nothing seems to be easier than to get another commitment again-and-again; not formal commitment, but practice in reality would be a more meritorious goal. One has to keep in mind, however, that punishments are meted out by humans against other humans, and it is a question whether emotionally toned favorable or unfavorable conceptions about some persons, groups, or ideas, one of our most terrifying weaknesses, can ever be wiped out from our nature. Probably no lawmaking is conceiveable without manipulated justice, and the outcome of a criminal case (the punishment) will always be dependent on the judges' perception of the power's prescribed values and instilled biases and prejudices.

Viewing the crime problem from a critical or radical angle (the two seem now to be the same, since it has been explained more than once that a "critical" mode of inquiry is a "radical philosophy") is also a topic or form of contemporary criminology. Those who profess critical or radical criminology are, generally speaking, the ones who actually attack not so much the traditional criminology, rather, they conspicuously take a stand against the present structure of the society—yet without proposing an alternative, and most without having personally experienced another social system. They suggest breaking with the ideology of the age and they contend that "critical thinking" is the ability to think negatively; nevertheless, they do not recommend positive action or some kind of panacea for the crime problem. Destruction has a merit only if construction follows. These critics or radicals also appear to believe that they represent a "new" criminology and they usually fail to admit that they did have critical and even radical criminological ancestors— yet, there is the difference that a century ago both the critics and the radicals (at that time they could be distinguished) did offer options. While in our time the critics or radicals assume that criminologists automatically serve the interests of the state, they do not realize or they do not want to see that in all social systems criminology is necessarily serving the prevailing law, that is, the expression of the interests of the ruling power. Ferri and his nineteenth century contemporaries were quite critical in analyzing criminology of their own time and have proposed a great number of reform ideas; moreover, Ferri himself had leaned heavily toward socialistic ideas, and by the end of the nineteenth century he had joined the Socialist Labor Party which caused him to lose his university position. Turati (1883), Battaglia (1886), Marro (1887), Colajanni (1889), Lux (1892), Denis (1893), Loria (1894), Niceforo (1897), Salillas (1901), Nordau (1902), and Bonger (1899–1905) are only a few names of the very many who, well before our present radicals, denounced capitalism and placed themselves openly and solidly with Marxist doctrines where they suggested the way to find the answer to the crime problem. Yet, the "critical or radical" stand—claimed as a new trend, but in fact an old idea—is an issue in our contemporary criminology. However, it will need theoretical elaboration and practical experience.

Political crime is somewhat cautiously gaining its place among the contemporary criminological problems; as it appears, officials and the official criminal law have shown reluctance to accept it as a crime type. For example, the report of the American National Commission on the Causes and Prevention of Violence in 1969 devoted several thousand printed pages to the many facets of violence; but, despite the fact that the bulk of this report dealt with assassinations of office holders and other violent crimes clearly of a political character, the general problem of political crime and the concept of the political criminal were not discussed. It happened only in the early years of the 70's that contemporary criminology listed political crime among the current criminological issues, and even then political crime became a topic of discussions as if it were the new treatment of a new criminal phenomenon. It may be true that in our age the problem of political crime is more of a topical issue than it may have been in the past; yet, one has to recognize that it is one of the oldest of all crime types, and from the Greeks and Romans down to the present day, it is indeed almost impossible to catalog them. Also, it should be remembered that Filangieri (1788), Lombroso (1876), Ferri (1881), Garofalo (1885), Colajanni (1889), Proal (1898), Maxwell (1914), and Parmele (1918) are again only examples from a series of the writers in the past who have already submitted the political criminality in their analyses. However, the subject matter is so heavily entangled with other problems that there is still ample room for further examinations in contemporary criminology.

Organized crime has occupied for many years an important area in contemporary criminology, yet we are still not sure whether it is a globally overarching international or nationwide organization, or if it represents only a number of smaller sized independent groupings of criminals for more efficient criminal performance, or, maybe it is a part of our culture that is bound to the larger organization of our society. Should we mean by "organized crime" a limited number of criminally oriented families whose conviction is close to the impossible in view of the extremely diffuse territory that is used by them for their inordinately broad criminal activities, or the narrowly understood small scale gangs, syndicates, and rackets whose prosecution and disruption are difficult due to their skillful banding together, or the criminally geared organizations made up by criminals and pseudo conformist elements who are entrenched in our culture and dominate almost the whole machinery of social life and therefore their prosecution and dissolution can hardly be hoped? It is so often heard, mainly from newly elected officials, that fighting against "organized crime" should be one of the most important tasks of securing law and order, but what organized crime really means has always been just vaguely indicated. Again, contemporary criminology is not dealing with a specifically American criminal phenomenon, and not with any novelty, since organized crime in its different forms had been known and studied for a long time before it became a part of the American crime problem. "Crews" or "crues," described by Green (1592) as "wicked companions," or, as they had been called from the seventeenth century, "gangs," that is criminals who banded together by associated ideas, have existed and functioned for centuries. Bournet (1884), Kocher and Paoli (1888), and Tarde (1890) are only examples of those who analyzed this dangerous brigandage practiced in England, France, Spain, Greece, Hungary, and in Italy in Corsica, Calabria, and Sicily; moreover, they wrote about the powerful aristocracy of crime, the "Maffia." The "maffiosi" have allegedly often played a historic role; and as chronicles tell us how King Ferdinand of Naples did it during the French Revolution, kings and emperors recognized the importance of these criminals and had dealings with them. The American "Maffia," or "Cosa Nostra" as it is now called, seems to be an imported criminal type, yet it is still in need of definitional classification. Before contemporary criminology vows to combat it, clarification of what we mean by organized crime should be badly desired; as it is conceived and analyzed in our time, at least by many writers, it appears to be somewhat enigmatic and puzzling.

White-collar crime, if organized crime could be understood as a societally all encompassing criminal phenomenon, appears to be a close relative of organized crime; and if white-collar crime could be interpreted as deeprooted and imbedded in our culture, it may be the case that organized crime plays a significant role in the activities of white-collar criminals. If it were correct to assume that some businessmen legally violate the law, certain automobile merchants legally break the rules, there are home maintenance and repairmen who have fraudulent yet formally legal practices, advertisement of goods and merchandise is often deceptive, tax returns are occasionally prepared with the intent to cheat, health hucksters are persuading sufferers to try unnecessary cures, there are landlords who find a way to violate rent control regulations, guarantees of machines are not rarely misleading, and many, many more legally circumvented crimes uninterruptedly occur in the ordinary conduct of our daily functioning where the strong and powerful constantly face the weak and powerless in the great variety of social situations, then, maybe, the issue of morality should enter the picture, and, perhaps, white-collar crime would not even be a crime in its true sense. If so, white-collar "crime" might be a part of the culture; it is accepted or at least tolerated by the weak and powerless by simply using those defensive mechanisms which, in a limited range, are at their disposal; and, since culturally approved behaviors and customs can hardly be qualified as crimes, contemporary criminology actually should not pay attention to them. White-collor crimes, although not known with this name, have been constantly experienced throughout the social history of man, and if contemporary criminology regards them as "crimes" and problems, it agrees with the ancient Romans who viewed similar acts as crimes because their normal sense and right conscience censured such acts. While in modern criminology Sutherland baptized these conducts "white-collar crimes," they may find their convenient place in Garofalo's (1891) "natural crime" category. It is an important goal of contemporary criminology, by all means with the assistance of ethics, to classify whether white-collar crime is a crime or not; and if it is, should it be regarded as a specified and unified criminal offense or only as a mode of committing already defined offenses.

Burglary, one of those forms of theft which is almost always committed by some sort of force, is a justified concern of contemporary criminology; after all, in the United States a burglary is committed roughly in every ten seconds and, in terms of frequency, it may be rated as second of all serious crimes. In the long past, along with robbery and similar crimes, it was the ordinary offense of professional criminals; but, as Joly (1888), von Liszt (1892), Manouvrier (1893), Ferriani (1899), Bonger (1905), and others analyzed it, by the end of the nineteenth century it had shown a decline and has been largely replaced by fraud and other intellectually or psychologically performed crimes against property all over the world. At the wake of force and violence, burglary has gradually returned to the arena of crimes. Moreover, it has taken, mainly in residential areas, a prominent position. Its rate is going up so fast that, for example, in five years, from 1969 to 1974 the residence burglaries at nighttime increased by 60 percent and in daytime by 67 percent; in 1974 an estimated total of over 3 million burglaries had occurred. From the criminological point of view, it is a crime of opportunity, committed by both amateurs and professionals with our having little knowledge about the burglar as a criminal personality; otherwise, it is primarily a problem that should belong to the field of law enforcement. It is not clear that what sociological, psychological, economic, or other forces make one a burglar and it is even less clear why the police are not doing more for the protection of the millions of prospective victims. Shoplifting appears to be related to burglary since it seems to be characteristic to those times when theft with force has shown a decline and theft without force has taken its place. This change, however, proved to be only temporary because while burglary and robbery have returned to the scene of crime, shoplifting has remained there with them. It has, however, proved to be an ever increasing disturbance of law and order. It is also a crime of opportunity, and since Boucicaut founded the "Bon Marché" store in Paris in 1852, following its modern selling system, and more and more department stores have been established, thefts committed in these shopping places have rapidly increased. Again, shoplifting is not a new problem to which contemporary criminology is exposed; Dubuisson (1902), Thiekötter (1932), and Schmidt (1939) are only a few of those who devoted much attention to its analysis before the Second World War. As with the case of the burglar, we know but little about the shoplifter and his motivation. Why does one shoplift only occasionally? why persistently? why professionally? why without being in need? why as a psychopathic personality and why as a totally normal individual? why only small values? why mostly females? why without class stratification? —these and many other questions are awaiting answers.

Hijacking, skyjacking, and violence, they may go arm-in-arm, are also not novelties, except their modes of execution and technologically refined performance. Those "highwaymen," the holdup criminals who robbed travelers along public roads on horseback, are the ancestors of the hijackers and skyjackers of our time. No period of human history has been lacking murders, assaults, rapes, robberies, and all kinds of violent crimes against both persons and property; civilization only changed the methods and used instruments from rough modes and primitive tools to more cunning performances with more polished facilities to prevent them. Frègier (1840), du Camp (1869), Krauss (1884), Garofalo (1885), Prins (1886), or Olrik (1894) are again only a few nineteenth century examples of those many who a century ago discussed the violence of criminals. However, while violent methods of achieving criminally what one wants have declined for many decades in favor of shrewd and artful ways of committing crimes, in our contemporary world, violence has returned to the scene of the crime problem, perhaps, even more forcefully than ever before. This seems to be the case not only when goals of political nature are at stake (when hijackings, skyjackings, and violence in general should be taken care of by politicians to bring peace to this earth), but also when ordinary crimes disrupt the peace of the society (when contemporary criminology should take the initiative).

Deterrence, again, is an age old controversial issue that has occupied the mind of great many thinkers of the past. As is well known, the first defense of the victim against crime was revenge in different forms such as private revenge when the lonely man himself and without help took revenge on his attacker, blood revenge when the victim's blood relatives came to his help in the revenge taking, superstitious revenge when the Church took over the action to execute God's revenge, social revenge that was said to be the expression of the societal outrage over the crime, and others. Society, however, mainly from the eighteenth century, wanted to pride itself with showing humanitarian sentiments; therefore, the repelling term of "revenge" has been substituted with the word "deterrence" with the aim of involving some psychological connotation. First, the cruelty of the penal consequence did not really change, only its label did. By deterrence, it has been meant that the infliction of punishment should serve as an impressive example for the future conduct of the offender as well as for potential wrongdoers, and thus crime could be prevented. The death penalty, corporal punishment, imprisonment, and other punishments have been supposed to deter from crime those who thought of satisfying their aspirations through violating the law. Before long, however, deterrence had been detached from revenge, and conceptually it really became understood as using penal instruments to discourage or to hinder crime by fear. Yet, with Holtzendorff's words, even so the penal system has become bankrupt. Primarily Ferri, but others also, as early as in the nineteenth century, were searching for the means of social protection with penal consequences other than punishment; Ferri proposed "penal substitutes." Although his ideas (as is the case with so many classical proposals) have not become realities, a strong trend was started to humanize deterrence, mixed with what is called "treatment" and "correction," to the extent that capital punishment has been abolished at many places. Moreover, in contemporary America even the termination of imprisonment has been proposed. Nevertheless, this other extreme too has suffered "bankruptcy," and now, parallel with the mitigating extremism, contemporary criminology again has to be exposed to voices claiming deterrence. To deter persons from the commission of crime, one of Beccaria's (1764) main proposals is voiced by influential sources today again. This rather confused contemporary approach to a workable system has developed the idea of *diversion from criminal justice system* which, heavily loaded with unsolved theoretical problems, essentially attempts to pull out the offender from the administration of criminal law and makes efforts to resolve the crime problem largely outside the traditional penal procedure. Apart from the fact that these diversional experiments are apt to make criminal law indiscernible from civil law, they pose to contemporary criminology the thwarting question of how to find out if circumventing penal procedures can transform criminals into law abiding members of the society.

Behavior modification, a harsh intrusion upon man's freedom of will, appears to be in sharp contrast to all proposals for avoiding force in treating criminals in order to change the lawbreakers. Psychosurgery, electroconvulsive treatment, administration of drugs, and other interventions to master and control the convicted individual's behavior, regardless of his personality and previous free life experiences, may be able to build obedient puppets of the society, but they do not seem to reform law violators to be freely constructive members of their social environment. Behavior therapies are manyfold, but even the mildest procedures do appear as artificially influencing the human subjects to conform with the law, rather than as teaching them to understand why they should conform. Well before this contemporary approach to corrections, sterilizations were performed to prevent the development of criminal family trees, castrations were carried out to hinder sex crimes, and, even before that, the thief's arm was cut from his body to make him unable to steal, not to mention those treatment methods which may be applicable on psychotics as if it were the case that criminals are mentally sick. These and other forcible and brutal interventions are not much different from certain present day behavior modifying methods, at least not in their neglecting the societal factors which, even after the behavior modifying treatment has been "successfully" completed, may reintroduce the offender to his criminal activities. But, this drastic therapeutical correction is not even as simple as that. Behavior modification, regardless of its promise or failure, and this is where contemporary criminology should ponder this question that seems to be supported from many corners, is supposed to struggle with a number of crucial theoretical and ethical problems. One of them is whether we humans have or do not have a freedom of will and to what extent, do we have the right to this mental freedom, and are we supposed to submit ourselves to a personality—changing procedure (that has alarmed the world in situations where it was called "brainwashing")? Another example of the theoretical puzzles is whether medical science should take over the administration of crime problem, and on what grounds and with what justification. As it appears, the idea of behavior modification should be a justified concern of contemporary criminology.

Prison labor, as a rehabilitative tool, like the other issues, should not be regarded as a new problem to contemporary criminology. The general public is for making the prisoners work hard as a punishment; prison administrators seem to believe in the reforming aspects of prison labor, also they hope that by having working and busy inmates the peace of the institutions might be easier to secure; legalistically oriented experts and many pseudoexperts claim that work in the prison is not part of the punishment, and that prison labor is an exploitation of the convicted persons, and also that the cheap labor could be an unfair competition to legitimate industry. From the time of galley slavery, as forced labor, to our time, the issue is subject to often fervent debates. The history of incarceration demonstrates the hesitancy over the justification of prison labor and the problem of how to do it. First, the contract system was tried out by leaving the work of the prisoners to outside contractors, and the prison administration kept only the responsibility of guarding the inmates. A variation of this procedure was that the contractor furnished the raw materials and received from the institution the final product. Then, the contractor accepted the full responsibility for the prisoners, including their maintenance and discipline. Later on, the state directed the prisoners' work and sold the products on open market, giving a small share of the profit to the working inmates. A variation of this system was that the final products could be sold only to state offices and also that the prisoners have been permitted to work only in agriculture, road building, and other services to the public. The controversy is still going on, although as early as in the eighteenth century Pope Clement XI at San Michele in Rome, Hippolyte Vilain in Ghent, or in the renovated Walnut Street Jail in Philadelphia it has appeared clear that prison labor if combined with education can prove to be a significant rehabilitative system. Probably not so much the labor itself, but the attitude toward work is the factor that counts, and maybe John Howard (1777) was correct in suggesting that "make men diligent, and they will be honest." Contemporary criminology could do a valuable service by elaborating on these ideas.

The social consequences of conviction or stigma is also an old problem, yet it claims its revival in contemporary criminology. It is not only the question of how poorly the prison prepares the prisoner for living freely and normally upon his release, but it is mainly the issue of how the society receives the discharged prisoner. In the past, mutilation, branding, stocks and pillory, and other devices were used not only as forms of corporal punishment, but they also served the society as identifications to know who the criminals were; they represented a kind of warning against the punished persons. In our time, the centuries old belief that we should beware of those who have been found guilty in a crime has not changed. The ex-convicts do not carry any longer some appropriate mark on their forehead, yet "humanized" methods make them recognizable. The loss of civil rights, being hounded by the police, keeping their record, questioning by prospective employers, and other sundry methods fortify the asumption that our judges were wrong and our penal system failed; "therefore" no person who ever was convicted can be trusted by those members of society who happened to avoid being involved as accused individuals in the machinery of the administration of criminal law. The ex-convict always remains at disadvantage against others; actually, in this sense, all guilty persons receive a life sentence. This public belief clearly encourages the discharged prisoners, who are thus deprived from normal life in any case, to continue their criminal activities. To reeducate the public might be a formidable task of contemporary criminology, but failing to accomplish success in this respect would guide us to recognize at least one factor of recidivism.

Compensation to victims of crime is the last of the selected issues for the care of contemporary criminology. If one looks at the legal systems of different countries, one seeks in vain a country where a victim of crime enjoys a certain expectation of full restitution of his loss or compensation for his injury. In the rare cases where there is state compensation, the system is either not fully effective, or does not work at all; where there is no system of state compensation, the victim is, in general, faced with the insufficient remedies offered by civil procedure and civil execution. While the punishment of crime is regarded as the concern of the state, the injurious result of the crime, that is to say, the damage to the victim, is regarded almost as a private matter. It recalls man in the early days of social development when, left alone in his struggle for existence, he himself had to meet attacks from outside and to fight alone against fellow-creatures who caused him harm. The victim of today cannot even seek satisfaction himself, since the law of the state forbids him to take the law into his own hands. In the days of his forefathers, restitution or compensation was a living practice, and it is perhaps worth noting that our barbarian ancestors were wiser and more just than we are today, for they adopted the theory of restitution to the injured, whereas we have abandoned this practice, to the detriment of all concerned. And this was wiser in principle, more reformatory in its influence, more deterrent in its tendency, and more economic to the community, than the modern practice. Since in our time England has begun to revive the Medieval practice of restitution or compensation, slowly and gradually more and more countries have introduced legislative steps for the satisfaction of the victims of crime. It would be an exaggeration to say that what was so successful in the Middle Ages has been successfully reestablished in our time. Contemporary criminology appears to have a long way to go before achieving what was accomplished centuries ago.

Again, this is not all that could carry the heading "contemporary criminology"; they represent only selected issues. And again, all this is not a set of problems which would be characteristic to criminological novelties of our time; they are old problems which have no answer as yet but are timely in calling the attention of contemporary criminology. Tomorrow other old or new problems may emerge.

Part One
Contemporary Views on Criminology

Introduction

The constantly and rapidly rising crime rate and the widespread variety of criminal offenses have made the American crime problem a fundamental social problem. The fear that any of us may become a victim of others' lawbreaking has developed a justified obsession of most members of the society. We all feel haunted and harassed in our daily work and peaceful life by the fear of crime. James Brooks contends that this fear is irrational, yet it is real. He suggests that it should be heeded by public policy-makers who would be better equipped to neutralize it if they had a better understanding of its causes and a better recognition of its undesirable consequences.

This fear might be mitigated by Eugene Doleschal and Nora Klapmuts' recommendation that more studies to reveal the hidden crimes be made. After all, as they quote from a report of the Council of Europe, "what makes a person 'criminal' is not the fact that he has committed a crime (because noncriminals have done that also), but the fact that he was caught, tried, convicted and punished." To draw on the findings of hidden crime studies and studies of the selection of offenders for punishment would, as they propose, develop a "new criminology." The "new criminologists," they suggest, should view the crime problem from a perspective that would place only minimal importance on the search for the causes.

Indeed, as it has been analyzed by Gresham Sykes, in the last one or two decades American criminology has witnessed a transformation of the interpretation of criminal behavior. Topics, such as the operations of the police and others, which have received relatively little attention in the past, began to be examined by an increasing number of criminologists. "Radical" and "critical" criminology have appeared in the arena of criminological thinking and Sykes submits these distinct changes to his scrutinizing analysis.

Chapter One

The Fear of Crime in the United States

James Brooks

The fear of crime has recently become more pervasive. To an objective investigator of this phenomenon, much of it is irrational. But the fear exists. Regardless of the reasons for being fearful, fear itself is a reality that policy-makers must consider. The lessening of fear thus becomes an important step in a comprehensive effort to combat crime and the effects of crime.

Certain kinds of crime—the "personal" crimes—produce more intense alarm than others. "The crimes that concern Americans the most are those that affect their personal safety—at home, at work, or in the streets. The most frequent and serious of these crimes of violence against the person are willful homicide, forcible rape, aggravated assault, and robbery." [1] How does it come about that "offenses involving physical assaults against the person are the most feared crimes" and that "the greatest concern is expressed about those in which a weapon is used"? [2] One explanation finds an answer in xenophobia:

Reprinted, with permission of the National Council on Crime and Delinquency, from *Crime and Delinquency*, July 1974, pp. 241–244.

The fear of crimes of violence is not a simple fear of injury or death or even of all crimes of violence, but, at bottom, a fear of strangers. The personal injury that Americans risk daily from sources other than crime are enormously greater. The annual rate of all Index offenses involving either violence or the threat of violence is 1.8 per 1,000 Americans. This is minute relative to the total accidental injuries calling for medical attention or restricted activity of 1 day or more, as reported by the Public Health Service. A recent study of emergency medical care found the quality, numbers, and distribution of ambulances and other emergency services severely deficient, and estimated that as many as 20,000 Americans die unnecessarily each year as a result of improper emergency care. The means necessary for correcting this situation are very clear and would probably yield greater immediate return in reducing death than would expenditures for reducing the incidence of crimes of violence. But a different personal significance is attached to deaths due to the willful acts of felons as compared to the incompetence of poor equipment of emergency medical personnel.[3]

It would appear, then, to be more logical for Americans to direct their worry and fear toward inadequate or too few ambulances. But these deficiencies do not seem to concern the general public. The man in the street is most afraid of being victimized by a criminal stranger. A disproportionate amount of the thought given to crime in general is concentrated on crimes of violence. One of the stimulants that nourish this fear is the mass media's lurid portrayal of the victim of crime. "The available data indicate that for most people, attitudes about serious crimes and crime trends come largely from vicarious sources."[4] So, while most people are not themselves victims of crime and do not know anyone who has been the victim of crime, they feel threatened because they have seen on television or heard on the radio or read in newspapers and magazines case histories and depictions of violent crime. Their emotions and anxieties become aroused and fed with each day's reports of new victims of crime. Although the chances of one's becoming a victim of crime might be statistically remote, the prevailing reaction seems to be, "It could have been me" or "Next time it might be me." Since this attitude is not completely rational, it cannot be neutralized completely by rational rebuttals. It remains a force to contend with.

Aside from the undeniable realities of crime itself, the manner of reporting them actually contributes to an unjustified fear of crime. The fashion in America seems to require dramatic flair even in the preparation and presentation of crime statistics.

Considering the current public sensitivity about crime and violence, the following comparison to European countries is significant.

"The publication of criminal statistics [in England and Scandinavia] is not regarded as a dramatic act to mobilize public awareness against the danger of rape, murder and other kinds of crimes, but it is regarded as a regular kind of source of information, bringing to the knowledge of those who are interested—unfortunately very few—what is going on in this vast amount of crime.

"Our [England's] criminal statistics in comparison to your publications differ as much as—if I may bluntly say so—an old English cup of tea compares with a dry Martini on the rocks. They [British statistics] are very prosaic, very quiet. And this in some ways makes them less attractive to read. But it does produce them for the public." [5]

There are other deficiencies as well in the reporting of crime in the United States that possibly contribute to the widespread belief in a much greater incidence of crime than is actually the case. This is not to say that crime is not a very serious problem in the United States but rather to suggest that generally held perceptions of reality can be at least as important as reality itself in the way they influence a person assessing his own well-being. It may be doubly important when the realities of crime are not determined.

The consequences of fear of criminal attack seem to be exclusively detrimental for the individual and for society; the ways in which this fear is externalized can be viewed only as damaging. It is not an exaggeration to suggest that the feeling of well-being among the citizenry is in danger of being perhaps fatally eroded by this fear. Already, there are indications that preferred life styles are being modified to preserve some feeling of safety.

This fear leads many people to give up activities they would normally undertake particularly when it may involve going out on the streets or into parks and other public places at night. The costs of this fear are not only economic, though a burdensome price may be paid by many poor people in high crime rate areas who feel compelled to purchase protective locks, bars, and alarms, who reject an attractive night job because of fear of traversing the streets or who pay the expense of taxi transportation under the same circumstances. In the long run more damaging than costs are the loss of opportunities for pleasure and cultural enrichment, the reduction of the level of sociability and mutual trust, and perhaps even more important, the possibility that people will come to lose faith in the trustworthiness and stability of the social and moral order of the society.[6]

This is as fundamental an impact as one can imagine; its significance should not be understated. Because of this fear, a most unhealthy state of affairs has arisen and promises to worsen. "Watch the people," advises a policeman in Washington, D.C.; "see how they walk quickly and with a purpose. There's no casual strolling. People don't come into this town at night unless they have a specific destination in mind. They go straight to it and then go home as fast as possible."[7] It is not only the nighttime visitor who is deterred; more and more, the daytime visitor also tends to avoid the downtown area. A survey undertaken by the Metropolitan Washington Council of Governments showed that "65 per cent of the city's largely white suburban residents visit the downtown area less than once a month, and 15 per cent come downtown less than once a year. Asked their chief worry, the large majority of those surveyed responded: 'Crime.' "[8] Such is the condition of society. The manifestations of fear are beginning to permeate our existence. They take the form of "the locked doors, the empty streets, the growing number of guns bought for self-protection, the signs on public buses that say: 'Driver does not carry cash.' "[9]

With increasing crime rates and the accompanying perceptions of what this increase means to the individual, we are experiencing also an increase in societal costs other than those that are the direct result of victimization. "What economists label opportunity costs for feeling safe probably are far greater economic burdens of crime for these citizens than the direct costs of victimization. With these precautions go . . . the psychic costs of living in an atmosphere of anxiety."[10]

Insofar as crimes against individual citizens are concerned, then, it is suspected that "the immediate consequences are of much less moment than are people's intense reactions to the perceived crime situation."[11] It is important for public policy-makers to be aware of this distinction and to make reduction of the fear of crime an object of attention, just as reducing the incidence of crime is an object of attention. If they do not act appropriately on this knowledge, the result may be an extraordinary anomaly: the fear of crime will increase at the same time that the incidence of crime may decline. A reduction in the incidence of crime will not automatically be accompanied by a corresponding reduction in the fear of crime.

So little attention has been paid to this aspect of crime and its effects that we do not know just what tactics might be most effective in combating the fear of crime. But it should be emphasized that this aspect of the general problem of crime will require its own special attention and solutions. Because of its irrational qualities, it may be more difficult to combat than criminality itself.

NOTES

1. President's Commission on Law Enforcement and Administration of Justice, *The Challenge of Crime in a Free Society* (Washington, D.C.: U.S. Government Printing Office, 1967), p. 18.

2. President's Commission on Law Enforcement and Administration of Justice, *Task Force Report: Crime and Its Impact—An Assessment* (Washington, D.C.: U.S. Government Printing Office, 1967), p. 87.

3. *Id.,* p. 88.

4. *Id.,* p. 86.

5. National Commission on the Causes and Prevention of Violence, *Crime of Violence,* Vol 11, Staff Report, by Donald J. Mulvhill and Melvin M. Tumin with Lynn A. Curtis (Washington, D.C.: U.S. Government Printing Office, 1969), p. 35 quoting statement of Leon Radzinowicz. Hearings before the Commission (September 26, 1968), p. 642.

6. *Task Force Report, op. cit. supra* note 2, p. 94.

7. *Wall Street Journal* (February 11, 1970), p. 1, col. 1.

8. *Ibid.*

9. *Daily Congressional Record,* 92nd Congress, 1st Session, (1971) CXVII, No. 17, S1419.

10. Albert D. Biderman, Louise A. Johnson, Jennie McIntyre and Adrianne W. Weir, *Report on a Pilot Study in the District of Columbia on Victimization and Attitudes toward Law Enforcement,* Bureau of Social Science Research, Inc. (Washington, D.C.: U.S. Government Printing Office, 1967), p. 159.

11. *Id.,* p. 160.

Chapter Two

Toward a New Criminology

Eugene Doleschal
Nora Klapmuts

In *The Greening of America* Charles Reich traces the historical development of three levels of consciousness in America.[1]

Consciousness I was characterized by a system of beliefs that held that success comes to those of moral character who work hard and practice self-denial.

Consciousness II, often associated with liberalism, created the corporate state and an America in which the individual had to make his way in a world directed by others. It demanded sacrifices for a common good, the arrangement of things in a rational hierarchy of authority and responsibility, and the dedication of each individual to goals beyond himself.

Consciousness III maintains that the individual is the true reality, that it is a crime to become an instrument designed to accomplish an extrinsic end, to be alienated from oneself, to defer meaning to the future. It sees a society that is unjust to its poor and its minorities, run for the benefit of a privileged few, lacking in democracy and liberty, ugly and artificial.

. . .

Reprinted, with permission of the National Council on Crime and Delinquency, from *Crime and Delinquency Literature*, Vol. 5, No. 4, 1973, pp. 607–626.

STAGES OF CRIMINOLOGY

The development of criminology and, with it, trends in the administration of criminal justice, parallel Reich's three levels of consciousness both historically and in basic assumptions. A distinct stage of criminology can be found in each of Reich's levels as a logical and integral part of each level.

. . .

Criminology I: The Classical School

The founding father of the first phase of modern criminology—the classical school—was Cesare Beccaria, whose *Treatise on Crimes and Punishments* established a standardized system of justice with a "tariff" to fit the severity of punishment to the gravity of the crime. Partly under his influence, eighteenth and nineteenth century criminal justice gave meaning and definition to such terms as penology, retribution, deterrence, and criminal responsibility, and to the criminal's ability to distinguish right from wrong. Criminology I, the classical school, was predominantly a servant and defender of society against its criminal predators and placed the blame for crime . . . on the "moral turpitude" and lack of will power of the individual offender. Its method of crime control was punishment and incapacitation of the criminal. . . .

The classical school maintained that punishment is a deterrent and that it should cause enough fear, over and above the pleasure derived from the crime, to inhibit deviant behavior. Its proponents thought that punishment should be humane and reformative and were responsible for the substitution of imprisonment for corporal punishment and torture. The classical school was a system of universal, abstract justice based on the assumption of free will.[2]

Those who still support the classical system of criminal justice believe that punishment should fit the crime and that criminals should be made to pay for their crimes. They demand a "crackdown" on criminals and protest their "mollycoddling" by courts and the penal system. They ignore the evidence that the most successful criminal predators are its cultural heroes (e.g., industrial robber barons) and that the mechanisms of crime control often perpetrate the most harmful crimes.

Criminology II: The Positivist School

Criminology II began late in the nineteenth century. The positivists challenged the idea of free will and maintained that the treatment must fit the criminal. The positivists view man and his behavior as determined and regard criminals as ill or deprived. The role of penology is to provide the offender with treatment and a cure for his deviance.[3]

Modern correction is experiencing the full impact of the positivist school in its efforts to "treat" and "rehabilitate" the criminal. Treatment approaches have taken myriad forms, including individual psychotherapy and counseling, group therapy, vocational training, and intensive community intervention and supervision. Some treaters recognize no limits to the extent they may go in attempting to rehabilitate the offender.[4] To the treatment spokesmen, whatever is wrong with correctional policies today could be corrected by expanding and intensifying treatment, by using more individualized treatment (finding exactly the "right" treatment for each offender), or by treating the offender in a more normal, noninstitutional environment. There are some who continue to assert, in reference to past efforts that have failed, that treatment has never really been given a fair chance. So strong is the faith in the potential of treatment that repeated efforts are made to find effective approaches to offender rehabilitation even in the face of growing evidence that criminality and recidivism apparently cannot be "cured."

The primary underlying assumption of the treatment model is that criminal or delinquent behavior is merely a symptom of underlying maladjustment. Theories about the *causes* of such maladjustment changed over the years from a belief in the biological or psychological abnormality of deviants to a focus on the offender as a product of social dysfunctions, culture conflict, unavailable opportunities, or poverty and slum living. But while the implications for correction of offenders changed (from attempting to alter the criminal personality to trying to compensate for lacks in his social situation), the focus of attention remained the offender, and correction still worked to change him or his life-situation to prevent repetition of his criminal behavior.

Criminology III: The Interactionist School

Still largely unknown to the majority of correctional practitioners today, a new criminological and correctional philosophy is slowly gaining acceptance both in the United States and abroad. Originating in Scandinavia, the new philosophy rejects the treatment ideology on several grounds, including the practical grounds of ineffectiveness: the magic pill to cure recidivism cannot be found because the "ailment" does not exist. True successes in rehabilitation have been virtually nonexistent. A survey of all studies of correctional treatment published between 1945 and 1967 found that the present array of correctional treatment efforts has no appreciable effect—either positive or negative—on the recidivism rates of convicted offenders.[5] In another review of numerous correctional programs, Robison and Smith concluded that there is no evidence to support claims of superior rehabilitative efficacy of any correctional alternative over another.[6] This conclusion is supported by the most sophisticated research studies: generally, the more rigorously scientific the methodology the less likely is success to be reported.

The treatment ideology is rejected on legal grounds as enforced treatment has led to the disregard of civil liberties and as it has come to be viewed as often more punitive than under the classical system of punishment. The treatment philosophy clearly has not resulted in more humanitarian handling of the offender.[7]

Most important, the ideology of treatment to fit the offender is being rejected because studies of "hidden" or undetected crime of the past decade have challenged the traditional distinction between criminals and noncriminals, showing that those who become officially known as criminals are merely a small biased sample of the universe of persons who commit crimes selected to fulfill a scapegoat function. In a report to the directors of criminological research institutes of the Council of Europe, B. Kutchinsky sums it up as follows:

What makes a person "criminal" is not the fact that he has committed a crime (because non-criminals have done that also) but the fact that he was caught, tried, convicted and punished.[8]

HIDDEN CRIME STUDIES

A large number of self-report studies of crime have concluded that close to 100 per cent of all persons have committed some kind of offense, although few have been arrested.[9] In a substantial portion of the offenses revealed by these studies, the crime was so serious that it could have resulted in a sentence of imprisonment if the offender had been arrested.

Most of the studies examined the relationship of social class to crime and delinquency. While the evidence is contradictory, most recent studies come to the conclusion that persons of all classes commit crimes and that no social class is responsible for a disproportionate share of crimes committed.

. . .

In support of recent studies, research found that the relationship between social status and delinquent behavior was weak except that *higher-status white boys were more delinquent than lower-status white boys.* The greater seriousness of the higher-status boys' delinquent behavior stemmed from their committing proportionally more thefts, joy riding, and (surprisingly) assaults. The frequency much more than the seriousness of delinquent behavior was positively associated with getting caught. Getting caught was thus to a large extent a chance occurrence.

A study of risk ratios in juvenile delinquency, or factors associated with detection by police and court action, found that while frequency of delinquent behavior was positively associated with getting caught, neither frequency nor seriousness of behavior was related to social class.[10] In other words, despite the preponderance of lower-class persons in official records, the lower classes neither commit offenses more often nor commit more serious offenses. Studies in Sweden, Norway, and Finland discovered a similar discrepancy a decade ago.[11] It appears that while persons of all social classes commit crimes, those who are caught up in the criminal justice system are primarily lower class. Kutchinsky observes that "it is becoming increasingly clear that most criminals are created through a process of discriminatory selection, ostracizing stigmatization, and dehumanizing punishments."[12]

The discovery that crime and delinquency do not vary significantly from one social group to another while the vast majority of inmates of correctional institutions are lower class has led criminologists to take a closer look at the way in which offenders are selected for arrest, prosecution, and punishment.

SELECTION OF OFFENDERS FOR PUNISHMENT

It is common knowledge among most students of crime and delinquency that the officially designated criminal is the final product of a long process of selection. Studies of this selection process support hidden crime studies in consistently demonstrating that certain groups and certain classes of persons are overrepresented while others are underrepresented in the criminal justice system. Those caught up in the system are overwhelmingly the poor, the lower class, members of minority groups, immigrants, foreigners, persons of low intelligence, and others who are in some way at a disadvantage. Those who have a good chance of escaping the system are the affluent criminals, corporate criminals, white-collar criminals, professional criminals, organized criminals, and intelligent criminals. In general, the most successful criminals . . . escape the system while the less successful are caught. If, as hidden crime studies have indicated, only a small proportion of persons who commit crimes are eventually caught and punished and if these are usually the least successful, then the criminal justice system expends most of its resources on a small group of individuals whose offenses are relatively less significant.

Using examples drawn from criminal statistics and from reports of court proceedings, Dennis Chapman demonstrates how society, through the legal system, selects for punishment a scapegoat group drawn from a much wider population of antisocial individuals. This group, composed of working-class men lacking education, influence, and resources, is liable to penalties of imprisonment and desocialization from which members of the middle and upper classes are relatively immune, even though they may engage in behavior that, defined in operational terms, is identical in its social effects. This very selective bias in the legal system means that most studies of crime and the offender take as their starting point a stereotype of the "criminal" that is a social and legal artifact.[13]

Throughout the world one of the main determinants in the process of selection for punishment is socio-economic status. A study of white-collar offenders known to police in Helsinki in 1955 examined the relationship between the socio-economic status of the suspect and the decisions of the police, the prosecutor, and the judge.[14] Like many American studies of this relationship, this study found that a person of higher socio-economic status had a significantly greater chance of having his case adjusted informally by the police, of avoiding prosecution even if referred to court, and of not being sentenced. Only 26 per cent of offenders from the higher socio-economic group were sentenced by the courts, while 57 per cent of the lower-status offenders were involved in judicial processing to the final stage of sentencing.

In the United States and a few other countries the social class factor is complicated by race. An American study of the effect of race on sentencing analyzed the disparities between the sentences of whites and those of Negroes in the South. Utilizing 1,205 cases drawn from the prison and parole records of seven Southern states, it arrived at this simple conclusion:

> There is a significant absolute disparity between the sentences received by black offenders and those received by white offenders. . . . Careful analysis of the data failed to reveal any general factor which would account for the disparity other than race.[15]

Typical of American studies is one of 3,475 Philadelphia delinquents that found that blacks and members of lower socio-economic groups were likely to receive more severe dispositions than whites and the more affluent even when the appropriate legal variables were held constant.[16]

The process of selection for punishment is arbitrary but apparently not random. Many of the numerous studies on this subject point out the influence of the police, the prosecutor, and the judge upon the selection process. Studies of discretionary decision-making on the part of criminal justice officials have shown that some of the factors that affect the selection process are quite subtle. A rather revealing study, by Nathan Goldman, of police discretion in Pennsylvania indicates that systematic selective biases influence the decision to process an alleged juvenile offender through the court. Goldman found that, in addition to the policeman's own private attitudes and experience and his concern for status and prestige in the community, the attitudes of the community toward the offense, the offender, and his family also affect the decision of the officer in his reporting of juvenile offenses. The availability of a juvenile offender for official recording, and for research on delinquency, thus depends on the responsiveness of the police officer to a series of collective social pressures and personal attitudes. The policeman's interpretation of these pressures will determine the composition of that sample of juvenile offenders who will become officially recognized from among all those known to him.[17]

Numerous studies of the process of selection in specific types of offenses have also been made with similar results. A study of drunken driving, for instance, demonstrated that minority-group members, the lower class, males, and youth are consistently more likely to be convicted of driving while intoxicated than are whites, the upper class, and older persons.[18] A study of the corporate and judicial disposition of employees involved in embezzlement found that when the amount stolen was held constant, more lower status employees than higher status employees were prosecuted, indicating that offenders with whom the enforcers could more easily identify were treated sympathetically.[19] A German study of selection for prosecution and punishment of shoplifters found that only 2 per cent of shoplifters are eventually subjected to a legal sanction and these 2 per cent are not representative of the total sample. Of one hundred shoplifters, fewer than five are detected. Of every one hundred detected, fewer than fifty are reported to authorities. Of one hundred reported, eighty are punished. At all stages of the selection process from detection to punishment, certain groups were consistently more likely to be processed to the next stage: foreigners, adults, and members of the working class. For example, while 8 per cent of thefts were committed by foreign workers, 15 per cent of those reported to the authorities were foreign workers.[20] Another study of public reactions to shoplifting consisted of a field experiment in which rigged shoplifting events were enacted in the presence of store customers who were in a position to observe and react to the shoplifting incidents. It was found that while sex of shoplifter or of store customer had little effect on reporting levels, appearance of shoplifter exerted a major independent effect on reporting levels. A highly significant relationship was found between "hippie" appearance of the person acting as shoplifter and willingness on the part of store customers to report the incident. The study concludes that the imputation of deviance not only resides in the fact of deviance itself but also depends heavily on the meanings that the observer attaches to the behavior and the actor. Willingness to report deviant acts can be assumed to depend on the "deviate's" other social identities, a significant clue to identity being provided by appearance.[21]

Studies of the types of offenders who escape punishment and how they are selected are also numerous. It is well known that organized criminals are among the economically most successful. How they escape detection and punishment through bribery, threats, loopholes in the law, and society's apathy and ambivalence has been aptly described by Donald Cressey in *Theft of the Nation*.[22]

Similar in his success is the professional criminal. A British study notes that offenders who make a full-time job of crime and who establish relationships and networks in the pursuance of their common occupational interests operate at an economic cost to the community that is disproportionately high relative to their numbers. On the basis of two pilot studies it was estimated that there is one full-time professional criminal for every ten thousand inhabitants in Britain.[23] In a city of one million, 102 full-time offenders were analyzed. A very large proportion was found to be both able and successful in their criminal occupation—i.e., making a lot more money than they would have made in such legal occupations as are open to them and successful in avoiding court appearance, conviction, and imprisonment. This study makes the important point that the major skill of the professional criminal, avoiding detection and imprisonment, suggests a serious distortion in criminological research, which consistently studies those offenders who are caught and punished. The offenders most available for study are the persistent criminal failures who have little in common with the able and successful professional criminal.

No sociological studies of corporate criminals are reported in the literature but the selective, discriminatory system of justice in favor of the rich is amply documented. U.S. Senator Philip Hart observes from his questioning of corporate criminals that, for the affluent and influential, loopholes in the law are so abundant that it takes determination to avoid them. Corporate criminals are availed of a host of quiet settlement procedures that the government never employs to keep a burglar out of prison. Discriminatory justice in favor of the rich occurs at all stages of criminal justice. Upper-class crimes generally result in civil damage suits, cease-and-desist orders, license revocations, and fines. The upper classes, simply because they have access to government decision-makers, can also influence the development of the very statutes that regulate upper-class behavior.[24]

A review of studies of juvenile offenders of high intelligence concludes that the comparative rarity of known bright delinquents is the result of differential immunity accorded them by reason of their higher intelligence. It is suggested that they are more skillful in escaping detection and that their high intelligence may influence the police in deciding not to arrest. Intelligent delinquents share largely the same criminological, educational, and general social characteristics as the majority of other delinquents but they differ in important respects: they are rarely encountered, they are treated differently by the courts, and they are more often presented as emotionally disturbed. These delinquents are more readily adjudged psychiatrically disturbed because of their greater verbal fluency and ability to communicate with psychiatrists.[25]

These studies, and many others like them, have suggested that any approach to crime that concentrates on the characteristics of the convicted criminal, the "causes" of his behavior, or his treatment aimed at preventing further convictions is likely to be unproductive. If the population of officially labeled criminals is as unrepresentative of the crime problem as these studies indicate, a very large portion of criminological literature is leading us up a dead-end street.

TOWARD A NEW CRIMINOLOGY

While most criminologists today are preoccupied with such traditional concerns as the offender, his characteristics, and his classification and treatment, a few have begun to move in a totally different direction, which if it proves productive, may radically change both criminology and correction. The new criminology has drawn on the findings of hidden crime studies and studies of the selection of offenders for punishment. The most recent of these have found that, while the vast majority of persons who are caught and punished are lower class, the commission of crime does not vary significantly from one social group to another. In effect, it is primarily the poor and the powerless who are caught.

The work of several criminologists serves to illustrate the direction that criminology has taken. What these criminologists have in common is a de-emphasis of the importance of the individual offender as an object of study and a focus on the role of society in creating and maintaining crime and criminals for a necessary function. A crucial implication of these theories is that society is currently operating at cross-purposes: society apparently has a need to designate certain individuals as criminal and certain behaviors as crime at the same time that it tries to prevent such behavior and to punish or "treat" persons who engage in it.

Patrik Törnudd believes that the low utility of criminological research is attributable to the failure of traditional criminologists to view crime as a necessary social function.[26] He believes that society *needs* crime, or at least a certain amount of behavior that is publicly defined as deviant. Crime serves three major functions: social integration, norm reinforcement, and innovation. (1) The identification of acts as criminal allows a harmless channeling of aggressions, while at the same time reinforcing group solidarity and other social values. The quotation, "Nothing unites a nation as much as its murderers," describes this mechanism. (2) Norms are needed to uphold social organization. To maintain norm conformity, continuous reinforcement must take place. Each public denunciation of an identified act is a reminder of the norm's existence and importance. (3) Fundamental moral innovations call for deviance manifested in action, with the attendant conflict (crime) a necessary element of the process. Crime, according to Törnudd, also fulfills a number of lesser functions, including self-regulating deviance for instrumental purposes: e.g., theft of bread by a hungry person.

With respect to prevention of crime, Törnudd suggests that the range of permissible crime can be viewed as a dynamic equilibrium in which society can settle for differing levels of crime at the cost of, among other things, production, the speed of social change, and solidarity. If crime is necessary and normal, then any measure of crime must take into account the degree of necessity.

Törnudd recommends that, instead of searching for the "causes" of crime, criminologists should formulate their research strategies and communicate their results with respect to (a) fluctuations in the level of crime or (b) the process that determines the selection of offenses and offenders for punishment.

Inkeri Anttila views crime as the visible expression of a balance among conflicting social pressures [27] and points out that treating the offender will never solve the crime problem since criminals serve a useful purpose as scapegoats of the social system.[28] Although the treatment approach to correction was a breakthrough in its time, the undesirable aspects of the approach have become evident as the concept of treatment of offenders has come to dominate the correctional system. Equating offenders with the sick, Anttila argues, is a fallacy when the "sick" and the "doctor" are in conflict and when the treatment does not bring about a cure. This fallacy has led to an acute problem of legal rights and safeguards because of the absence of treatment predictability and a frequent disproportion between the seriousness of a crime and the intensity of treatment. Preoccupation with the individual offender blinds the treaters to the existence of social evils that are much more urgent targets for society's crime control efforts. The treatment system, says Anttila, must not be used to camouflage social injustices and delay vital reforms. It is more urgent to repeal obsolete laws and to eliminate arbitrary decision-making and discrimination against the socially powerless.

While the elimination of crime is not a realistic goal, Anttila believes that we can strive for social balance and influence the structure and gravity of crime. This has important policy implications: For every crime problem it becomes as important to examine the possibilities of changing society's control of crime (to the point of decriminalization) as it is to change the offender. This social balance, Anttila says, has an inner logic of its own that does not permit decriminalization of previously proscribed behavior to go too far and does not permit the number of criminal laws, crimes, and criminals to fall below a certain level.

Projecting into the future, Anttila suggests that alternatives to traditional punishment and treatment will perhaps include efforts to affect the standard of living of the offender or to express, in some subtle way, society's disapproval of certain types of harmful behavior. This prediction appears reasonable if one accepts the hypothesis that the proportion of persons sentenced for traditional crimes will decrease while the proportion of persons sentenced for tax and business fraud, polluting the environment, and misuse of public office will increase.[29] A systems-change model of crime control is already operative in traffic insurance legislation: insurance eases the suffering inflicted on the victim and satisfies society with an economic sanction in the form of raised insurance premiums, even in cases of criminal negligence. Such financial charges and other economic sanctions can, in many cases, take the place of traditional punishment.[30]

Another criminologist, Raimo Lahti, points out that Scandinavian criminology no longer searches for the causes of crime in the characteristics of criminals or their environment. The question asked is not why some individuals become criminal but why they are identified as criminals in a selective process. Mere reduction of crime can no longer be accepted as an objective. Crime reduction must be sought at the lowest possible cost and with due regard to equity and justice. Society, as owner of the largest resources, must accept primary responsibility for the reduction of the costs of crime.

For the future, Lahti predicts that a value- and cost-conscious school of thinking will probably gain influence in the decision-making process concerning crime. This means that when several alternatives are available, the costs of these solutions and their applicability will be compared with different values and the decision will be based on this comparison. It will frequently be more expedient to develop measures to prevent opportunities for crime than to deal with offenders.[31]

Applied criminology, according to Marc LeBlanc, runs the risk of becoming an instrument of control, especially as criminology is transformed into a technological science. This danger is compounded by the fact that crime is a political concept: since each political regime defines its own criminality, criminology can easily become a political tool. The distinction between crime and deviance, between concern and control, between punishment and treatment, between criminology and repression, is always politically defined.[32]

Dennis Chapman has presented . . . a new theory of crime, incorporating many of the research findings on hidden crime and the selection of offenders for punishment. The main theses of his theory can be summarized as follows:

(1) Apart from the fact of conviction there are no differences between criminals and noncriminals. Criminal behavior is general but the incidence of conviction is controlled in part by chance and in part by social processes that divide society into criminal and noncriminal classes, the former corresponding roughly to the poor and under-privileged. (2) The social system operates to select individuals from a larger universe of individuals with identical behaviors. (3) *Behavior that has a disapproved form (crime) also has objectively identical forms that are neutral or approved.* The choice among disapproved, tolerated, and approved forms of behavior may depend on chance, knowledge, learning, or training. The designation of certain actions as permitted, tolerated, or condemned in different circumstances is arbitrary. (4) Different social groups are treated differently for behaviors that are objectively identical. Certain persons and groups are immune from selection as criminals, primarily because of the protective institutional environments in which they live. (5) Crime is a functional part of the social system. Identification of the criminal class and its social ostracism permits the guilt of others to be symbolically discharged and reduces social class hostility by deflecting aggression that might otherwise be directed toward those in power. A special part of the official ideology functions to prevent the designated criminal from escaping from his sacrificial role and institutional record-keeping maintains his identity. (6) The legal system is a crime-creating institution: once created, an institution develops a dynamic of its own and becomes involved in the behavior with which it is concerned as a participant, and in special circumstances as an instigator. It may do this in response to social pressures.[33]

These statements raise many complex issues, including the plurality of the moral and legal order, the conflict between society's belief system and its goal system, and the conflict between groups with power and groups without power. Unlike other crime theories, this "theory of the stereotype," as Chapman calls it, begins not with the person and his characteristics or behaviors but with the moral order and the law. It sees society, not the criminal, as the main problem. It asks why a legislature decides than an action must be punished. While much law is in the public interest, it still reflects the distribution of power in society and much legislation (or the absence of it) serves the interests of particular classes, groups, or organizations. These laws are then selectively administered by the police and the courts. The differential distribution of privacy is one of the crucial variables in this process: the affluent are immune since most of their behavior occurs in private. Poor urban areas, on the other hand, are heavily policed, thus producing high arrest rates—a classic example of the self-fulfilling prophecy. Defense against a legal charge depends not on innocence but on power, social connections, knowledge of the law, and financial resources, all of which are unequally distributed. Following conviction the discriminatory process continues along class lines, with the rich more likely to escape imprisonment and more likely than the poor to appeal the conviction and the sentence. Finally, the theory is concerned with removing the stigma. The first step in this direction, says Chapman, is to rid ourselves of all we have been led to believe on the subject. It calls for better understanding of the range of behavior we have designated criminal and the futility of punishment for most types of behavior.

Even a brief review of the thinking of these criminologists indicates that the new criminology is more than just another theory of the labeling process. Labeling theory has contributed to the knowledge on which the new criminology is based. Studies of the labeling process have pointed out that criminal labels are dispensed in such a manner that persons who are expected to be the most criminal (i.e., poorly educated, indigents, blacks) are given the greatest opportunity to develop a criminal identity or career. Labeling theorists have helped to turn attention away from the deviant acts of individuals and the causes of their deviance toward the criminogenic effects of negative societal responses to deviance. They have suggested that official action (imposition of a criminal label) may lock the person so stigmatized into a criminal career, thus creating more crime in the effort to prevent or deter it. They have also pointed out that the processes of labeling fulfill a social function: the identification of deviant "outsiders" functions to bring the labelers closer together.

The new criminology builds on the work of the labeling theorists, but it goes further. Labeling theorists still concentrate on the effects of labeling on the persons stigmatized, the impact of social processes on the individual. Labeling theory makes assumptions about the predisposing characteristics that lead an individual to commit his first offense and the changes in him resulting from his stigmatization. In other words, there is an implicit assumption of the existence of a group of criminals and delinquents or "predelinquents," some of whom are caught and labeled officially while others escape such labeling. The new criminology does not consider these concerns to be of critical importance, claiming that the concept of a criminal or criminally predisposed group is a social and legal artifact. The new criminologists consider a "criminal" to be anyone who is convicted of a crime, whether or not he has actually committed it, and include among "noncriminals" anyone who breaks the law but avoids detection.[34] It is processing by the criminal justice system that distinguishes the criminal from the noncriminal. This approach is concerned not only with the social rejection of some forms of behavior and the ostracism of some persons who engage in it, but also with the acceptance by society of other forms of the *same* behavior engaged in by other persons. It considers not only stigmatization and de-stigmatization but *non*stigmatization, showing us that while people of all classes and groups engage in some form of "appropriation of property of others without their consent" (theft), only certain forms of this conduct are wholly disapproved and only some kinds of persons are subject to penal or other sanctions for it.

CONCLUSION

Current public and official views of crime and criminals, and the "solutions" to the crime problem that derive from them, appear obsolete from the perspective of those who have begun to take criminology into new territory. The tents of Criminology III are not entirely new: In the early part of this century Emile Durkheim wrote that criminality is a normal element of every society, that society needs criminals to reinforce social norms, and that even a society of saints would have its social norms and its norm-breakers.[35] In the 1950's Aubert explained that each society organizes itself for the protection of the ruling classes against the socially inferior.[36] Criminologists today are rediscovering and expanding on these views, fortifying their arguments with the research evidence of the intervening years. Their theories point up the weaknesses and limitations of traditional conceptions of the crime problem which present crime as an aberration and criminals as a minority of ill, immoral, misguided, or improperly socialized persons who are somehow different from the average citizen. The orthodox view encourages the belief that if we could just find out what is *wrong* with people who offend against society these people could be rehabilitated to become useful and productive citizens like the rest of us.

The new criminologists view the crime problem from a wholly

different perspective. They consider the search for the "causes" of crime and a "cure" for the criminal a waste of time since official crime and the detected criminal are produced and maintained by social forces that have little or nothing to do with the harmfulness of actual behavior. The most successful criminals (those realizing the greatest economic gain) are rarely caught, rarely prosecuted, and rarely punished. When punished, they are punished less severely. These are persons with power or access to power, the rich, and the intelligent. The less successful criminals are more likely to be caught, prosecuted, and punished. When punished, they are punished more severely. They are the powerless, the poor, and the unintelligent.

The new criminology concentrates not on the officially designated criminal but on (1) the *definition* of crime—the decision to make, for instance, intoxication by marijuana or other drugs criminal while intoxication by alcohol (the drug of those who make the laws) is noncriminal; and (2) the *selection* of certain lawbreakers for identification as criminals—for example, the decision to arrest, prosecute, and imprison the lower-class man who steals a hundred dollars and to deal informally with the upper-class embezzler of thousands of dollars by quiet settlement to avoid damaging his reputation.

The new criminology views crime as an integral part of society—a normal, not a pathological, kind of human behavior. It assumes that crime cannot be eliminated—although its structure and form might be affected by changes in crime control policy,[37] and that crime in some form serves useful purposes in integrating what is known as law-abiding society and in defining its boundaries. Most of all, it points out that deviance is a relative concept, that what we call "crime" and "criminals" are more or less arbitrarily defined classes of acts and actors rather than the clear-cut distinctions implied by the labels "criminal" and "noncriminal." Although people and behaviors are viewed as one or the other, in reality the classifications of criminal and noncriminal shade into each other with no sharp lines of demarcation. The distinctions made between them are arbitrary but apparently not random; criminal labels are usually dispensed in ways that uphold the established order and do not threaten the lives and life styles of the classes or groups with power and influence.

That crime and delinquency are political concepts has frequently been noted. . . . Richard Quincy writes that crime has become a political weapon that is used to the advantage of those who control the processes of government. The state . . . has used its power through the law to define as criminal what it regards as a threat to the social and political order. This has always been true—there are few acts, no matter how heinous, that have not at one time or under some circumstances been tolerated or approved; and there are few acts, no matter how petty, that have not at some time been considered punishable offenses. . . . The influence of official conceptions of the crime problem is evident in the recent focus on "crime in the streets." This type of crime having been officially identified as *the* major crime problem, both public concern and the bulk of government crime control resources are directed against the perpetrators of street crimes. In another time or place, the crime problem might just as well be identified as environmental pollution, misuse of public money, or large-scale embezzlement, fraud, or other actions that adversely affect large numbers of people.

The political nature of crime-control policies is most obvious with respect to juveniles and the laws of juvenile delinquency. Children and young people represent a class of persons who, despite their large numbers, have little or no power in society. Most of them cannot vote and cannot make or change the laws that affect them. Their own norms and values, to the extent that they differ from those of the adult world, are not embodied in the law. For example, while leaving his parents' home may be quite legitimate from a juvenile's point of view and that of his peers, in the statutes it is called "running away" and is punishable by measures that are often quite severe. A wide range of other activities and behaviors, relatively harmless or completely justified from a youthful point of view, can lead to a lengthy period of incarceration for the juvenile unfortunate enough to be caught. Consideration of the juvenile justice system in operation has led Langley, Graves, and Norris to propose that juvenile delinquency be viewed as "a community-enacted, legally based political procedure for controlling and altering youthful behavior that is disruptive to an orderly adult way of life." They suggest that juvenile delinquency be defined as "behavior that the state deems necessary to control and to alter through the political structure of the community." [38]

Adult crime could easily be defined in the same way. Our prisons are full of people whose particular offenses are disruptive to an orderly middle- or upper-class way of life. Theirs are the crude offenses, less socially acceptable than the more subtle white-collar crimes, even though the white-collar criminal may inflict more social harm or monetary loss. The "real"criminals, according to official ideology, are in prison or under some other form of correctional supervision. The vast majority of them lack the power to influence the law-making process in their own favor and, without skill, knowledge, or social influence, they are easily caught and punished. They are the criminal failures and society's scapegoats. They have, of course, committed real crimes for which their punishment is authorized by statute. But so have the great many who go free.

While these facts are acknowledged by a growing number of modern criminologists, traditional views of crime and criminals are still predominant in both correctional practice and criminological research, especially in the United States. Because of this, much criminological thinking and research is handicapped and is falling behind. The prestigious President's Crime Commission stated what was then (1967) and still is widely accepted as fact: "Delinquency is a *lower-class* phenomenon." And standard reference works on criminal procedure suggest that prosecutors refrain from prosecuting in cases where the offender comes from a "respectable" background [39]—implying that prosecution for a crime may be harmful to middle-class lives. Most crime and delinquency research deals with that small proportion of criminals who have failed at crime and are caught.[40] The causes of criminal behavior are thus assumed to lie somewhere in the psyche or the social and family background of the criminal failure. Yet the biased nature of the official criminal population suggests that the study of this group may be productive only to the extent that it indicates what it is about its members that leads to their selection for criminal justice processing.

In addition to the important implications for criminology theory and research—that the focus of attention should shift from the stigmatized to the stigmatizers and that more attention be directed toward crime and deviance as part of the normal functioning of society—the new criminology raises issues for criminal justice that suggest the need for a dramatic reordering of priorities. It appears that society has been bearing down heavily on a hapless group of secondary offenders who have been unsuccessful in escaping justice, while tolerating or helplessly watching the depredations of the more successful criminals.

One approach to reform of our system of crime control, consistent with the new criminology and geared toward providing equal justice, might be first to redefine crimes operationally and then to decide which kinds of operationally defined kinds of behavior are widely believed to be the most harmful. If, as seems to be the case, there is a general consensus that violence against persons (e.g., murder, assault, etc.) is the kind of behavior that society most abhors, then crime control efforts should be directed not against "street crime" (which by circumstance is almost exclusively the domain of the lower classes) but against personal violence in whatever form it takes. Upper-class and official violence should not be disguised by euphemism, nor should its perpetrators be excused because their credentials imply that violence was either justifiable or merely an aberration from a normally "respectable" life style. Conversely, if upper-class economic crimes (e.g., embezzlement, fraud, tax evasion, etc.) are fairly well tolerated and absorbed by society and the economy, then surely it is both unnecessary and unfair to punish so severely the economic crimes (theft, larceny, robbery without violence, burglary, etc.) of the less advantaged.

Any society concerned not only with law and order but with justice for all must first decide which are the serious crimes, which crimes cause the greatest social harm, and then commit itself to the equal distribution of punishment for all kinds of classes of persons who engage in such behaviors. Until we can achieve such a just redirection of crime control and correctional efforts, we should at least be aware that our present system, upheld by our most cherished notions of what is a criminal and what is a crime, is set up and operated in ways that work to the distinct advantage of certain social groups and classes and to the clear disadvantage of others. The research and theory of Criminology III can help us to understand why this is so, what functions are served by this arrangement and by alternative ones, and what can reasonably be expected in the way of productive change.

NOTES

1. Charles A. Reich, *The Greening of America* (New York: 1970).

2. Herbert Bloch and Gilbert Geis, *Man, Crime, and Society* (New York: 1962), pp. 84–87.

3. *Id.*, pp. 87–90.

4. Inkeri Anttila, "Punishment versus Treatment—Is There a Third Alternative?" *Abstracts on Criminology and Penology*, 12(7): (1972), pp. 287–290.

5. Douglas S. Lipton, Robert Martinson, and Judith Wilks, *Effectiveness of Correctional Treatment: A Survey of Treatment Evaluations* (New York: State Office of Crime Control Planning, 1970).

6. James Robison and Gerald Smith, "The Effectiveness of Correctional Programs," *Crime and Delinquency*, 17(1) (1971), pp. 67–80.

7. *Supra* note 4.

8. Council of Europe, Ninth Conference of Directors of Criminological Research Institutes, *Perception of Deviance and Criminality* (Strasbourg: 1971), pp. 75–79.

9. Eugene Doleschal, "Hidden Crime," *Crime and Delinquency Literature*, 2(5) (1970), pp. 546–572.

10. Nanci Koser Wilson, *Risk Ratios in Juvenile Delinquency* (Ann Arbor, Mich.: University Microfilms, 1972).

11. *Supra* note 9.

12. *Op. cit. supra* note 8.

13. Dennis Chapman, "The Stereotype of the Criminal and the Social Consequences," *International Journal of Criminology and Penology,* 1 (1) (1973), pp. 15–30.

14. "White Collar Crimes and Status Selectivity in the Law Enforcement System" (Research Report No. 120), Institute of Sociology, University of Helsinki (1969).

15. "Race Makes the Difference," Southern Regional Council (Atlanta, Ga., 1969).

16. Terence Patrick Thornberry, *Punishment and Crime: The Effect of Legal Dispositions on Subsequent Criminal Behavior* (Ann Arbor, Mich.: University Microfilms, 1972).

17. Nathan Goldman, *The Differential Selection of Juvenile Offenders for Court Appearance* (New York: National Council on Crime and Delinquency, 1963).

18. Ross L. Purdy, *Factors in the Conviction of Law Violators: The Drinking Driver* (Ann Arbor, Mich.: University Microfilms, 1971).

19. Gerald Robin, "The Corporate and Judicial Disposition of Employee Thieves," *Wisconsin Law Review,* (3): (1967), pp. 685–702.

20. Erhard Blankenburg, "Die Selektivität rechtlicher Sanktionen: eine empirische Untersuchung von Ladendiebstählen," *Kölner Zeitschrift für Soziologie und Sozialpsychologie,* 21(4) (1969), pp. 805–829.

21. Darrell J. Steffensmeier and Robert M. Terry, "Deviance and Respectability: An Observational Study of Reactions to Shoplifting," *Social Forces,* 51(4) (1973), pp. 417–426.

22. Donald R. Cressey, *Theft of the Nation* (New York: Harper & Row, 1969).

23. J. A. Mack, "The Able Criminal," *British Journal of Criminology,* 12(1): (1972), pp. 44–54.

24. Philip A. Hart, "Swindling and Knavery, Inc." *Playboy* (August 1972), pp. 155–62.

25. Dennis Gath and Gavin Tennent, "High Intelligence and Delinquency—a Review," *British Journal of Criminology,* 12(2): (1972), pp. 174–181.

26. Patrik Törnudd, "The Futility of Searching for Causes of Crime," *Scandinavian Studies in Criminology,* Vol. 3 (Oslo, Universitetsforlaget, 1971), pp. 23–33.

27. Inkeri Anttila, "Conservative and Radical Criminal Policy in the Nordic Countries," *Scandinavian Studies in Criminology,* Vol. 3 (Oslo, Universitetsforlaget, 1971), pp. 9–21.

28. *Supra* note 4.

29. *Ibid.*

30. *Supra* note 27.

31. Raimo Lahti, "On the Reduction and Distribution of the Costs of Crime: Observations on the Objectives and the Means of Criminal Policy," *Jurisprudentia,* no vol. (1) (1972), pp. 298–313.

32. Marc LeBlanc, "Theorie-Recherche-Pratique: Une Interaction à Developper," *Canadian Journal of Criminology and Correction,* 15(1) (1973), pp. 13–24.

33. *Supra* note 13.

34. *Ibid.*

35. Emile Durkheim, *Rules of Sociological Method* (Glencoe, Ill.: Free Press, 1950), pp. 65–73.

36. V. Aubert, *On Straffens sosiale funksjon* (Oslo: 1954).

37. *Supra* note 4.

38. M. H. Langley, H. R. Graves, and B. Norris, "The Juvenile Court and Individualized Treatment," *Crime and Delinquency,* 18(1) (1972), pp. 79–92.

39. *Struggle for Justice: A Report on Crime and Punishment in America,* prepared for American Friends Service Committee (New York, 1971), p. 107.

40. There is evidence to suggest that the emphasis of American researchers on the individual offender and their use of official sources of data have been heavily influenced by the concerns of those who fund research, particularly the government, and some evidence that this may change. John F. Galliher and James L. McCartney, "The Influence of Funding Agencies on Juvenile Delinquency Research," *Social Problems,* 21(1): (1973), pp. 77–90.

Chapter Three

The Rise of
Critical Criminology

Gresham M. Sykes

I.

In the last ten to fifteen years, criminology in the United States has witnessed a transformation of one of its most fundamental paradigms for interpreting criminal behavior. The theory, methods and applications of criminology have all been exposed to a new scrutiny, and there seems to be little doubt that the field will be involved in an intricate controversy for many years to come.

. . .

In the social turbulence of the 1960's, institutions of higher education were at the center of the storm. Students supplied much of the motive force, and the university frequently served as a stage for, as well as a target of, conflict. The university, however, is more than a place or a social organization. It is also a collection of academic disciplines, and these too felt the tremors of the time. Sociology, in particular, was subjected to a barrage of criticism from a variety of sources, and it is within that framework that we need to examine the change that has overtaken criminology.

Reprinted by special permission of the *Journal of Criminal Law and Criminology* © 1974 by Northwestern University School of Law, Vol. 65, No. 2, pp. 206–213.

It was the special claim of sociology . . . that the discipline had largely freed itself from social philosophy. If the status of sociology as a science was not exactly clear, there was no doubt about its dedication to scientific methods and objectivity.[1] Sociology, it was said, was value-free.

It was precisely this point, however, that served as the focus of attack for a number of students and teachers.[2] Sociology, they argued, was still contaminated by the bias and subjectivity of particular interest groups in society. The claim to the cool neutrality of science was a sham. This was especially evident in the area of sociological theory. Social structure, it was said, had been interpreted in terms of consensus, but it was really conflict that lay at the heart of social organization. People in positions of power had traditionally been analyzed in terms of bureaucratic roles aimed at the rational accomplishment of organizational objectives. In reality, people in positions of power were motivated largely by their own selfish interests. A great variety of social problems had been viewed by sociology as flowing from individual pathologies. In fact, however, this approach merely disguised the extent to which the existing social system was at fault, and thus helped to buttress the status quo. Sociology had long been wedded to an evolutionary model of social change, whereas the truth of the matter was that real social change came about not through small increments but through far more radical leaps.

This debate, which broke out into the open in the sixties, involved a great many of the intellectual specialties of sociology, but it was particularly evident in the field of criminology. The study of crime, its causes and its cure, had long been regarded as a borrower rather than a lender when it came to the intellectual substance of the social sciences. It had seemed a bit marginal to the major concerns of a science of society, from the viewpoint of many sociologists —perhaps because of its connections with the study of social problems, which many sociologists had viewed as being too deeply enmeshed in value judgments. Now, however, the growing argument about the objectivity of sociology suddenly found many of its crucial themes exemplified in how academic criminology had handled the subject of crime.

II.

As a special field of knowledge, criminology had its origins in the attempt to reform the criminal law of the eighteenth century.

Bentham, Romilly and Beccaria were all children of the Enlightenment, and they shared the objective of making the law a more just, humane and rational instrument of the state. With the rise of the Positivist School in the nineteenth century, however, with its optimistic faith in science, criminology began to move away from the domain of legal thinkers—a movement that became particularly marked in the United States after 1900.[3] In some parts of Europe, and in Latin America, criminology maintained its links with jurisprudence, but in the United States we witnessed a peculiar split. Criminal law became a subject matter for lawyers and law schools; criminology, on the other hand, turned up in the liberal arts curriculum of almost every college and university, largely a creature of the social sciences and particularly sociology.

In some ways, this might have seemed to be a reasonable division of labor. A knowledge of the criminal law was, after all, a part of the lawyer's professional training, even if, until fairly recently, it tended to lack the eclat that attached to areas of law that were potentially more financially productive. The lawyer's interest in the criminal law was apt to center on the nature of the legal rules and their interpretation by the courts; and his concern with why people break the rules and what happens to them after they leave the courtroom was likely to be rather fleeting. These were questions, however, that fell naturally into the theoretical and conceptual framework of the sociologist. Often enough, he had neither the training nor the inclination to enter the thoughtways of the legal scholar to pursue the law's meaning of *mens rea,* search and seizure and conspiracy.[4]

It is possible that this matter of thoughtways was as important as any special taste in subject matter in the mutual neglect exhibited by criminologists and scholars of criminal law. The study of the law, it has been said, is organized for action, while the social sciences are organized for the accumulation of knowledge; and this aphorism points to a fundamental conflict between the intellectual discipline of law and sociology that helped to keep their practitioners apart. As Robert Merton has indicated, sociologists are guided in their work by the scientific ethos, not in terms of an individual ethical choice, but as a matter of institutionalized professional norms. The search for knowledge is to be undertaken in a spirit of neutrality, and the scientist must have the same passion for proving his hypotheses wrong as for proving them right. The validity of ideas is to be established by impersonal standards of proof; and learned authority must stand on an equal footing with the brashest newcomer when it comes to the empirical testings of facts. Scientific knowledge must be shared with one's colleagues, and no information is to be kept secret because it might bring an advantage or because it might be disturbing. Finally, the scientist is supposed to be under the sway of an organized skepticism that accepts no conclusion as final, no fact as forever proven. Every issue can be reopened and reexamined.[5]

These norms may not always be followed by social scientists as they go about their work, but in a rough way they do guide much scientific behavior, including the behavior of sociologists. The settling of legal disputes, however, is cut on a very different pattern. Lawyers are typically involved as partisans with a far from disinterested concern in the outcome of a case. At law, much is made of the weight of authority, and the discrediting of arguments on an *ad hominem* basis is a familiar occurrence. Information may be withheld on the grounds of privileged communication or with the idea that it would distort the reasoning of the triers of fact. There is a strong impulse to settle cases quickly and not to reopen old disputes.

These differences in the intellectual styles of professional work in sociology and in law appear to have greatly increased the difficulty of exchanging ideas between the two fields, and reinforced their separate development. In any event, the fact that criminal law and criminology tended to remain in separate academic compartments over much of the recent past led to a number of unfortunate consequences. First, many aspects of the criminal law's operation, such as arrest procedures, the activities of the grand jury, trials, and the statutory revision of the criminal law, often remained outside the purview of criminologists. Some attention was given to these matters, it is true, but the bulk of the attention of academic criminology was devoted to questions of crime causation and corrections. One need but review textbooks in criminology of ten or twenty years ago to be struck by the short shrift frequently accorded the criminal law and other issues that loom large in the eyes of the legal scholar and that are, in fact, vital to understanding the relationship between crime and society. Second, the concept of crime was apt to remain singularly crude as the social scientist pursued his goal of building an explanatory schema for criminal behavior. A great variety of acts were frequently lumped together under headings such as "norm violation" and "delinquency," and the careful refinements of legal thought were shoved to one side. Many of the distinctions were quite irrelevant, it is true, from the viewpoint of the social sciences, for they were based on the needs of prosecution, an outmoded concept of man as a hedonistic calculator, and arbitrary, inconsistent categories such as felonies and misdemeanors. But the law at least recognized that "crime" was far from a homogeneous form of behavior, while criminology exhibited a disquieting tendency to speak of crime and the criminal in general. A greater interplay between the two fields might have stimuated efforts to build useful typologies. Third, the fact that the two fields had so little to do with one another meant that many of the findings emerging from criminology received a less than sympathetic ear from those more closely tied to the criminal law. Serious doubts about the effectiveness of juvenile services, prisons, probation and so on were expressed by criminologists, but their voices seldom seemed to carry beyond the groves of academe.

III.

In the late fifties and early sixties, a distinct change began to make its appearance. Topics that had long received relatively little attention in criminology (such as the day-to-day operations of the police) began to be examined by increasing numbers of sociologists. The crude classifications of earlier years began to give way to the empirical study of relatively specific types of criminal activity. The criminal law, which had been taken as a fixed parameter for so long by so many criminologists, began to be examined with a much more inquiring turn of mind. In short, the rather narrow viewpoint of criminology in the United States began to be enlarged and much of its proper subject matter—long left to others—began to be addressed at a serious and systematic level. The change, however, was not mainly because the criminal law and criminology had somehow found a way to end their long estrangement, although this played some part. Rather, a major reason for the shift appears to have been rooted in the same social forces that were modifying sociology as an academic discipline. By the beginning of the 1970's, it was evident that a new strain of thought had entered American criminology, challenging many of its basic assumptions.

Some have spoken of a "radical criminology," but the term is misleading since it suggests a particular ideological underpinning that probably does not exist. I think "critical criminology" is a somewhat better term, at least for the purposes of this discussion, keeping in mind that all such summary phrases can obscure as well as illuminate.

The themes involved in this new orientation can be roughly summarized as follows:

First, there is a profound skepticism accorded any individualistic theory of crime causation. It is not merely biological theories and psychological theories of personality maladjustment that have been abandoned. Sociological theories, dependent on notions of the individual's "defects" due to inadequate socialization or peer group pressures, are also viewed with a wary eye. The problem has become not one of identifying the objectively determined characteristics that separate the criminal and non-criminal, but of why some persons and not others are stigmatized with the label of "criminal" in a social process. "If preconceptions are to be avoided," writes Austin Turk, "a criminal is most accurately defined as any individual who is identified as such. . . ." [6] The roots of this idea in labeling theory are clear enough. A number of writers in criminology today, however, have pushed the idea within a hairline of the claim that the only important reality is the act of labeling—and not because labeling ignores who is a criminal and who is not, but because we are all criminals.

Second, what I have called "critical criminology" is marked by a profound shift in the interpretation of motives behind the actions of the agencies that deal with crime. Many writers, of course, had long been pointing out that the "criminal-processing system" was often harsh and unfair, and, more specifically, that the poor and members of minority groups suffered from an acute disadvantage. Few criminologists, however, were willing to go so far as to claim that the system was inherently unjust. Rather, the usual argument was that our legal agencies were frequently defective due to lack of funds, unenlightened policies, and individual stupidity, prejudice and corruption. Now, however, among a large number of writers, the imputation of motives is of a different order: The operation of legal agencies is commonly interpreted as 1) the self-conscious use of the law to maintain the status quo for those who hold the power in society; or 2) activity aimed at maintaining organization self-interests, with "careerism" as both the carrot and the stick. If the system is unjust, then, we are not to look for relatively minor structural defects or random individual faults. Rather, the criminal law and its enforcement are largely instruments deliberately designed for the control of one social class by another.[7]

Third, the rightfulness of the criminal law had been questioned infrequently in the work of American criminologists, even if they were willing to admit that its application sometimes left something to be desired. The insanity plea, the definition of juvenile delinquency, the death sentence, the prohibition of gambling— these areas and a few others were open to vigorous critical scrutiny. By and large, however, the great bulk of the criminal law was taken as expressing a widely shared set of values. In any event, the question of "rightfulness" was not a suitable topic for the social sciences. In the last decade or so, however, there was a growing number of criminologists who found that assumption unrealistic. We could no longer accept the idea presented by Michael and Adler some forty years ago . . . that most of the people in any community would probably agree that most of the behavior which is proscribed by their criminal law is socially undesirable. According to the emerging "critical criminology," the criminal law should not be viewed as the collective moral judgments of society promulgated by a government that was defined as legitimate by almost all people. Instead, our society was best seen as a *Gebeitsverband,* a territorial group living under a regime imposed by a ruling few in the manner of a conquered province.[8] The argument was not that murder, rape and robbery had suddenly become respectable but that popular attitudes toward the sanctity of property, the sanctity of the physical person, and the rather puritanical morality embedded in the law were far less uniform than American criminology had been willing to admit.

Fourth, American criminologists had long been skeptical of the accuracy of official crime statistics which they nonetheless accepted, reluctantly, as a major source of data for their field. The Uniform Crime Reports of the Federal Bureau of Investigation were, after all, "the only game in town," as far as national figures on criminal behavior were concerned. If the use of other official statistics derived from cities, states and particular legal agencies were almost always coupled with disclaimers; still, they were used.

The problem with these statistics, as criminologists were quick to point out, was that they could lead to either overestimation or an underestimation of the total amount of crime in any given year, but no one could be sure which was the case. Furthermore, the components of the total crime rate might be in error, and some of the components might be too high while others were too low. The data were based on thousands of local police jurisdictions throughout the country, and even the FBI refused to vouch for their accuracy.

It was clear that a part of the difficulty was the fact that the police had a stake in the amount of crime recorded in official records: if the crime rate went down, the police could win public acclaim for their efficiency in dealing with the crime problem; if the crime rate went up, the police could demand greater financial and political support as they fought their battle with the underworld. This issue, however, was apt to be treated in a rather desultory fashion, in terms of developing a theory about the relationship between crime and society, or simply noted as one more difficulty placed in the path of securing precise data for the construction of a theory of crime causation. The essential task was to find ways to get "better" data, either by seeing to it that official statistics became more accurate, or by finding alternative ways to gather information about the true incidence of criminal behavior, such as self-reporting methods or sociological surveys using the reports of victims to uncover the amount of crime. Since the sixties, however, another view of the matter has become increasingly popular in criminological thought. Rather than dismissing the interest of law enforcement agencies in crime statistics as an unfortunate source of error, the collection and dissemination of information about the incidence of crime has become, for many, an important theoretical variable in its own right. The crime rate, writes Peter Manning, is "simply a construction of police activities," and the actual amount of crime is unknown and probably unknowable.[9] Whether there is more or less "actual" criminality . . . is not the issue. The crucial question is why societies and their agencies report, manufacture, or produce the volume of crime that they do.

The legitimacy of the rules embedded in the criminal law could no longer be taken for granted, then, and neither could the credibility of the government that reported on their violation. The most fruitful line of inquiry with regard to the causes of inaccuracy is not chance error or simple bias. Instead, we must look for a systematic distortion that is part of the machinery for social control.[10]

IV.

"Critical criminology" cannot, I think, be viewed as merely a matter of emphasis, with its major themes no more than bits and pieces of the conventional wisdom of the field. The set of ideas do form a coherent whole that is sufficiently different from much of American criminology of the period immediately before and after World War II to warrant the label "new." At the heart of this orientation lies the perspective of a stratified society in which the operation of the criminal law is a means of controlling the poor (and members of minority groups) by those in power who use the legal apparatus to 1) impose their particular morality and standards of good behavior on the entire society; 2) protect their property and physical safety from the depredations of the have-nots, even though the cost may be high in terms of the legal rights of those it perceives as a threat; and 3) extend the definition of illegal or criminal behavior to encompass those who might threaten the status quo. The middle classes or the lower-middle classes are drawn into this pattern of domination either because 1) they are led to believe they too have a stake in maintaining the status quo; or 2) they are made a part of agencies of social control and the rewards of organizational careers provide inducements for keeping the poor in their place.

The coercive aspects of this arrangement are hidden—at least in part—by labeling those who challenge the system as "deviants" or "criminals" when such labels carry connotations of social pathology, psychiatric illness and so on. If these interpretative schemes are insufficient to arouse widespread distaste for the rule-breaker as "bad" or "tainted," official statistics can serve to create a sense of a more direct and personal danger in the form of a crime wave that will convince many people (including many of the people in the lower classes) that draconian measures are justified.

The poor, according to this viewpoint, may or may not break the legal rules more often than others, although they will certainly be arrested more often and treated more harshly in order to prevent more extensive nonconformity. In a sense, they are expendable in the interest of general deterrence. In any event, they are probably driven in the direction of illegal behavior, even if they do not actually engage in it, because 1) the rules imposed on them from above have little relationship to the normative prescriptions of their own subculture; 2) the material frustrations of the lower classes in a consumer society where the fruits of affluence are publicized for all, but available only to some, prove almost unbearable; and 3) there is generated among the lower classes a deep hostility to a social order in which they are not allowed to participate and had little hand in the making.

The perspective sketched in above would seem to fit well with a radical view of American society, or at least with an ideological position on the left side of the political spectrum. While this might possibly account for the attention the perspective has received from some writers in the field of criminology (and some students with a very jaundiced view of the capitalist-industrial social order), I would very much doubt that critical criminology can be neatly linked to any special political position.[11]

At the same time, it does not appear that this new viewpoint in criminology simply grew out of the existing ideas in the field in some sort of automatic process where pure logic breeds uncontaminated by the concerns and passions of the times. Nor does it appear that a flood of new data burst upon the field, requiring a new theoretical synthesis. Instead, as I have suggested at the beginning of this article, it seems likely that the emergence of critical criminology is a part of the intellectual ferment taking place in sociology in general, and both have much of their source in the socio-historical forces at work in the 1960's.

Among the many elements that have been involved, there are at least three social-historical changes that appear to have played a major role. First, the impact of the Vietnam war on American society has yet to be thoroughly analyzed and assessed, but it is clear that it has had an influential part in the rise of a widespread cynicism concerning the institutions of government, the motives of those in power, and the credibility of official pronouncements. The authority of the state has been called into question, including the authority of the state made manifest in the law as its instrument. The good intentions —indeed, the good sense—of those running the apparatus of the state have, for many, become suspect. The truth of official statements, whether it be body counts or crime counts, is no longer easily accepted among many segments of the population. The notion of a Social Contract as the basis of government may have been long recognized as a fiction in American life, but it was also widely accepted as a metaphor expressing a belief in government by consent. In the 1960's, there were many people (including many in the social sciences) who felt that the metaphor was coming apart. Government was far more apt to be seen as manipulation and coercion, and the legal rules could be more easily interpreted, at least by some, as part of a social order imposed by a ruling elite. "Property is theft," said Proudhon in 1840. In the 1960's, his curt saying had taken on a new bite.

Second, the growth of a counter-culture in the United States in the last decade admittedly remains within the realm of those ideas that are far from precise. Yet, there seems no question that a shift in values and ideas did take place and that the use of drugs— particularly marijuana—was a major theme. The arguments about drugs have been repeated so often, the facts and theories elaborated upon in such familiar detail, that discussion of the subject has taken on the appearance of a litany. Nonetheless, for present purposes, it is important to point out that millions of people engaged in behavior they regarded as harmless, but that was defined by society as a crime— not a minor or relatively harmless breach of the law, according to the authorities, but a serious, dangerous offense. Whatever may have been the consequences in terms of popular attitudes toward the law and law-enforcement agencies, another reaction was let loose, namely, a long skeptical look at traditional ideas about the nature of the criminal and the causes of criminal behavior.

In addition, as a consumer-oriented middle class wedded to

establishment values emerged as a favorite whipping boy in the analysis of what was wrong with American life, evidence of white-collar crime took on a new prominence.[12] Far from being a form of behavior largely confined to those at the bottom of the social heap, crime was everywhere. "If you are a typical American citizen," says Erik Olin Wright, "chances are that in your life you have committed some crime for which you could have been sent to jail or prison." [13] If this were true, and if the people caught up and punished by the system of criminal justice were so largely drawn from the lower classes, then the machinery of the criminal law must be far from fair or impartial. If you were labeled a criminal, something more than criminal behavior must be involved.

Third, the rise of political protest in the 1960's took on a variety of forms, ranging from heated discussions to bloody confrontations in the streets. It became clear that even the most dispassionate of observers would have to agree that in a number of instances the police power of the state had been used illegally to suppress political dissent. Some accounts, such as those dealing with the deliberate elimination of the Black Panther leadership, might be shown to have been slipshod in their facts; other accounts might be hopelessly confusing when it came to pinning down precisely the illegality of police actions. Enough evidence remained, however, to show that the police had been used in many instances beyond the limits of the law to silence political opposition. In addition, there were a large number of cases (more murky, perhaps, in terms of being able to disentangle the facts) in which it was believed that the law had acted legally to apprehend and punish a law breaker, but in which the law's actions were due to the individual's social and political beliefs rather than to his criminal behavior. The criminal law, in short, was seen by many as becoming more than a device for controlling run-of-the-mill criminality. It was becoming an arm of Leviathan, not as a matter of abstract theory, but as something directly experienced or immediately observed.[14]

It was the intellectual climate produced by these and similar social-historical events, I would argue, that played a major part in the rise of critical criminology, as much as any forces at work within the field of traditional criminology itself. The new perspective is touched by ideology, but not determined by it; incorporates points made before, but builds something different; and offers a new interpretation or point of view rather than a vast quantity of new data. All of this, of course, leaves untouched the issue of the potential contribution of this perspective to the study of crime and society.

V.

Is critical criminology valid? The question is really an un-answerable one, I believe, because what we are confronted with is not so much a body of precise, systematic theoretical propositions as a viewpoint, a perspective, or an orientation—terms that I have de-liberately used throughout the discussion. A theory states the rela-tionships among a number of variables that are well defined; a viewpoint, on the other hand, urges us to look in one direction rather than another, points to promising lines of inquiry, singles out one interpretation from a set of possible interpretations dealing with the same set of facts. In this sense, the viewpoint of critical criminology as it stands today probably cannot be said to be true or false. Rather, it is a bet on what empirical research and the-oretical development in the field will reveal in the future. In many ways, I think the bet is not a bad one.

However, before examining what some of the contributions of critical criminology might be, let us look briefly at its more obvious defects. In the first place, criminologists writing from this perspec-tive have a tendency to uncover the latent functions of the criminal law and its operation and then convert these latent functions into manifest ones—unfortunately, all too easily.[15] That is to say, the administration of the criminal law frequently works to the disad-vantage of the poor, members of minority groups and the unedu-cated. It is then assumed, often with little concrete evidence, that this, in fact, is the intended and recognized goal of those adminis-tering the criminal law. The task of sociological analysis, however, requires a good deal more than this rather superficial imputation of motive which is apt to degenerate into glib cynicism.

In the second place, a number of writers who are exploring the ideas we have presented under the heading of "critical crim-inology" often use a model of social stratification that is either overly simplified or ambiguous. We are frequently presented with the poor on the one hand, and the Establishment or those in power on the other, with a vaguely defined middle class being portrayed sometimes as another victim of injustice and sometimes as a co-opted agent of those on the top of the socio-economic scale. In reality, however, there is probably a great deal of variation in different socio-economic groups in attitudes toward the criminal law and its administration (such as lower class support of the police and upper class use of drugs); and, if this is true, the idea that the criminal law is predominantly something imposed from above has need to be substantially modified.

In the third place, we may all indeed be criminals, in the sense that most adults have committed an act at one time or another that would be called a crime by the criminal law. This does not mean, however, that we are all murderers, rapists, robbers, burglars and auto thieves. Persistent criminals or criminals considered serious may be singled out for the law's attention without reducing a criminal conviction to a mere label that has no connection with an objective reality. Labeling theory in sociology has never quite come to grips with the relationship between the dynamics of the labeling process and the realities of the behavior being categorized. . . . If critical criminology is to make a significant contribution to a sociology of crime, it will need to avoid the error of believing that because the legal stigma of crimes does not match the occurrence of crime-in-general in the population, the stigma is necessarily based on irrelevant factors such as income and race. Certain patterns of criminal behavior may still have much to do with the matter.

While recognizing these strictures, I think it can be argued that "critical criminology" holds out the promise of having a profound impact on our thinking about crime and society. It forces an inquiry into precisely how the normative content of the criminal law is internalized in different segments of society, and how norm-holding is actually related to behavior. It makes us examine how the legal apparatus designed for the control of crime takes on a life of its own, and begins to pursue objectives that may have little to do with modifying the crime rate. It directs needed attention to the relationship between the political order and nonconformity, thus revitalizing one of sociology's most profound themes, the relationship between the individual and the state. And it impels us, once again, to analyze equality before the law as a basic element of a democratic society. As T. H. Marshall has pointed out, much of the history of the last 250 years or so in Western societies can be seen as an attempt to achieve citizenship for all, which he defines as a kind of basic human equality associated with the concept of full membership in a community.[16] The concept of legal equality emerged in the eighteenth century, the concept of political equality in the nineteenth, and the concept of social equality in the twentieth. But none of the gains can be taken for granted, for they can be lost as well as won. In the administration of the criminal law in our society today, there is ample evidence that our ideals of equality before the law are being compromised by the facts of income and race in an industrial, highly bureaucratized social order. If a "critical criminology" can help us solve that issue, while still confronting the need to control crime, it will contribute a great deal.

NOTES

1. See, e.g., Mazyur, *The Littlest Science,* 3 AM. SOCIOLOGIST 195 (1968).

2. See, e.g., Gouldner, *Anti-Minotaur: The Myth of a Value-Free Sociology,* 9 SOCIAL PROBLEMS 199 (1962).

3. See H. MANNHEIM, COMPARATIVE CRIMINOLOGY (1965).

4. See R. QUINNEY, THE PROBLEM OF CRIME (1970).

5. See R. MERTON, SOCIAL THEORY AND SOCIAL STRUCTURE (1949).

6. A. TURK, CRIMINALITY AND THE LEGAL ORDER (1969).

7. See, e.g., J. DOUGLAS, CRIME AND JUSTICE IN AMERICAN SOCIETY xviii (J. Douglas ed. 1971): If there were no groups trying to control the activities of other groups, and capable of exercising sufficient power to try to enforce their wills upon those other groups through the legislative processes, there would be no laws making some activities 'crimes' and there could, consequently, be no 'criminals'. . . .

[C]riminal laws are specifically enacted by the middle and upper class to place the poorer classes under the more direct control of the police.

8. See M. WEBER, THE THEORY OF SOCIAL AND ECONOMIC ORGANIZATION 337 (T. Parsons ed. 1947).

9. Manning, *The Police: Mandate, Strategies, and Appearances,* in CRIME AND JUSTICE IN AMERICAN SOCIETY 169 (J. Douglas ed. 1971).

10. See Biderman and Reiss, Jr., *On Exploring the 'Dark Figure' of Crime,* 374 ANNALS 15 (1967): Any set of crime statistics, including those of the survey, involves some evaluative, institutional processing of people's reports. Concepts, definitions, quantitative models, and theories must be adjusted to the fact that the data are not some objectively observable universe of 'criminal acts,' but rather those events defined, captured and processed as such by some institutional mechanism.

11. In the current intellectual climate, there are a great many pressures to identify particular scientific ideas with particular ideological positions. Ideas and ideology, however, still exhibit a peculiar independence despite strident claims that they must go together; and if some criminologists believe that the viewpoint of critical criminology is something that must be considered, there is no iron necessity that ties them to either a liberal or a conservative stance. For an illuminating examination of the issue in another field, see Herrnstein, *On Challenging an Orthodoxy,* 55 COMMENTARY 52 (1973).

12. It should be pointed out, to underline the idea that these ideas were not the sole property of a particular ideological position, that attacks on the middle class style of life often came from the Right as well as the Left, with much discussion of the perils of a lower middle class moving into affluence.

13. E. WRIGHT, THE POLITICS OF PUNISHMENT 3 (1973).

14. *See* T. BECKER, POLITICAL TRIALS (1971).

15. I am here following the usage provided by Robert Merton, who defines manifest functions as the objective consequences of social action intended and recognized by the actors involved, whereas latent functions are consequences that are neither intended nor recognized. *See* R. MERTON, *supra* note 5, at ch. 1.

16. T. H. MARSHALL, CITIZENSHIP AND SOCIAL CLASS (1950).

Part Two
*Contemporary
Approach to
Political Crime*

Introduction

Political crime is one of the most neglected subject matters of criminology. Although it might be regarded as the oldest crime type and no era of man's social history can pride itself in not having suffered it in one form or another and despite the fact that in our contemporary world the rate of political crime and the brutality of its commission are growingly alarming, even contemporary criminology has paid but little attention to its analysis. Louis Proal wrote about it, emphasizing its historical perspectives, by the end of the nineteenth century. Yet, his thoughts are still fresh even in our time, and the profile he depicted might be seen as if it were drawn by the contemporay criminologist.

Still, while we may "feel" it, criminal law and criminology have not defined what political crime really is. Stephen Schafer attempts to demonstrate the difference between ordinary and political crimes, and, at the same time, to show the difficulties of this distinction by pointing out the relativity of political crimes. The similarity of political crime with heroism and then again with pseudopolitical crime poses barriers to clear insight.

What the personality characteristics of a social political criminal type, the political assassin, are can be sensed by Conrad V. Hassel's discussion. Physical appearance, psychological peculiarities, psychiatric state of mind, family background, and other characteristics are presented in his effort to picture who the political criminal actually is and also what challenge this offender poses to the law enforcement community.

Much depends on the socio-political structure of the society, as John M. Steiner contends, since if the ordinary man can not see any alternatives and experiences, his only way of survival is to adjust to all constraints; he might be ready to serve the prevailing power and its ideology, even if this involves violence and injustices.

Chapter Four

Political Crime

Louis Proal

. . .

Lord Brougham has affirmed that "sobriety, integrity, love of the public good, and disinterestedness, virtues foreign to a court, spring up naturally on a democratic soil." Virtues never spring up naturally; it is only vices that spring up without effort as weeds do; virtues, like useful plants, require to be cultivated if they are to spring up on democratic soil. Corruption is prevalent under all forms of government. Tribunes of the people are corruptible as well as senators. During the last years of the Roman Republic they showed themselves every whit as greedy as the patricians for the gold of Jugurtha. The King of Numidia made grants to begin with to all whose influence in the Senate was great; the moment his emissaries made gold to gleam before their eyes, the senators were fascinated by the huge sums offered them. Jugurtha, however, did not overlook the tribunes of the people, for he had advised his emissaries "to try the effect of gold upon all consciences." Babius, a tribune of the people, was no more incorruptible than Calpurnius or Scaurus. All, patricians and plebeians alike, were glad to be bribed, and Jugurtha, on leaving Rome, dis-

Reprinted by permission of Patterson Smith Publishing Corp.

gusted at so much greed, could not refrain from exclaiming: "Venal city, that will speedily perish if it finds a buyer."

Aristophanes in his admirable comedies has scourged not only the impudence of demagogues, but their venality as well. A pork-butcher, addressing Cleon, says to him: "You resemble those who fish for eels; in clear water they catch nothing, but if they only stir up the mud they make a good haul; in the same way it is only in times of trouble that you line your pockets . . ." The people: "Ah! rogue, so this is how you rob me, I who loaded you with crowns and presents." Cleon: *"I stole in the public interest."* The people: "Quickly return me that crown." Cleon: "Good-bye, crown; . . . so another is going to possess you; assuredly he will not be a greater thief, but perhaps he will be luckier. . . . I admit that I am a thief. Do you allow that you are another?" Cleon's rival has no scruples in making the admission; he hastens to add that he has been guilty of perjury as well, and that, being the greater rogue of the two, he deserves to come off best. "To steal, to commit perjury," he says, "that is the way to reach a high position." These being his principles, a brilliant future had been predicted him while he was young. "There is the stuff of a statesman in him."

It would seem that when a man is called upon to take part in the conduct of public affairs the sentiment of his responsibility and his concern for the public good should raise him morally to the level required by his situation. Unhappily, considered closely, many great politicians from the moral standpoint are very petty; their lives often offer the spectacle of irregularities and vices that create astonishment, and that contrast with the fine sentiments with which they adorn their speeches. Disinterestedness is not, as a rule, a virtue of statesmen. But there have been politicians who have become famous solely because they were honest.

. . .

[However,] the [Roman] governors who pillaged the provinces set aside a portion of their ill-gotten gain for the judges before whom they would have to appear to answer for their crimes. Verres declared that he had distributed in this fashion what three years of his Sicilian pretorship had brought him in; that he considered himself fortunate if the product of a single year remained for himself, and that he had reserved for his judges that of the third year, the best and the most fruitful.

. . .

Political corruption also existed in Athens and even at the most glorious period of its history, the century of Pericles. Politicians were wont "to occupy themselves with the conduct of public affairs with the intention of making money out of their posts and of pushing their own interests." The orators Stratocles and Democlides "used to invite each other to proceed to their golden harvest, referring mockingly in these terms to the rostrum whence they addressed the people."

. . .

The politicians of the period kept up their popularity by gifts to the people; corrupt themselves, they were the corrupters of others. Pericles himself, as the author of the measure by which those who attended the public deliberations, the public games, and even the fêtes received payment, introduced corrupt habits into Athens, which, in the end, caused the democracy to degenerate into a demagogy. The people kept honest citizens out of the public functions, reserving them for the demagogues who flattered them and made them distributions of money.

. . .

England also has traversed periods of corruption. The most precise details are found in the Memoirs of Commines, touching the venality of the chief personages in England under the reign of Edward. Louis XI. paid "some sixteen thousand pensions to ministers, great persons, and courtiers." Lord Hastings, the Lord Chamberlain, let himself be bought like so many others by the King of France; "he raised great difficulties before he would become a pensioner of the King," because he was already in receipt of a pension of a thousand crowns from the Duke of Burgundy, but yielding to the pressure brought to bear upon him by Commines, he was induced to accept the offers of Louis XI., who had him offered double what the Duke of Burgundy was giving him. Louis XI. ordered Pierre Claret, his steward, to remit him two thousand crowns, and to demand a receipt, "so that in the time to come it should be patent and known how the Lord Chamberlain, Chancellor, Admiral and Equerry of England, with many others, had been the pensioners of the King of France." Pierre Claret had an interview with the Lord Chamberlain in private. "After having said to him what was necessary on the part of the King, he handed him the two thousand crowns in gold, for money was never given great foreign personages in any other form." The emissary of Louis XI. asked Lord Hastings for a receipt, or at least for a brief letter, so that he might not be suspected by his master of having kept the money for himself. The Lord Chamberlain, however, replied: "This gift comes to me of the good pleasure of the King, your master, and not at my request; if you wish me to take it, you will place it here in my sleeve, and there will be no letter or witnesses, for I do not wish that by my fault it shall be said, 'The Lord Chamberlain of England has been the pensioner of the King of France,' nor that my receipts be found in his office of accounts."

Chancellor Bacon was also guilty of peculation, and was a corrupt magistrate. Brought up before the House of Lords, he confessed his errors in these terms: "After examination of the accusation made against me, sounding my conscience, and recalling my conduct as far back as I am able, I confess fully and sincerely that I have been guilty of corruption. I renounce any attempt to defend myself, and abandon myself to the clemency and mercy of your Lordships." A commission of the House of Lords waited upon Bacon to inquire whether he was really the author of the letter containing these confessions, which he then renewed, saying: "My Lords, I am indeed the author of this letter in which I accuse myself. The letter is my work, the work of my hand and of my heart. I implore your Lordships to be full of pity for a poor broken reed."

Seven Kings of England bought the votes of Members of Parliament at the price of a pension.

. . .

The Dutch Deputies and the great Polish nobles were no more incorruptible than were the Ministers. "Amongst the Dutch," says Louis XIV., "there were several Deputies to whom I caused pensions to be paid. I gave considerable pensions, too, to several Polish nobles, in order that I might dispose of their votes at the election which was in prospect. I had pensioners in Ireland, whose work was to stir up the Catholics against the English. I was further in treaty with certain refugees from England, to whom I promised important sums, that they might revive the activity of what remained of the Cromwell faction. I gave the King of Denmark one hundred thousand crowns to induce him to join the league against the King of England, and later I presented the Queen, his wife, with a necklace of pearls; I gave another necklace to the Electress of Brandenburg, and made the Queen of Sweden an important present, having no doubt but that these princesses, overlooking the general interests of their States, would feel themselves honoured in their own persons by the pains I took to secure their friendship. Being aware of the influence enjoyed in Sweden by the Chancellor, and that the Prince of Anhalt and the Count of Schwerin had the ear of the Elector of Brandenburg, it was my wish to secure their good offices by my liberality." It is clear that Louis XIV. spared no expense to procure himself allies in the foreign courts. "It often happens," he says, "that moderate sums, dispensed opportunely and with judgment, keep States from incomparably greater outlays and losses. In the absence of support it was possible to acquire at small cost, it is sometimes necessary to raise great armies. A neighbour, who might have been made our friend with a slight expenditure, sometimes costs us very dearly when he becomes our enemy." When engaged in a negotiation with the House of Austria, in the interest of the Duke d'Enghien, he purchased the good offices of a high functionary attached to the person of the Emperor for 100,000 crowns.

Corruption continued to be prevalent in England after the revolution of 1688. Numerous scandals cropped up in the course of 1695.

· · ·

The English Members of Parliament who sold their votes paid heavily for their seats. Lord Chesterfield wrote to his son (letter of the 19th December, 1767) that he had entered into negotiations with an agent for the sale of rotten boroughs for the purchase of a seat in Parliament, and that he had offered him £2,500, but had received the reply that it was no longer possible to find a borough at the price, the rich Indian merchants having bought up all that were in the market at much higher prices. The purchase of a borough was a speculation; seats were bought that votes might be sold. The electioneering agents even attempted to procure a quotation for seats on the Stock Exchange, and it actually came about that a tariff was established for certain boroughs. The spectacle was witnessed of boroughs offering themselves to the candidate who bid the most. Oxford offered to elect the candidate who would pay the debts of the town, and concluded the bargain with the Duke of Marlborough.

According to Lord John Russell £5,000 was paid for a seat in Parliament during the early years of the 19th century. Wilberforce admitted that his elections had cost him £8,000. The rotten boroughs were suppressed in 1832. Electoral and political corruption have since diminished, but they have not disappeared. In 1878, two English men of business boasted in public that they possessed infallible means of influencing the members of a committee entrusted with the examination of a Bill.

· · ·

Numerous were the Ministers who were convicted of peculation under the old régime. Numerous, too, were the courts of justice instituted with the object of forcing the financiers to disgorge the money of which they had robbed the Treasury.

· · ·

On 25th April, 1328, Pierre Rémi, principal treasurer to Charles the Handsome, was hanged, under Philip of Valois, for malversations committed in Guyenne and for "great thefts of royal moneys"; in a few years he had amassed one million two hundred thousand francs, which represents twenty millions of modern French money. He was hanged on the gibbet of Montfaucon, which he caused to be reconstructed, and the King regained possession by confiscation of what he had been robbed. In 1409 Jean de Montague, who had enriched himself in the financial administration, was condemned to be beheaded. During the reign of Charles VII., Jean de Xaintoings, Receiver-General of Finances, was arrested for having dissipated and wrongly employed the moneys of the King, extensive sums of which it was proven he had stolen. He was also declared guilty of forgery. Still he was only condemned to a few years' imprisonment and to the confiscation of all his possessions.

. . .

Marshal de Marillac, sentenced to death under Richelieu for peculation, could not understand such severity. "A man of my station condemned to death for peculation!" he cried. Richelieu showed himself pitiless. He considered the art of finance as one of the principal parts of politics; it is the more indispensable in a State, he adds, in that money is the soul of all affairs. A commonwealth is only strong in proportion to the richness of the public treasury. Mazarin was far less severe upon those guilty of peculation: it is known that he was not above reproach himself, and that he left behind him after his death a fortune of 50 millions, which would represent 200 millions to-day.

. . .

In the preamble to the decree announcing the institution of the Chamber of Justice of 1661, the King declared: "In these recent times, a small number of persons have built up rapid and prodigious fortunes by illegitimate means. Their immense acquisitions, their insolent pomp, their boundless opulence, offer an example calculated to corrupt all the maxims of public honesty." The persons referred to in the preamble of the edict were the financiers, who occupied a prominent position in the society of the 17th century, La Bruyère depicts them buying titles of nobility and marrying their daughters to courtiers. "If a financier is unsuccessful the courtiers say of him he is a commoner, a nobody, a vulgar fellow; if he is successful they demand the hand of his daughter. . . . A very rich man may . . . introduce a duke into his family and make a nobleman of his son. . . ."

. . .

The spectacle of the nobility manœuvring to be invited to the houses of financiers is not peculiar to our own time.

. . .

A new and very severe decree against peculation was issued in 1701; it ordained that those convicted of this crime should suffer the death penalty. Nevertheless the depredations of the financiers continued.

At the death of Louis XIV. public opinion again demanded the repression of the abuses committed by the financiers. A new Chamber of Justice was instituted in March, 1716. It gave the judges who were to compose the chamber power to pass capital and penal sentences, and to impose fines. It was authorised, too, to take proceedings against persons of every kind, of whatever birth and station, who should have been guilty of peculation. These severe dispositions did not last, and a decree dated September 18th of the same year, 1716, permitted capital and penal sentences to be transmuted into fines. In the end the Chamber of Justice concerned itself with decreeing taxes rather than with anything else.

· · ·

The history of the Chambers of Justice comes to an end here, but the history of crimes of corruption does not terminate with it. On the contrary, under the Regent with Law and the Cardinal Dubois, and under Louis XV., corruption continues on a growing scale. The King himself speculated in wheat, and was one of the shareholders in the notorious company of the "compact of famine," which brought about the artificial famines of 1768 and 1769. The corrupt practices of this period are so generally known that I consider it useless to relate them over again.

It is easier for a people to carry through a political revolution than a moral revolution, to change its régime than to change its conscience. During the Revolution the politicians continued to make money, and the financiers did not cease to league themselves with the politicians. The most passionate demagogues combined business with politics.

· · ·

To rehabilitate these demagogues it has been stated that many of them died poor, but this poverty is no proof of their morality. They died poor because they dissipated their ill-acquired riches; their hands were empty but not clean; their pockets were emptied as soon as they were filled.

Corruption under the Directory attained still further development. The type of the politicians of this period is Barras, an avaricious, unprincipled rake, who pledged himself to all parties and had a finger in every conspiracy. Bonaparte called him the most corrupt of the corrupt.

· · ·

Political morality improved under the Empire and the Restoration. The passion for military glory, the reawakening of the religious sentiment, and later the love of political liberty raised the moral level. Devotion to the national flag silenced the love of riches; the feelings uppermost in the minds of the soldiers of the Empire were esteem for courage and the sentiment of honour; consideration and honours were the reward of military virtues. Napoleon I. had a liking for honest men. Still he more than once endeavoured to corrupt men, and he took for his Ministers men of dubious honesty, such as Fouché and Talleyrand. At the close of his reign he regretted his action and said: For the future I wish to have none but honest men about me.

. . .

Chapter Five

The Relativity of Political Crimes

Stephen Schafer

DISTINCTION BETWEEN ORDINARY AND POLITICAL CRIMES

In the broadest sense, it may be argued that all crimes are political crimes inasmuch as all prohibitions with penal sanctions represent the defense of a given value system, or morality, in which the prevailing social power believes. Taking this to the very extreme, even a bank robbery, a shoplifting, or a rape is a political crime. After all, making such acts criminal offenses is a protection of the interests, values, and beliefs of the lawmaking power, actually the political-social system, which regards certain things as right and worthy of safeguarding with the threat of penal consequences.[1]

Whatever is called crime in law, by definition, constitutes a legal relationship between the official state and the members of the society. But this seemingly administrative and formalistic legal relationship is in its real essence a political relationship, since it pertains to the terms of existence between the state, as a political power, and

Reprinted by permission of MacMillan Publishing Co., Inc. (The Free Press), from *The Political Criminal*, 1974, pp. 19–37.

the members of the society who live under this power, or rather, to the place and role of these men in their state. That is, it defines what is permitted and what is prohibited them in their political society. Thus, the legal relationship between the state and its members is an ideological-societal relationship where the the stipulations of criminal law serve as safeguards of the various values of the ideology that the state power wants to see implemented. While it is not uncommon to meet arguments which strive admirably to propose that the political state power is for creating conditions to implement the values and goals of the society, the brutal reality suggests that the power creates the societal values and goals and enforces the conditions in which they are fulfilled.

Human behaviors that are qualified as crimes by the law, therefore, represent counterideological-societal conditions declared as nondesirable by the social-political state power. The interests, values, and beliefs of this power, whatever its operational structure may be, are expressed through legal norms. Among these norms are the rules and definitions of criminal law which, in order to enable the state to exercise control over accentuated ideological issues, declare certain acts to be crimes. In the definition of crimes, then, the state power's political ideology is translated into legal terms. Bank robbery, shoplifting, and rape, to mention examples, are crimes because the political state power ideologically believes in protecting other people's money, in allowing honest customers to browse through displayed goods in stores, and in protecting the bodily or sexual integrity of females. From this point of view, David Riesman's question, "Who has the power?" [2] and the contention of C. Wright Mills that the power is in the hands of an exploitative elite [3] are irrelevant, since all types of social powers are political powers and all have some kind of ideology mirrored by the criminal law.

When the political state power expresses its ideology, or value system, through the regulations of the criminal code, it determines the "norms of action" *(norma agendi)* and, at the same time, authorizes the executive organs of the state to apply penal sanctions in order to enforce the observance of these norms or, in other words, the acceptance of the value system. The question of which specific values or interests are so protected is dependent upon the legislators, as the political agents of the state power who conceive and pass criminal laws.

Since the analysis of what political crime is requires a conceptual rather than a definitional approach,[4] the general notion of political offenses might reasonably be equated with the concept of ordinary crimes. Whether it be treason, murder, drug use, embezzlement, homosexuality, arson, or whatever, ultimately and in the final examination, each is determined to be a crime by the legislators' philosophical, ideological, and political postures that construct in the form of law "the formal expression of the value system of the prevailing social power." [5] Asuming this is so, the distinction between ordinary and political crimes becomes difficult to determine since all crimes might be viewed from the concept of political orientation and as ideological in nature. Thus, all crimes may be qualified as political crimes.

As a matter of fact, the more pronounced the ideology of the political-social power, and the less possible the participation of ordinary men and social groups in the decision-making processes, then the easier it is to see that all crimes are of a political nature. In the heavily ideological political structure, the concept of criminal responsibility is spelled out more vividly, the ideological basis of all crime definitions is less concealed, and the suprauniversalistic interpretation of the crime problem is more openly admitted. In this suprauniversalistic understanding of crime, the political-social power emphasizes the political ideology so that it stands above not only individual interests, but also above the conventional group interests of the society (that is, the interests of the "universe"). [6]

While in other types of political structures the ideological foundations of the so-called ordinary crimes are not so apparent, and these crimes are most often seen only as disturbances of legally protected individual interests, in the suprauniversalistically oriented societies criminal law offers direct protection and care not so much to individuals or groups, but outrightly to the ideas of the ideology itself.

The German *Täterstrafrecht* (criminal law as it involves the criminal) in the Third Reich, for example, tended to disregard the rigidly formalistic definition of crimes and to establish the degree of responsibility in accordance with the political personality of the criminal, even if he was the perpetrator of a traditionally "ordinary" crime. This proposition, to some extent, separated the criminal from his objective relation to his crime and victim and subjected his human conduct to a judgment directed by the supreme ideology. This approach attempted to find what was called the "normative type" of criminal, and the penal consequences of his responsibility would be decided by the deviation of his personality—and not his actions—from the ideologically saturated and politically interpreted norm. Capital punishment under this concept would not necessarily be inflicted on a person who actually committed a murder, but on any individual who, in view of his total personality, should be regarded as a "murderer type," regardless of whether he committed a homicide or not.

This concept ideologized the interpretation of all crimes so extensively that the criminal act and its legal definition were no more than aids to the political evaluation of crimes. It suggested that the *Volksanschauung* (public view) cannot be satisfied with a simple "symptom" (that is, the criminal offense), because the criminal is not always what one particular crime makes him appear to be. Eric Wolf claimed that "political liberalism and religious naturalism" are over, and therefore the "ethically indifferent positivistic individualism" should be replaced by "phenomenological personalism." [7] Wolf as well as Georg Dahm,[8] the pioneers of this normative typology, emphasized an ideological understanding of crime, in fact of all crimes, and proposed that the *Volksanchauung* should operate to control "disobedience and resistance" against the "national socialistic state."

In this kind of elastic concept, which so strongly disregards any distinction between ordinary and political crimes, not the personal drama of the criminal and his victim, but the drama of the offender and the ideology is of paramount importance, and all crimes are actually confused with political sins. In this suprauniversalistic concept of crime, the virtual absence of ordinary offenses has substituted for the personal victim the idea of a victimized ideology. The net result of this exaggeration by which all crimes are seen as having political origins is, necessarily, the suppression of legal arguments, and it may ultimately make the judicial agents of the political-social power the definers of what a crime actually is.

· · ·

When Martitz claimed that the term "political crime" is an expression of the political language, and not the language of the law,[9] he did not pay attention to the real world's cruel fact that the language of the law in truth is the political language.

Indeed, criminal laws do not even distinguish between ordinary and political crimes, criminal codes just talk about crimes in general, even if the definition of one or another crime indicates the element of "political" motives, and only a few codes, if any, qualify certain criminal offenses explicitly as political crimes. The term "political crime," as commonly used, is not the offspring of criminal law. It is in fact a somewhat artificial and arbitrary product of international law which facilitates the processes of extradition and the possibility of offering asylum for certain fugitive criminals. How much of these crimes, then, demonstrates political motivation, and how much displays the components of a so-called ordinary crime, is a question that does not clearly lead to a general classification that would distinctly differentiate between the ordinary and political violations of law. The catalog of political crimes only shows that hardly any of them lack at least a portion of the act that would be judged as an ordinary criminal offense if they were not committed from political motives. This dioecious nature of political crimes prompted Heinrich Lammasch to call them relative offenses.[10]

However, in view of the political-ideological cradle of all crimes, it might be more appropriate to see the common or ordinary offenses as relative political crimes, as opposed to the absolute political crimes where the target of the lawbreaking is the ruling power's value system as a whole, rather than a part or an issue of it. Shoplifting and robbery, for example, are criminal attacks against the value attached to private property, and even abortion and homosexuality are assaults only against single issues of the political power's ideology. The political nature of these kinds of crimes is only occasionally conspicuous; thus, these "ordinary" crimes may be tentatively called "relative political crimes." But where the unlawful battery of the criminal is aimed at the sum total of the lawfully prevailing ideology or value system, or at least at one of its representative or critical institutions, for the sake of approaching the concept of the political criminal, and through that the problem of morality and crime, the violation of the legal norm might be called an "absolute political crime."

LAWMAKING AND JUSTICE

The absolute political criminals, that is, those who inflict a criminal blow upon the ideology as a whole or who at least attempt to assault it, almost always act in the name of what they think is justice. They believe in an ideal universal concept of justice, often confused with morality, that would symbolize an unqualified, unconditional, and self-existent fairness, as they conceive it, and they usually refuse to accept the thesis which suggests that justice means only what those who are in power agree to make it mean.[11] They believe in the unjust nature of the prevailing value system and the law that reflects it, and they tend to reject hearing Northrop's question: Is there any objectively determinable standard, in other words an "is" other than the living law against which the goodness or badness of the living law can be measured?[12]

The political criminal is both appalled and perturbed by the a priorism, subjectivism, and complacency of the lawmakers, with their enthusiasm for sitting in armchairs and laying down the social-political power's law about the functioning of the human mind, the human predicament, and so forth, and their rationales for doing so.

However, hardly any political criminal can be persuaded to assume that he himself would not act otherwise, should he be the one who is sitting in this armchair in the event that his crime, aimed at replacing other people's justice with his own, is successful.

The discrepancy between the ruling power and the political criminal on the nature of lawmaking and justice is a disconcerting theme common to all ages. The quest for an answer (incidentally, often neglected by sociological criminology in the search for social crime factors) has failed to achieve a comforting resolution. It offers only a frustrating and depressing experience to both parties as well as to those students of sociology and criminology who are interested in the puzzle of lawmaking and justice, or better, in the justice of lawmaking.

Law, in view of its representing the governing value system, is a political phenomenon. And, perhaps, the depth of this petulant disagreement on the meaning of the battered idea of justice between the ruling power and the absolute political criminal calls for the challenge of the tempering assumption that the two positions are logically not incompatible, appearances notwithstanding, since no lawmaking is really conceivable without manipulated justice. It is a familiar ground to students of the sociology of law that although the procedure of a trial, so the myth runs, is designed by neutral rules to find the truth, the judges are likely to confuse the combat against crime, which is their business, and the fight against broader social menace, which is not. The courtroom is almost always stuffed with the ruling power's value system, and the outcome of a case is dependent on the judges' perception of these values.

The painful pivot of the question to keep in mind is that both the bearer of the social-political power and the political criminal are men. Therefore, the man-committed crimes in general, and naturally among them the so-called political crimes, are dependent upon the man-made law, and, thus, as long as the existing power prevails, its understanding of justice, as ritually declared, is "right" and consequently must not be attacked beyond certain limits.[13] Since by definition the "conservatives" tend to conserve this justice, the "radicals" are those who attempt to change it, and thus are usually, or rather necessarily, the political criminals.

This idea probably motivated Havelock Ellis to suggest that the word criminal in the expression "political criminal" is a euphemism to spell out the suppression of a small minority by the majority.[14] And while Hugo Grotius, from the opposite point of view, cited Tertullian, who proposed that every man is by birth a soldier with a mission to combat criminals guilty of treason, Louis Proal, a judge of the Court of Appeal at Aix, cited the anarchist Valliant, who proposed that the citizen has the same rights whether acting in self-defense against the tyrant or against an enemy.[15]

The question, of course, is who are the "radicals" and "anarchists" and who are the "conservatives," and which of them, and in what circumstances, are really the political criminals. The question inevitably leads to the problem of the relativity of law and justice, and, consequently, to the riddle of relativity in the concept of "absolute political crime," a characteristic that is only rarely obvious in the changing nature of "relative political crimes," or, as they are commonly called, "ordinary crimes." Ultimately it is a question that guides us to the understanding of man, should he be the powerful or the powerless—a multidimensional being whose consciousness, morality, justice, and freedom can be approached from different points of view, none of which can claim to be the only legitimate one.[16]

Perhaps this consideration led Havelock Ellis to contend that the word criminal in the term "political criminal" is "an abuse of language," and to suggest that such a concept may be necessary only to ensure the supremacy of a government, just as the concept of heresy is necessary to ensure the supremacy of the Church. The political criminal of our time or place, he argued, may be the hero, martyr, or saint of another age or land.[17] A monarch, for example, is the incarnate personification of conservation, and yet, as Maurice Parmelee contrasted, Charles I in England and Louis XVI in France were beheaded as political criminals. And, as he continued, although "there is perhaps nothing in human culture more archaic than religion," under the French Revolution the clergy were proscribed as criminals.[18] To mention a more modern example, the abrupt and rapid changes in the lawmaking power structure at the time of the Hungarian revolution in 1956 resulted in criminals becoming heroes and then again criminals, and law-abiding citizens turning into criminals and then again into conformists—all within eight days.[19]

These few examples may sufficiently demonstrate that there is great complexity in the structure of the idea of justice and that the assessor of the battle between the lawmaking ruling power and the political criminal cannot safely determine which of them is supported by justice. The history of the philosophy of law, from the earliest beliefs in divine or superhuman commands to contemporary models of social engineering, could not reflect an agreement in a universally valid formulation of what justice should really mean.

When the political criminal assaults the ruling power's justice by claiming that it is unjust and by contending that his own justice *is* just, he might be right, but only in a relative sense. All laws are formulated on the unspoken assumption that they are just and represent the right justice, even though they may not appear so to all members of the society and especially not to the political criminal. The laws are just and they reflect justice: This has to be learned by all aspirants of political crimes, at least insofar as they are defined by the ruling social-political power and so long as the existing power prevails. . . . Cicero told the story of a captured pirate who defended himself before Alexander the Great by saying that he did exactly what the great conqueror did but that he was to be punished as a pirate rather than a conqueror just because he operated with a small boat rather than a large armada.[20]

Of course, the case of the pirate is not as simple as that. The question of who or what has the right to declare what right is, or who can claim his justice as just, is a centuries-old problem that has been studied by jurists as well as by sociologists. Perhaps one of the reasons for their long-standing disagreement in finding an answer is that lawyers are too close to the problem and sociologists are too distant from it, and both seem to be reluctant to meet in the domain of legal philosophy or in what is called the sociology of law. By the way, at this point it is difficult not to let slip the suggestion that one of the decisive factors in the impasse on the general crime problem is our contemporary sociological criminologists' hesitancy to relate their etiological research to the speculations and findings of the philosophy of law and the norm system. Of course, much more is involved in the idea of law than sheer obedience and blind acceptance of the power-conceived justice, and usually a rich and complex interplay among individuals, groups, and conflicting values takes place before a law is created. Yet, in the ultimate analysis, the definition and interpretation of justice, and lawmaking accordingly, are always monopolies in the exclusive possession and under the exclusive control of the social-political power.

The greatest obstacle to understanding this tenet is our reluctance to accept that what we think of as right and just does not necessarily represent the only correct view. We tend to think in terms of a single immutable truth and conclude that therefore there is only one possible system of justice. The claim that the social system and its law are just and fair rests upon the dubious hypothesis that there is only one just and fair code of values.

NOTES

1. A somewhat similar stand was taken by Maurice Parmelee in *Criminology* (New York, 1918), p. 92. Thorsten Sellin's "culture conflict"

theory in *Culture Conflict and Crime* (Social Science Research Council, New York, 1938) may also not be far from supporting such a contention. The Soviet concept of "social danger" strongly leans toward such an understanding.

2. David Riesman, "Who Has the Power?" in Reinhard Bendix and Seymour M. Lipset (eds.), *Class, Status and Power* (New York, 1966).

3. C. Wright Mills, *The Power Elite* (New York, 1956).

4. William Thomas Mallison, "Political Crimes in International Law: Concepts and Consequences," *Newsletter* of the American Section of the Association Internationale de Droit Pénale, no. 9 (December 1971), Washington, D.C., p. 10.

5. Stephen Schafer, *Theories in Criminology: Past and Present Philosophies of the Crime Problem* (New York, 1969), p. 17.

6. Stephen Schafer, *The Victim and His Criminal: A Study in Functional Responsibility* (New York, 1968), pp. 33–36.

7. Eric Wolf, *Vom Wesen des Täters* (Berlin, 1932); "Richtiges Recht im nationalsozialistischen Staat," *Freiburger Universitätsreden*, vol. 13 (1934).

8. Georg Dahm, "Die Erneuerung der Ehrenstrafrecht," *Deutsche Juristenzeitung*, 1934, *Der Tätertyp im Strafrecht* (Leipzig, 1940).

9. Fr. Martitz, *Internationale Rechtschilfe in Strafsachen* (Leipzig, 1888/1897), vol. I, p. 139.

10. Heinrich Lammasch, *Das Recht der Auslieferung wegen politscher Verbrechen* (Vienna, 1884); *Auslieferungspflicht und Asylrecht* (Leipzig, 1887).

11. Schafer, *Theories, op. cit.,* p. xi.

12. Filmer Stuart Cuckow Northrop, "Ethical Relativism in the Light of Recent Legal Science," *Journal of Philosophy,* vol. 51 (Nov. 10, 1955), pp. 649–662.

13. Schafer, *Theories, op. cit.,* p. 14.

14. Havelock Ellis, *The Criminal* (5th ed., New York, n.d.; preface to 4th ed., dated 1910), p. 2.

15. Louis Proal, *Political Crime,* trans. unknown (New York, 1898), pp. 50–51, first published under the title *La criminalité politique* (Paris, 1895). To regard the state as criminal and the members of the society as victims is the crux of the problem and philosophically a high controversial contention that leads to the problems of the natural law and to the assumption that there exists only a single justice.

16. See Schafer, *Theories, op. cit.,* p. 11; also the general tone in Pratima Bowers, *Consciousness and Freedom* (London, 1971).

17. Ellis, *op. cit.,* pp. 1–2.

18. Parmelee, *op. cit.,* p. 461.

19. Stephen Schafer, "The Concept of the Political Criminal," *The Journal of Criminal Law, Criminology and Police Science,* vol. 62, no. 3 (1971), p. 381. Adapted by special permission.

20. Cicero, *De Republica,* III. 12.

Chapter Six

The Political Assassin

Conrad V. Hassel

Over the past decade, scenes which have seared most permanently the consciousness of millions of Americans include: a prancing,
riderless black horse, boots lashed backwards in the stirrups, a mule-
drawn casket, and arrogant fanatics firing weapons at national leaders.
These events were trapped on merciless television screens as Americans
watched the unfolding tableau again and again in total disbelief.

Shock, grief, anger and helplessness characterized the private
emotions of the American people over the assassinations or attempted
assassinations of presidents and other political and civic leaders.
These emotions resulted in speculation concerning a possible tragic
flaw in the American character—a streak of uncontrollable violence
which must vent itself in the periodic national trauma of political
assassination.

Public reactions to these incidents varied. There was a sense
of profound shock, not only in the United States, but throughout
the world. The killing of Martin Luther King resulted in rioting
in some cities. However, one factor remained constant: the inability

Reprinted by permission of the *Journal of Police Science and Administration*, Vol. 2, #4, 1974, pp. 399–403.

of large segments of the public to accept that the act of assassination was the work of a single, usually insignificant individual.

To many it was more satisfying and indeed more logical to believe the crimes were the act of a highly intelligent, uniquely evil conspiracy, perhaps directed by a foreign power or some subversive domestic group bent on overthrowing the government. It was difficult to accept the grace of a Kennedy, the oratory of Martin Luther King, or the force and energy of a George Wallace being extinguished by any but the most powerful and evil of forces. It was even more tragic and grotesque when the perpetrators of such acts were an Oswald, a Ray, and a Bremer.

Unwillingness to accept the fact that insignificant little men can be the instruments of such profound tragedy is demonstrated by the debate concerning the alleged conspiracy in the assassination of Abraham Lincoln. This debate has continued for over 100 years, as will the arguments over the deaths of John F. Kennedy and Martin Luther King.

One can only speculate concerning the course of American history had Lincoln, McKinley, and the brothers Kennedy not been slain. What can be said about the men who conceived, planned and carried out these truly devastating acts? What did they look like? Who were they? A study of the assassins or attempted assassins of Andrew Jackson, 1835; Abraham Lincoln, 1865; James A. Garfield, 1881; William McKinley, 1901; Theodore Roosevelt, 1921; Franklin D. Roosevelt, 1933; Harry S Truman, 1950; and John F. Kennedy in 1963 shows that most were white, short and slight of build.[1] These same characteristics seems to fit the killer of Robert Kennedy and the would-be slayer of George Wallace.

So many major political assassins have been short and slight of build that it is probably a factor in the composite social and psychological makeup of this type of killer. This is not to place the political assassin into a particular biological or body structure group, or to say that short, slightly built white males have a particular penchant for political murder, but when taken into consideration with the other factors which contribute to the assassin's behavior, being small, in a position to be looked down upon, seems to be an important characteristic.

Of the eight presidential assassins listed above, only John Wilkes Booth could be said to be of average stature. The rest were small men.[2] The assassin generally feels that he has been treated unfairly by the world around him. Add to this attitude the extra insult of biological accident—his size—and one has a potentially volatile mixture.

Unlike physical appearance, there seems to be no common denominator relating to socio-economic class. Most of the political assassins or attempted assassins (and with these could be included Sirhan Sirhan and Arthur Bremer) came from the working class. The exceptions were Charles J. Guiteau, the killer of President James A. Garfield, John Wilkes Booth and John N. Schrank, who attempted to murder President Theodore Roosevelt. These three men were from the middle class. Guiteau was a sometime lawyer and writer of religious tracts; Booth was a member of a prominent family of successful actors who had some small success in this calling; and Schrank was a New York tavern owner.[3]

The ages of the nine assassins or attempted assassins were between 24 and 40, as were Sirhan, Bremer and Ray.[4] The age factor is of doubtful relevance, since nationally, few crimes of violence are committed by persons over 40. Most of the assassins had reached maturity at the time of the act, indicating a fully developed personality and a longstanding mental or emotional problem.

In an effort to discern a common denominator among all the assassins, some salient factor of their individual environment that would link them all to some common pattern, one factor appears to be glaringly obvious: none of them had a stable masculine figure with whom to identify during childhood.[5] This particular symptom extends far beyond assassins. Studies of those who have threatened the lives of politically prominent persons reveal that most "had domineering mothers and weak and ineffectual fathers."[6]

John Wilkes Booth was raised almost exclusively by his mother. John N. Schrank, who shot Theodore Roosevelt, lost his father at age seven. Oswald's father died just after Oswald was born.[7] The fathers of Ray and Sirhan beat their sons, deserted their homes and left their families to fend for themselves.[8]

Beyond the two factors of physical appearance and lack of father image, other similarities become more speculative. The least speculative of these common factors is the apparent lack of any meaningful relationship with members of the opposite sex. Oswald's wife, Marina, accused him of impotence two months before he killed Kennedy; neither Ray nor Sirhan ever had a girl friend; Bremer's relationship with the one girl he sometimes dated was quite platonic and he never had sexual relations with her;[9] and Lawrence, who attempted to kill Andrew Jackson, never married. Leon Czolgosz, who shot William McKinley, and Guiseppe Zangara, who killed Mayor Clinton Cermak of Chicago while attempting to kill Franklin D. Roosevelt, actively avoided the company of women. Booth and Guiteau did have casual sexual liaisons with women, but none that appeared to be of a lasting nature.[10]

The obvious psychological theory that springs from the interpersonal relationships of the assassins is that they were motivated by hatred of a father who had neglected, deserted, or otherwise mistreated them. They projected this hatred into rage against an ultimate authority figure, such as a president or strong political or civic figure, thereby sowing the ultimate seeds of assassination.[11] Although logical and to some degree satisfying, such an explanation is oversimplistic. Most of the assassins not only had poor relationships with women, but also with other men. Only two of those who either killed or attempted to kill presidents were involved in anything that could remotely be called a conspiracy. Booth gathered around him a few inadequate persons, at least one of whom appeared to have been a mental defective, and the attempted assassins of Harry S Truman, Oscar Collazo and Griselio Torresola, planned the attempt poorly and it was foredoomed to failure.[12] The rest of the assassins were loners, at least as far as the evidence presently shows.

It is generally agreed that most, if not all, of the assassins thus far alluded to were mentally ill to the point of severe psychosis. This is not to say that they were legally "insane," which is, after all, a legal and not a medical or psychiatric definition. Many, in fact, could not be categorized as falling within any of the legal definitions of insanity.

Beyond the fact of possible psychosis, the particular mental derangement is less easily definable. Two major categories of psychosis are generally suggested: paranoia and paranoid schizophrenia. The difference between the two is as much a difference in degree as in kind. In both illnesses, the patient suffers from delusions, i.e., he thinks he is someone he is not or he thinks he is being persecuted. In the case of paranoid schizophrenic, the delusions are less well organized, more fantastic and accompanied by hallucinations, e.g., voices of the people who are persecuting him or commands from God. The paranoid schizophrenic becomes more and more disorganized,[13] while the paranoiac, except for his delusions, retains his personality relatively intact.[14]

Sirhan Sirhan was diagnosed by experts a paranoid schizophrenic,[15] Zangara as paranoiac,[16] Guiteau as paranoid schizophrenic,[17] Lawrence, Schrank, Czolgosz, and Oswald as probably paranoid or paranoid schizophrenic.[18] Some experts have diagnosed all the assassins or attempted assassins of U.S. presidents as paranoid schizophrenic except for Callazo and Torresola.[19]

Leaving precise clinical definitions aside, it is clear that all the assassins acted under some delusion strong enough to lead to murder. Whether such delusions were aided and abetted by hallucinations is a point of academic debate. John Wilkes Booth believed himself to be the instrument of God, as did Guiteau, whose mission was to save the public by killing President Garfield. Czolgosz killed McKinley because he believed McKinley was the enemy of the working people. Zangara blamed the capitalists for his lack of schooling and his intestinal disorders and believed he would get even with them by killing Franklin Roosevelt.[20] Richard Lawrence, who made an attempt on the life of Andrew Jackson, believed he was Richard III of England and the United States owed him large sums of money. John Schrank believed that Theodore Roosevelt had murdered President McKinley and tried to avenge McKinley by killing Roosevelt.[21] Sirhan Sirhan believed himself an Arab patriot and killed Robert Kennedy because Kennedy had proposed sending 50 military aircraft to Israel.[22] None of these delusions would be calculated to attract any large political movement. It is difficult to conceive that they would have sufficient appeal for even a small conspiracy. Perhaps one reason why these men, with such visions of the world, are so dangerous and often successful in their murderous schemes, is the pure irrationality of their thought processes, which makes it extremely difficult for rational men to predict their actions and thus to defend against them.

In a paper submitted to the National Commission on the Causes and Prevention of Violence, Dr. Doris Y. Wilkinson sought to apply the theory of the achievement-expectancy gap. She theorized the political assassin has an unrealistic expectancy of high achievement in society, but because of his lack of intelligence, social status, education or other factors, he is unable to achieve his expected goal. Upon realizing that he cannot achieve the status to which he believes he is entitled, the psychic trauma somehow becomes politicized and he attacks that person who, in his mind, has achieved that status.[23]

This theory supports the father hate idea in that the killer already harbors ill will against authority. It also seems to fit well with Booth's expectation that he would be thought of as a hero after killing Lincoln; with Oswald's dream of becoming premier of Cuba and his disappointment when he found that the Russians did not welcome him as a hero and were not anxious to have him as a Soviet citizen; with Sirhan's expectation of becoming a diplomat but lacking the ability to complete college; and Bremer's fantasizing about being a great writer but being able to hold only menial employment as a janitor or busboy.[24]

The achievement-expectancy gap theory also tends to explain the lack of blacks, Chicanos, or American-Indians among the murderers of the politically prominent. Since some members of these minority groups have a low expectancy of achievement because of the lack of success of other members of their ethnic groups, they do not experience the psychic trauma associated with failure to achieve an unrealistic goal. In the face of failure, "the system" can be blamed. Such thinking provides a convenient safety valve for aggression, with the result that such aggression does not become directed to a Wallace or a Kennedy.[25]

Added to the general family pathology of the assassin is the fact that the paranoid personality is often overwhelmed by anxiety and feelings of worthlessness. The paranoid can only preserve a feeling of integrity by severely distorting reality.[26] The volatile mixture of the assassin is thus complete. His general hatred for authority finds release in a paranoid delusion, a murderous, anxiety-relieving attack on a politically prominent person.

Recent studies have suggested a further complication in the possible underlying causes of the paranoid personality, specifically the paranoid schizophrenic. Dr. Jacques S. Gottlieb, a respected biochemist, told the 1972 convention of the American Psychiatric Association at Dallas that he had found a possible connection between schizophrenia and an unstable enzyme in the emotional center of the brain.[27] If a biological base for this mental abberration is established, the schizophrenic may be amenable to control through medication.

It is clear that political, and, particularly, presidential assassinations, have not been the product of rational political motives, even though the assassin himself may have felt his reasons were political.[28] The assassin's motive resulted from a misperception of reality; his view of the world was severely out of focus.

It is a tribute to the American system and further evidence of the lack of any real sinister conspiracy in the assassinations that our institutions suffered no fundamental disruption by the assassinations. In fact, there has seemed to have been no substantial change in the direction of public policy as a result of the loss of a president. If it is the killer's intent to change the thrust of presidential policy, the opposite result is obtained, since bills doubtful of passage prior to the assassination are quickly pushed through the Congress almost as a tribute to the murdered President.

Numerous suggestions have been made for the protection of presidents and other politically prominent persons, ranging from innovative protective devices to sophisticated data-retrieving computers in which information concerning unstable individuals could be stored.[29] However, the American propensity to deify many public officials, especially the president, and the need for charisma, which seems to be an indispensable part of every successful politician's appeal, tend to make them extremely appealing targets to the mentally deranged person with a grudge against authority.

It has been suggested that the functions of the office rather than the occupant's personality should be emphasized; that maximum use should be made of television; and that public appearances should be limited. However, the nature of the American system has encouraged personality politics, at least since the slogan "Tippecanoe and Tyler too" was coined in 1840. It does not appear that this style of politics will change fundamentally; it is what the American public wants and expects from its political leaders.

There is considerable doubt concerning the charge that there is a basic streak of violence in the American character when the United States is compared to such countries as Mexico, France, China, Japan, Italy, Bulgaria, Germany, Egypt, Iraq, Cuba, Iran, and Poland, all of which have had many more assassinations than the United States since 1918.[30]

A great challenge is posed to the law enforcement community by the lone assassin. The determined gunman, overwhelmed by his failures and seeking revenge for his insignificance by destroying what to his mind is the symbol of all that is oppressive to him, is a formidable threat. This is especially true if he is willing to sacrifice his own life to accomplish his goal. There appears to be no way for a free and open society to completely rid itself of this threat without placing severe limitations on the present style of political campaigning in the United States.

NOTES

1. James F. Kirkman, Sheldon Leirf, and William J. Crofty, *Staff Report to the National Commission on the Causes and Prevention of Violence*, Vol. 8, "Assassination and Political Violence" (U.S. Government Printing Office, Washington, D.C., 1969), p. 66.

2. David N. Daniels, M.D., Marshal F. Gilula, and Frank M. Ochberg, *Violence and the Struggle for Existence* (1972), p. 292. Work of the Committee on Violence of the Department of Psychiatry, Stanford University School of Medicine.

3. *Supra* note 1, pp. 50–60.

4. *Supra* note 2, p. 292.

5. David Abrahamsen, M.D. *The Murdering Mind* (1973), p. 18–19.

6. *Supra* note 1, p. 67.

7. *Supra* note 1, p. 62.

8. *Supra* note 5, p. 20.

9. *Supra* note 5, p. 21.

10. *Supra* note 1, pp. 49–57.

11. *Supra* note 5, p. 19.

12. *Supra* note 1, pp. 58–61.

13. Robert W. White, *The Abnormal Personality* (1964), p. 511.

14. James C. Coleman, *Abnormal Psychology and Modern Life* (4th ed. 1972), p. 276.

15. *Supra* note 14, p. 276.

16. John M. McDonald, *The Murderer and His Victim* (1961), p. 54.

17. *Supra* note 16, p. 51.

18. *Supra* note 2, pp. 298–299.

19. *Supra* note 1, p. 62.

20. *Supra* note 16, pp. 49–54.

21. *Supra* note. 16, pp. 291–299.

22. *Supra* note 14, p. 276.

23. *Supra* note 1, p. 66.

24. *Supra* note 5, pp. 22–23.

25. *Supra* note 1, p. 66.

26. Seymour Halleck, M.D., *Psychiatry and the Dilemmas of Crime* (1967), p. 171.

27. Remarks of Dr. Jacques S. Gottlieb given at a special symposium at a meeting of the American Psychiatric Association, April (1972), Dallas, Texas.

28. *Supra* note 1, p. 110.

29. *Supra* note 1, pp. 94–95.

30. *Supra* note 1, p. 117.

Chapter Seven

Power, Ideology and Political Crime

John M. Steiner

TOWARDS A NEW CONCEPTUALISATION OF POWER

Prudent students of history will find that sincerity expressed in violence, in the guise of a civil but nonetheless ideologically entrenched wish to bring about radical socio-political change, has invariably been costly in human lives. Advocates of such change only rarely adhere to the blueprint of behaviour purportedly designed to bring about the realisation of the proposed change. The Crusaders, the Jacobins, the Bolsheviks, the Fascists, the Nazis and the Maoists were by and large misguided by their "sincere belief" in their respective causes. They all claimed to obey "superior principles" (with their corresponding concept of law and order) to the utter disregard of existing "mundane" morality and with complete disrespect for human life which they allegedly set out to improve. In point of fact, time after time ideology has been used as an excuse, license and vehicle for the application of unconstrained power politics. Furthermore, it is a com-

Reprinted by permission of the *International Journal of Criminology & Penology*, Vol. 1, #1, 1973, pp. 5–14.

mon occurrence that ideological (myth) systems are planned and developed to suit the creator's personal needs. Equally frequently, they are subsequently adjusted better to serve the interests of the actors who, then, will apply them. . . . Indeed, the method by which an initial cause is advanced is invariably the most important factor in setting the stage for future action and in the subsequent adoption of policies once the system becomes established. One of the lessons which could have been learned by now is that the number of violent prophets a society can absorb with impunity is limited. Observations of this kind were made by Machiavelli in his treatise, *The Prince*.[1] The methods by which "causes" were advanced and institutionalised are, of course, primarily dependent upon the leadership's astuteness and ability to mobilise power in terms of "popular" support for such causes. But the concept of power itself remains unclear without the recognition that power is a product of social interaction only and not a mere attribute of the actor. In this context, domination of others can be understood as an attempt to free oneself from oppressive interdependency relations by simply reversing them. The will to power, then, the wish to dominate others, can be viewed as a striving for greater independence and autonomy from others by forming interdependency patterns which the originator and his associates deem or experience as being more favourable (to them). In short, power becomes reality if a power-dependence relationship is established,[2] that is to say, if a potential power holder is in a position to secure and fill a vacant power role (in time and space) which enables him to structure the scope and radius of action of those who will submit to him. Thus a dependency relationship will become an essential basis for the perpetuation of a power position. This, in turn, will enhance the image, and the degree of freedom, of the actor holding power if he is successful in safeguarding his status by harnessing a hierarchical chain of command by bureaucratic and institutional means. In other words, his power position will enable him better to control and structure his environment and thereby improve the chances to satisfy his individual needs, as reflected in his goal aspirations.[3] So, for example, by virtue of his acquired power role, the actor will receive recognition in the form of material and non-material rewards which will be reflected in the realisation of an aspired life-style. The power role will also place him in the limelight, which for many a power holder can become a source of satisfaction *per se*.[4]

This novel experience can stimulate in the actor ecstatic joy (or elation, a synonym used by Hannah Arendt) in response to a drift in emphasis to different areas of the actor's personality structure.[5] As a consequence of the newly acquired and more acceptable or satisfying identity as a power holder, the actor's self-image and social perspective will subsequently alter.[6] When the actor has been adequately prepared to play a specific power role (as, for example, in the case of the late President John F. Kennedy), elation will be kept to a minimum since he will not impute to the role more authority and influence than is in the interest of the people or warranted in a stable social order. Yet it should be understood that such a preparation itself does not ensure astute decision-making and does not produce a statesman out of an otherwise unqualified actor. However, if the legitimate social order is not stable, but is undergoing radical change, the possession of a power role may be a novel experience for the actor, and consequently he may lack the essential qualifications for the assumption of power and its corresponding responsibilities. In this instance, if it is a top leadership role (which is a relative concept in time and space), both the actor and his alters will mutually impute more authority and influence to the role than is traditionally ascribed to it. Hence, the actor may feel obliged to use his power to re-structure reality and, by doing so, serve as a significant model for others to follow.[7] So, for example, Hitler's expectations were treated as most important by the German people as long as the people were an actively involved, integral part of operative Nazi institutions. . . .

. . .

Unable to perceive the differences and ramifications between "realistic and non-realistic" social conflict,[8] top leaders will attempt to solve both types according to their social perspective and definition of the situation. If a non-violent solution either is not sought or cannot be found, an attempt will be made to resolve conflict by violent means or by re-structuring present realities. To accomplish this, policies and strategies will be promulgated and appropriate institutional channels found or, if not presently available, created, along with corresponding sets of social roles necessary for the realisation of such institutions or organisations. Low ranking officials at the end of the hierarchical chain of command will most likely be the ones to enact the orders passed down by the power élite. If, however, the initiated measures fail to resolve the conflict, and/or are rejected by the public at large as unacceptable, the low ranking officials who administered or implemented such measures in "good faith," upon explicit or implicit orders, and under considerable pressure, will usually be held responsible for the lack of success. After the Nuremberg Trial of the Nazi War Criminals (1945–46), conducted by the victorious Allies, the few high ranking, but lower echelon, policy making Nazi officials tried in German courts were sentenced to considerably lesser prison terms than many of their underlings. So, for example, we find that the lower ranking former SS staff members of concentration and destruction camps are chiefly held responsible for the massacres and are sentenced to long prison terms; this is done instead of bringing the roles of their superiors, the administrative initiators and high ranking desk-chair perpetrators, into proper context.[9]

. . .

Social institutions and organisations can indeed become pliable instruments in the hands of power holders who have developed expertise in the technique of harnessing power as a tool for the realisation of their designs. Thus, the absence of institutionalised (constitutional) checks and balances not only makes possible the rise of despotism but can also produce dependency relationships which are experienced by the submitting actors as excessive. Max Weber described this state as an "iron cage" of modern, bureaucratic society from which there is no breaking out.[10]

Only by a contextual understanding of a given social setting in which interaction takes place (which includes competition for the playing of power roles) can we better accept the recognition that

> Majors and Minors differ but in name
> Patriots and Ministers are much the same
> the only difference, after all their rout,
> is, that the one is in, the other out!

With these verses C. J. Weber, in 1836, wanted to point out to his compatriots the circular nature of the élitist social system.[11]

How can this be interpreted sociologically? It means that within a given socio-political structure social institutions will be created which in turn will produce specific types of leadership roles. These roles will be filled by individuals whose personality characteristics may be more suited for such positions and who will derive more satisfaction from playing them than others with different personality profiles. It would be unreasonable to assume that most of these individuals decide to play such roles merely because of a "situational accident." It is more likely that they are available and ready to play these power roles because of their very specific psychogenic needs. They are prevented from playing them because heretofore in the socio-cultural blueprint there had been no socially approved or institutionalised outlets for such roles on the sociogenic level.[12] Conversely, for example, members of the SS lost their power roles after the defeat of National Socialism because institutions such as the SS had become obsolete and therefore no longer provided a source for total leadership roles. Indeed, in the new democratic social setting, power roles with a coercive, intimidating or mass-destructive function had become dysfunctional. There was no longer any need to enforce social control by violent means or to restrict social interaction through rigid legal and social sanctions and tightly knit, hierarchically structured channels of communication. However, this is not to say that the personality structure of former members of the SS had undergone appreciable change in the democratic post-war German social setting. In fact, empirical evidence seems to indicate that this had not been the case.[13]

THE HISTORICAL SETTING OF THE NATIONAL SOCIALIST RISE TO POWER AND ITS SOCIOLOGICAL IMPLICATIONS

When we view history from a sociological perspective, we are primarily interested in those events that have set the stage for structurally-normative, relatively constant social paterns. One of the foremost and decisive factors is the concept of power which permits the ruling élite to impose social and ideological controls and new legal norms by which the means and degree of social contract and social sanction will be determined. In the case of National Socialism these social controls were not necessarily based on the basic needs of the people. Although Hitler's policies were at first actively supported by the public at large that had eagerly assumed a new identity as posited by Hitler's ideological rhetoric,[14] the scope of social interaction was solely determined by the "Führer" and by the Nazi élite after their power became more firmly entrenched.[15]

By virtue of its strategic social position the ruling élite is best equipped to harness, safeguard and perpetuate power. In practice, then, it can be observed that the interpretation and structuring of social reality tends to be largely determined by the current power élite. It is in their power to enact laws (the legal order being an intergral part of the social order) which will reflect and represent their view of the world, their interests, their values and social norms. Yet, the values expressed in such norms should by no means be viewed as simply the ones of an elect few, but rather as those held in common and shared with the group of people, subculture or class they represent, since, after all, the ruling élite is a product of the culture in which it has originated and in which a process of specific interaction has taken place. The power élite, however, defines and decides what does and what does not constitute deviant social behaviour. Essentially, law is made by the power élite with an eye to protecting its own interests and that of the class with which it is affiliated and from which it derives identity and support. Consequently, as Vilfredo Pareto already recognised, exploitation of fellow men by corrupt politicians and desk-chair perpetrators (white collar criminals) as a rule does not take place by breaking the law but by using it. This can be done because these laws primarily serve the interests of the privileged to the disadvantage and at the expense of the less—or under-privileged. In point of fact, they provide the nucleus for acts which can escalate into economic and political crime. Both types are integral components of what has become a historical reality as the ultimate crime, i.e., crime against the human status—genocide. Those who possess less can only be kept in place and exploited by those who possess more. By virtue of this fact, the latter are in a "superior" position to generate power potential which then is used to create social differentiation and inequality. Hence, in a society with a relatively rigid social stratification in which the power élite has little direct interaction with other segments of society, there will be no sharing of a common life-style. Consequently, there will be also an experience of mutual social distance, eventual alienation, conflict and an imbalanced dependence relationship between the lower and the upper social classes.[16] When power discontinues to be socially related, it ceases to be transmittable and thus becomes subject to challenge and seizure by a counter-élite. Subsequently, a power-circle will be closed again by the phase described by Pareto as the "circulation of élites." A case in point was provided by Hitler's National Socialism which brought about an escalation into destruction. A defunct post-World War I political élite was superseded by a new one, the Nazis. This counter-élite was able to muster the support of the drifting masses searching for a more effective and meaningful leadership. This counter-movement offered the people a popular political ideology (myth system) and, last but not least, social identity, deviant as it may have appeared to a non-involved, neutral observer.

Not only had joblessness and inflation threatened the existential security of the groping masses of Germans in search of an acceptable identity but the socio-political climate after the military defeat of 1918 was neither conducive nor geared adequately to preparing the citizen to participate in a democratic process of decision-making. The post-war socio-political structure of the Weimar Republic was not the product of a free choice made by the people, but had arisen out of the dictates imposed upon the defeated German nation by the victorious Allies. Moreover, in the primary sphere, the traditional

German family structure was designed to leave decision-making solely to the head of the family who, in turn, expected the leaders and administrators of the state to make social and political decisions for him. Hence, this primary social structure rendered the man in the street unequipped to assume co-responsibility, via reflective participation, in the formulation of those policies and the steering of those activities which had a decisive effect on society at large.

More specifically, on a sociogenic level (or, as Ferdinand Toennies defined it, *Gesellschafts* relationships,[17] this lack of active involvement resulted in an uneven power distribution and in dependency relationships which became increasingly "authority" centred and coercive, according to the formula: "All for the State; nothing outside the State; nothing against the State.[18] On the primary and psychogenic level (corresponding to Toennies's *Gemeinschafts* relationships),[19] the imbalanced dependency relationships tended to impair the chances of the individual to develop an autonomous, well-rounded, integrated personality structure that would facilitate harmonious social interaction and stimulate the capacity of concern for the well-being of fellow men.[20]

Thus we can say: When we view personality, from a social-psychological perspective, as a process and not as a mere system of inner traits, the analysis of politically deviant behaviour patterns takes on new dimensions. It is one thing to observe that a given individual is a political deviant or a Nazi, and another to state that he behaves deviantly under specific conditions. What constitutes politically deviant behaviour is not so much determined by the *Weltanschauung* held by an individual observer or by an outsider but is based on the consensus of those who have participated by way of interaction in the promulgation of social values and norms and on those segments of a populace which have a vested interest in the perpetuation of such norms. Cameron has suggested the search for the precipitating conditions. If, for example, fears, suspicions, threats and aggressive actions of paranoia-prone individuals heighten the anxiety of those around them, they "inevitably arouse defensive and retaliatory hostility in others.[21] Such a response tends to confirm their interpretation of the situation and promotes mutually aggressive tendencies. If, however, hostility-promoting responses are lacking and if, unlike Hitler, Mussolini, or Stalin, an objective statesman serves as a bridge to reality, the politically deviant-prone citizen "can begin to entertain doubts and consider alternative interpretations" [22] suggested by responsible cultural, social and political leaders. Only the most favourable social conditions can prevent hostile behaviour. There is good evidence that social structure, "class subcultures and variation in patterns of interaction are among the causes of this differential." [23]

In summary, we find that power-relationships are products of social interaction, structured by the reality of a given socio-political system. A power-relationship, therefore, is an integral part of a given socio-cultural blueprint and needs to be interpreted in the context of a time and space perspective, that is to say, all social phenomena created and interpreted by man are relative, tenuous and thus subject to change. Empirically, the functional importance of power can be best determined by the nature and number of significant dependence relationships a person or group of persons were able to establish in their interaction with others whereby the power status in terms of *exclusiveness* is advanced. [24]

In a final assessment of the foregoing thoughts, it can be found that if the socio-political structure is so constraining that the man in the street who becomes engulfed in it sees virtually no alternative but to assume the role assigned to him in order to survive existentially, he will serve those in power to enact the current administration's policies—even if they involve acts of injustice and violence. Such persons can be turned into SS—and party—men, . . . , and similar leading and supportive perpetrators who will be in no position to extricate themselves from the system without incurring severely felt social sanctions and penalties. [25] In other words, not only will these actors be rarely capable of deviating from social norms and dictates imposed on them, but they will be pressured into conformistic behaviour patterns, thus forming an integral link between policy makers and those who enact and perpetuate policies of intimidation, coercion and violence.

NOTES

1. N. Machiavelli, *The Prince* (translated and edited by T. G. Bergin). (New York, 1947) pp. 19–20, 23–26.

2. R. H. Emerson, Power-dependence relations. *American Sociological Review* (1972), 27, 31–37, 39–41. Also J. M. Steiner, *Social institutions and social change under national socialist rule: an analysis of a process of escalation into mass destruction.* Ph.D. Dissertation, University of Freiburg (1968), pp. 179–180.

3. From a careful study of biograms of power holders it becomes evident that compensation for low self-esteem is one of the important driving forces behind the search for power. This can be mitigated by a domination of others in which the individuality of those who submit is being effaced.

Cf. F. S. Perls, *Ego Hunger and Aggression* (New York, 1969), chapter XII, pp. 169–173. So, for example, Woodrow Wilson, in his Kansas address of May 1911, based in part on self-recognition, said the following:

> "The man with power, but without conscience, could, with an eloquent tongue, if he cared for nothing but his own power, put this whole country into a flame, because this whole country believes that something is wrong, and is eager to follow those who profess to be able to lead it away from its difficulties."

Quoted in F. Neumann, *Behemoth: The Structure and Function of National Socialism* (Toronto, 1942), p. 33. Cf. also A. L. George & J. L. George, *Woodrow Wilson and Colonel House* (New York, 1956); S. Freud & W. C. Bullitt, *Thomas Woodrow Wilson: Twenty-eighth President of the United States* (Boston, 1967).

Efforts to relate German family structures to political authoritarianism include: E. H. Erikson, *Childhood and Society* (New York, 1963), chapter IX, pp. 326–358. The legend of Hitler's childhood; J. M. Steiner, *op. cit.* Appendix XIV, pp. 368–370.

4. A stimulating portrayal of the process of a gradual change in the personality profile of power holders has been presented by L. Mnacko in his book, *Taste of Power* (New York, 1967), in which the author describes the rise and decline of a Communist statesman.

5. H. Gerth & C. W. Mills, *Character and Social Structure* (New York, 1964), pp. 96–97 and H. Arendt, *Eichmann in Jerusalem* (London, 1963), pp. 59, 42, 48, 50, 231. In referring to the function of personality structure, Mills observes the following:

> "Although men sometimes shape institutions, institutions always select and form men. In any given period we must balance the weight of the character or will or intelligence of individual men with the objective institutional structure which allows them to exercise these traits."

C. W. Mills, *The Power Elite* (London, 1969), p. 96. See also I. L. Horowitz, *The War Game* (New York, 1963), chapter 1, pp. 11–28, "Arms, policies and games."

6. In this context see Colonel B. C. Andrus (U.S. Army Retired), *I was the Nuremberg Jailer* (New York, 1970). A discriminative reader of Andrus's account will find that the victorious Allies' concern for human status and dignity, while sitting in judgment over the defeated top Nazi leaders, was, relatively speaking, not significantly different from that of the condemned while they had been in power. One of the basic notions underlying this attitude prevalent in Western societies, cultural differences notwithstanding, can be found in the traditional legal ethos expressed in the *lex talionis*.

7. Cf. G. H. Mead, *Mind, Self, and Society* (Chicago, 1934), pp. 154–156. See also B. N. Melzer, The social psychology of George Herbert Mead. In *The Sociology of Personality* (S. P. Spitzer Ed.) (New York, 1969), pp. 60–61.

Attention should also be drawn to the utilisation of biograms as helpful indicants of changes occurring in the power holder's self-image, identity, attitude and to other shifts taking place, not only in the actor's personality structure and social perspective after he has attained a high level of exclusiveness, but also in those of his followers who have formed a dependence relationship with him.

8. L. A. Coser, *The Functions of Social Conflict* (New York, 1968), pp. 48–55. Cf. also I. L. Horowitz, *op. cit.* Chapter 4, pp. 147–169. Conflict, consensus and cooperation.

9. See biograms and personal accounts (in this writer's personal archives) of former members of the SS currently serving life sentences in German penitentiaries. Cf. also J. M. Steiner, "Bureaucracy, totalitarianism, and political crime." In *Essays in Criminology*, Zum zehnjahrigen Bestehen der Deutschen Kriminologischen Gesellschaft und dem 50, Geburtstag ihres Präsidenten, Prof. Dr. Armand Mergen (Hamburg, Kriminalistik Verlag, 1969), pp. 35–38.

10. A. Mitzman, *The Iron Cage: An Historical Interpretation of Max Weber* (New York, 1970), *passim*. See also F. Kafka, *The Castle* and *The Trial, passim*.

11. Quoted by C. J. Weber, *Das Ritter-Wesen*, Vol. I (Stuttgart, Hallbergische Verlagshandlung, 1836), p. 42.

12. Durkheim asserts that a social fact must always be explained by a social fact. This concept of social facts corresponds to the organisation of behaviour at the sociogenic level and bears a stable relationship only to causes at that level. Relationships to other levels, though important while they exist, are less permanent and subject to greater fluctuation. Cf. E. Durkheim, *Les Regles de la Methode Sociologique* (Paris, Librairie Felix Alcan, 1927), pp. 120–137.

13. J. M. Steiner & J. Fahrenberg, Die Ausprägung autoritärer Einstellung bei ehemaliger Angehörigen der SS und der Wehrmacht *Kölner Zeitschrift für Soziologie und Sozial-Psychologie* (1970) 22, 551–566.

14. H. D. Duncan, Hitler's theory of rhetoric as a means toward social identification, *Communication and Social Order* (London, 1962), Chapter XII, pp. 225–236.

15. A. Speer, Erinnerungen (Berlin, Propylaen Verlag, 1969), *passim*.

16. J. M. Steiner, Ph.D. Thesis, *op. cit.,* pp. 179–180.

17. F. Toennies, *Community and Society* (translated by C. P. Loomis (New York, 1957), p. 191. Toennies's description of the ideal type of *Gesellschafts*—relationship involves strangers whose only principle in this interaction is: "What I do for you, I do only as a means to effect your simultaneous, previous, or later service for me. Actually and really I want and desire only this." *Ibid.*, p. 252.

18. J. Ortega y Gasset, *op. cit.*, p. 122.

19. F. Toennies, *op. cit.*, p. 191. Toennies's description of *Gemeinschafts*—relationships involves "concord" or "family spirit." He states: "All intimate, private, and exclusive living together, so we discover, is understood as life in *Gemeinschaft*." *Ibid.*, p. 33.

20. D. D. Winnicott, "The development of the capacity for concern," *Bulletin of the Menninger Clinic* (1963), 28, 167–176.

21. N. Cameron, "The paranoial pseudo-community revised," *American Journal of Sociology* (1959), 65, 58. Existential fear can be viewed as the expression of an unsatisfied need for survival and security in which the momentum of the unknown dominates. Fear is also artificially induced and manipulated by power holders, specifically in totalitarian societies, as, for example, the Soviet Union and Communist China, to bring about submission to their authority. It is used for Pavlovian conditioning, indoctrination, conversion or persuasion of recalcitrant non- or anti-communists. Such "mind reform," better known as brainwashing, produces a deliberately induced paranoid state which is maintained by a conditioned or controlled environment usually hermetically sealed by an "iron-bamboo curtain." See E. Hunter, *Brainwashing* (New York, 1961), pp. 224–243.

22. N. Cameron, *op. cit.*, p. 58.

23. J. M. Yinger, Research implications of a field view of personality. In *The Sociology of Personality* (S. P. Spitzer Ed.) (New York, 1969), Chapter 12, p. 180.

24. R. Dubin, *Pacific Sociological Review* (1963), 6, 16–22. Power function, and organization.

25. A. Everett *et al.* (New York, 1971).

Part Three

Contemporary Criminal Expressions

Introduction

In describing American crime, or crime in general, it is almost impossible to catalog the huge variety of all criminal expressions. It might be a degradation of the victim's suffering to contrast them in terms of importance; in fact, there are no petty crimes and from the point of view of the victim, all crimes are significant. Yet, there are some crimes in which contemporary criminology is particularly interested, perhaps because of their frequency and also in view of the difficulties in combatting them. One of these is organized crime, which according to Donald R. Cressey is a nationwide alliance of at least twenty-four tightly knit "families," mostly of Italian origin, whose criminal members function in the United States. Cressey proposes here that in coping with organized crime we have to have them disappear from our social system.

Another type of crime that is a focal concern of contemporary criminology is the white-collar crime, committed primarily by offenders in business and the professions. Gilbert Geis contends that a sense of injustice has often led to imprecations against the crimes and sins of members of the upper classes, those in government, business, and various professions, and contrasts the powerful with the powerless. Herbert Edelhertz suggests that the term "white-collar crime" is not well defined, he attempts to clear it and points to the impact of this class of crimes.

The great frequency of burglaries justifies John E. Conklin and Egon Bittner's analysis of burglary in suburbs; they call attention to the fact that our homes are not secure from the invasion by strangers.

Skyjacking, another of the modern crime types, has also alarmed contemporary criminologists, and Robert Chauncey finds that certainty of punishment would be a more effective deterrent than the severity of penalties. It is a violent crime and Daniel Glaser, Donald Kenefick, and Vincent O'Leary offer their analysis of the violent offender in general, and factors associated with his behavior and the classification of his different types in particular.

Chapter Eight

Coping with Organized Crime

Donald Cressey

None of the varieties of organized crime is against the law. Further, in most democratic nations it is not illegal for an individual or group of individuals rationally to plan, establish, develop, or administer an organization designed for the perpetration of crime—any more than it is illegal for detective-story writers and university students to sit around trying to invent 'the perfect crime.' Neither is it against the law for a person to occupy a position in the division of labour of an organization designed for the perpetration of crime. What is against the law in various jurisdictions is bet-taking, usury, extortion, burglary, receiving, robbery, murder, larceny and conspiracy to commit these and other specific crimes. Because 'organized crime' is merely a social category rather than a legal one, police and other governmental agencies do not even routinely compile information on it, as they do for other categories of crime, such as bicycle theft, buggery, and careless driving.

Careful studies of, say, robbery in London can be undertaken because police routinely maintain files on robbery. But attempts to conduct comparable studies of 'organized crime in Glasgow' or 'con-

Donald R. Cressey, *Criminal Organization* (New York: Harper & Row; London: Heinemann, 1972), pp. 81–106. Copyright © 1972 by Donald R. Cressey. Reprinted by permission of the publishers.

federated crime in New York' lead to frustration because, not being legal categories, there is no reason for police and prosecutors routinely and officially to assemble information on such subjects, or even to perceive them as proper objects of study. A sociologist's description of an automobile theft as 'organized crime,' 'professional crime,' 'crime craft,' 'project crime,' 'white-collar crime,' 'property crime,' 'dishonourable crime,' or 'idiotic crime,' cannot be of much concern to the police officer who is only directed to proceed against the individual criminal who stole the car.

The lack of legal and judicial concern for organized crime *as such* is more than the old 'problem of definition.' It is a fact of life which permits both New York Cosa Nostra leaders and London leaders of criminal working groups of robbers and extortionists to remain immune from arrest, prosecution, and imprisonment unless they themselves can be caught violating specific criminal laws. It is the problem of organized crime. If organized crime is to be controlled by traditional penal-law procedures, legislators must in the long run be able to define it and its principal variations at least as precisely as the varieties of burglary, automobile theft, robbery, and homicide are now defined in criminal statutes. Once defined, the behaviour conceivably could be prohibited by criminal law, as behaviour defined by burglary statutes is now prohibited. Were that the case, law-enforcement agencies could bring offenders to trial for committing organized crime, not merely for committing crimes that are organized.

It is becoming increasingly evident, however, that American legislators, at least, never will be able to surmount the fact that any effective legislative and law-enforcement approach to the problem of organized crime will in fact be unconstitutional and, thus, illegal. Organized crime, in all its varieties, flourishes in the United States because the criminal law cannot effectively be used to attack organizations. For sociological analysis and understanding, 'the problem of organized crime' is that of depicting criminal structures. But for control by the forces of the state, the problem is one of legal restraint.

. . .

The United States Constitution was in a manner of speaking designed to insure this less-than-optimal efficiency and effectiveness in the criminal justice process. The inefficiency, if it may be called that, is viewed by many as essential to the preservation of whatever is left of 'the land of the free and the home of the brave.'

. . .

Successful control will require methods for dealing with organizations rather than with individual criminals. But legislative attempts to implement this conclusion have frightened freedom lovers.

. . .

Another kind of proposed legislation takes a different tack. Here, the objective is not to outlaw the development of and participation in illicit divisions of labour. Instead, the law would specify that a person committing a crime while occupying a position in an illicit division of labour shall be subject to more severe punishment than a person committing the same crime while not participating in an illicit organization. There have been three major American proposals of this sort, all of them dealing with organized crime in terms so vague that even the distinguished lawyers and scholars who composed them must surely know they infringe on traditional freedoms.

First, the Model Penal Code, drafted by a committee of the American Bar Association, has a provision which could be used as the basis for imposing heavier penalties on organized criminals than on ordinary criminals. Yet the framers of the Code avoided the difficult task of defining precisely just who or what it is that is to be deterred by lengthy prison terms. The Code does not use organizational concepts. Instead, [it] . . . provides that a court may sentence a person who has been convicted of a felony to an extended prison term if 'the defendant is a professional criminal whose commitment for an extended term is necessary for protection of the public.' But, . . . 'professional' is necessarily a social concept, not a legal one, just as is 'organized.' Article 7 can hardly be said to advance either criminological knowledge or criminal justice administration by going on to provide, negatively:

> The Court shall not make such a finding unless the defendant is over twenty-one years of age and: (a) the circumstances of the crime show that the defendant has knowingly devoted himself to criminal activity as a major source of livelihood; or (b) the defendant has substantial income or resources not explained to be derived from a source other than criminal activity.

The first clause would be extremely difficult to prove in the case of a Cosa Nostra commissioner, an enforcer, a strategic planner, or a tactical planner because the villains, while occupying such specialist occupational positions, make it a point to commit no crime except conspiracies, which, of course, are extremely difficult to prove. Further, the device does not differentiate any felonies committed by a Cosa Nostra boss from any felonies committed by a pimp or a whorehouse madame. Neither does it differentiate a regular member of a working group of robbers from a full-time miscreant who makes a fair living breaking slot-machines or stealing cameras and radios from parked automobiles. Even worse, the clause does not differentiate between levels of 'livelihood.' If 'major' means more than fifty per cent, then the first twenty-five thousand stolen by a fifty-thousand-a-year corporation executive would not count, but the piddling sums stolen by a poor man whose livelihood is not very lively would get the man classed as a 'professional' if they made up more than half his income. The second clause of Article 7 would of course apply or not apply to any given defendant depending upon the definition of 'substantial.'

Unlike the Model Penal Code, the Model Sentencing Act, also drafted by a group of distinguished attorneys and judges, picks up the strong scent of organized crime. But then, like the Model Penal Code, the proposed legislation abandons the chase. Here, the critical concept is that of the 'dangerous offender.' The Model Sentencing Act stipulates that a thirty-year prison term shall be imposed on any felon who is so dangerous that the public must be protected from him and whose felony was committed as part of a 'continuing criminal activity in concert with one or more persons.' The legislation would leave to the discretion of prosecutors and judges the question of whether the felon is in fact 'dangerous.' But all felons are dangerous, by definition. More important, the only definition of organized crime or anything resembling it really suggested by the Act is 'continuing criminal activity in concert.' Unfortunately this phrase brings to mind only the orchestrated activities of pornographic players performing in The Royal Albert Hall. 'Law and order' enthusiasts could make the 'dangerous' criterion and the 'in concert' criterion apply to so-called 'subversive groups,' to civil rights leaders in Mississippi, and to student demonstrators in California, as well as to Cosa Nostra bosses and other participants in criminal organizations. 'Continuing criminal activity' is vague, but it could be measured in terms of the number of previous convictions, thus picking up habitual prisoners rather than habitual criminals.

Third, the President's Crime Commission made proposals whose principal contribution appears to be that of identifying the difficulty of defining organized crime for legal purposes. On a single page, the Commission used the phrase 'organized crime' or 'organized criminal activity' fourteen times without ever indicating precisely what was being discussed. It even used the phrase 'organized crime' in a legal sense, despite the fact that, as indicated, organized crime is not against the law. For example, the Commission recommended that witnesses be protected 'during the pendency of organized crime litigation' but it did not specify what kind of litigation was being considered. A prosecution for robbery, after all, is 'robbery litigation,' a prosecution for violation of an anti-gambling statute is 'gambling litigation,' and a prosecution for 'conspiracy to murder' is 'conspiracy litigation' or even 'murder litigation.' The Commission also mentioned local witnesses who 'fear organized crime reprisal,' but did not state how such reprisal differs from the reprisal of any criminal who is out to take private vengeance against one who bears witness against him.

More specifically, the Commission in its volume on the courts distinguished in what seemed to be a reasonable way between 'casual social gambling' or 'private gambling' and gambling activity which is a 'highly organized illicit business, involving large and sometimes national organizations dealing in billions of dollars a year.' After making this classical and popular distinction, the Commission went on to recommend that the criminal law and law-enforcement process be re-examined with a view to relieving 'private gambling and religious fund-raising enterprises' from criminal penalties, 'while seeking to bring the law to bear more effectively on the organized gambling promoter.' This should be accomplished, the Commission continued, 'by legislative definition rather than by haphazard and uneven application of police or prosecutorial discretion.' [1] But the Commission at this point gave not even a clue about what might be an appropriate 'legislative definition' of the 'highly organized illicit business' and the 'organized gambling promoters' it would control.

When the Crime Commission tried to distinguish street workers in illegal bet-taking operations from office supervisors and other management personnel, is got closer to the heart of the problem. Yet even here it continued to assume that common-sense terms like 'illegal business' could adequately and justly be used in the technical world of criminal justice administration. It recommended: 'Federal and state legislation should be enacted to provide for extended prison terms where the evidence, presentence report, or sentence hearing shows that a felony was committed as part of a continuing illegal business in which the convicted offender occupied a supervisory or other management position.' [2] Because most managers of illicit bet-taking businesses do not themselves take bets, and do not commit any other traditional crimes except the fuzzy one called 'conspiracy,' it is clear that the Commission was merely coughing, honking, and blowing its nose.

The United States Supreme Court has many times characterized as a first essential of justice that the terms of a penal statute creating a new offence be sufficiently explicit to inform those who are subject under it exactly what conduct will render them liable to the statute's penalties. For example, in holding a New Jersey criminal statute void for vagueness under the due-process clause of the American Constitution's Fourteenth Amendment, the Court said, 'No one may be required at the peril of life, liberty, or property to speculate as to the meaning of penal statutes. All are entitled to be informed as to what the State commands or forbids.' [3] The efforts to define organized crime in explicit legal terms which would satisfy this requirement have not, as indicated above, been a smashing success. It would appear wise to abandon this approach to the control of organized crime, 'professional crime,' and 'dangerous offenders.'

But this does not mean that criminologists and sociologists should abandon the study of illicit groups, businesses, and other organizations, or even that we should neglect our duty to define our terms precisely. Indeed, in the effort to understand organized crime we should elicit the assistance of engineers, economists, anthropologists, mathematicians, management experts, and anyone else with a knowledge of systems. It is not much of an exaggeration to say that the anthropological, sociological, business-administration and systems-analysis disciplines are all devoted exclusively to determining what phrases like 'in concert' and terms like 'organized' stand for.

In the last decade, systems experts—many of them engineers and physical scientists—have begun to show considerable interest in the organizational arrangements in police departments and other criminal-justice-administration agencies. Defence-research corporations, looking for new ways to turn a profit as the war business is drying up, are increasingly going into the crime business. Although much of their work merely transfers to the criminal justice area the tactics and gadgetry of war, some of it does not. For example, defence-research organizations in California and New York have made, and are making, careful analyses of the judicial process, from arrest to recidivism, and systems models of this process have been constructed. Similar work was done by the Science and Technology Task Force of the President's Crime Commission. [4]

Such attempts at systemization have been undertaken, by and large with a view to cost accounting, to improving data-gathering procedures, and to maximizing the flow of information about what happens to criminals after they commit their crimes. It is somewhat paradoxical to observe, in the light of this development, that the systems approach has not been utilized in the study of criminal organizations themselves. Information and concepts derived from such study would surely contribute greatly to our understanding of organized crime, and this understanding might in the long run permit policy makers to deal with organized crime by methods and stratagems which will not do violence to basic freedoms.

. . .

Yet those who ask the police to attack organized crime are in good company. The vast majority of the proposals for 'doing something' to halt Cosa Nostra's march toward monopoly in the United States have been based on the assumption that organized crime would be eradicated if only the police would attack it, or, at least, improve their defences against it. Because outlawing organizations has proved to be very difficult, and because 'special penalty' statutes necessarily deal at most with criminals that are organized rather than with criminal organizations, those who would bell the cat have found it difficult to go much beyond the proposition that for dealing with organized crime police should be given better law-enforcement equipment and software, such as wire-tapping and electronic bugging, computerized information-sharing systems, and co-operative regional 'strike forces.' [5] But such proposals also seem to presuppose that any law-enforcement action should take place with reference to organized criminals, not with reference to criminal organizations. For constitutional reasons having to do with civil liberties the police, like other criminal justice administrators, must necessarily devote most of their energy to dealing with organized criminals as if they were not organized. And, despite the improved tools and techniques recently laid on the American police, the chances that a Cosa Nostra member will be jailed for a crime are still much less than the chances that he will be hurt in an automobile accident.

. . .

The reactive and repressive system of law enforcement and criminal justice administration should not by itself be expected to rid a modern society of intelligent criminals who work together in criminal organizations. As long ago as the 1930s Rusche and Kirchheimer warned of the 'uselessness of shifting penal policies as a weapon against socially determined variations in the crime rate.' [6] This warning is coming to have special relevance for organized crime.

Speaking primarily of organized crime, William J. Keating, formerly Assistant District Attorney in New York City, has identified the limitations of the traditional law-enforcement approach in one sentence: 'Crime in our country is fought almost entirely on a complaint basis, after the horse is stolen, and preventive criminology is practiced only by one or two police departments and two or three well-staffed, privately financed citizens' anticrime commissions.' [7] By 'preventive criminology,' Keating means proactive methods in which the police attack crime by acting as detectives in their own behalf, without waiting for a citizen's complaint. In contrast to the time and energy involved when solitary men commit only simple crimes, or even when working groups of pickpockets participate in a day's work, it takes a relatively long time to assemble a confederation of criminals, an illegal gambling enterprise, or even a robbery or burglary organization—and then secretly to plan this organization's activities and co-ordinate the skills of its participants. The police, in response, 'rely more and more on informers from within the underworld and on infiltration into the underworld by "ghost squad" detectives.' [8] Radzinowicz has more elaborately made essentially this same point:

> When professionalism reaches the point where the planner or receiver keeps away from the scene of the crime, leaving the dirty work to others, something more is needed than fast cars, good communications and techniques for finding and analysing clues at the scene of the crime. Criminal intelligence bureaux in a number of police forces and regions are already keeping dossiers on some such suspects. Regional crime squads may concentrate much more in the future upon following up the careers of particular criminals and less upon investigating isolated crimes in the more conventional way.[9]

The practice of assembling intelligence information on the affairs of known criminals in the name of crime prevention is halfway between the traditional conception of the police as *reactive* defenders of the public and the newer conception of them as *proactive* attackers of criminals and potential criminals. Despite recent and widespread implementation by the police of the proactive conception in traffic and motoring cases, and in the currently popular 'doctrine of aggressive patrol' in high-crime-rate areas, 'preventive criminology' by the police in the organized crime field is severely limited by its threat to civil liberties. Further, when police proactively utilize informers, spies, wiretaps and electronic surveillance devices, criminals defensively add buffer positions and corrupter positions to their organizations, live as much as possible like respectable citizens, devise secret ways of communicating with their colleagues, and put informers, spies, wiretaps and electronic surveillance devices in police headquarters.

Since the days of national prohibition the American police have, with an increasingly efficient law-enforcement technology, tried to defend the society against individual criminals who are organized. They also have proactively assembled intelligence data on individual criminals who are organized. Yet criminal organizations have steadily increased their share of the nation's wealth. It is more than likely that there is a cause-and-effect relationship here. Perhaps the police and prosecutorial campaigns against organized criminals have only led to increased rationality of criminal organizations—to the establishment of efficient crime bureaucracies in which no man is indispensable, and which include positions for corrupters, corruptees, and enforcers.[10]

. . .

Once bureaucracies of criminals have been established, arrest and prosecution of the individuals participating in them is no longer an effective crime control measure. For example, the arrest, conviction, incarceration and deportation to Italy of New York's Charles Luciano only resulted in passing of Cosa Nostra leadership to Frank Costello. And neither the imprisonment of Cosa Nostra boss Vito Genovese in 1959, nor his death a few years later, had any discernible effect on the amount of crime committed by his 'family.' More generally, in the late 1920s Benito Mussolini, Fascist Premier of Italy, used dictatorial methods to execute, squash, and liquidate members of the Sicilian Mafia (some of them fled to the United States) but he did not destroy the organization, which had a new staff within a decade.

Such experiences should by now have taught us that when we ask the police to rid us of 'the organized crime problem' we are, by and large, only at most asking them to defend us from the lower-level forms of criminal organization. A campaign involving diligent detection and vigorous prosecution of criminals who commit crime said to be organized certainly will spook some of the criminals involved and decrease their individual profits. Such campaigns against members of criminal task forces, working parties and working groups sometimes even manage to dissolve or weaken the group itself. . . . Arrest of the tactical planners who lay about in restaurants and bars, as described by the President's Crime Commission in the quotation above should, similarly, be more effective than arresting other task force members even if the arrest deposes only the tactician and not his position.

But sooner or later we must acknowledge as outmoded and out of date the crime control ideology that merely asks criminal justice administrators to detect, arrest, convict, and punish criminals. It seems remarkable, at first blush, that police, legislators, and even lawyers and sociologists seem to be treating as rather unexpected 'phenomena' the fact that criminals are getting wiser and wiser, that systems of criminal organization are becoming increasingly rational, and that the criminal justice system is not equipped to cope with wise criminals and rational criminal organizations. Only a few moments of reflection will reveal that these conditions are related to more general changes recently occurring in Western societies.

Certainly we should know that as the level of education in a society increases, the level of education of its criminals will increase also, rendering obsolete any system of justice which is based on the assumption that criminals will be unaware of the frailties of the criminal justice system and that citizens generally will continue to revere 'the law' just because its administrators are dressed in uniforms, robes, wigs, and other trappings of office.

Certainly we should know that as communication systems improve, criminals will learn that the organizational weapons and techniques which bring success in legitimate affairs will also bring success in criminal affairs, rendering obsolete any police practices based on the assumption that police will be organized but criminals will not.

Certainly we should know that as we increasingly call for 'attacks' on criminals and for a 'war on crime,' criminals will learn to behave like squadrons of soldiers, rendering obsolete any system of justice based on the assumption that criminals will behave like individual deviants rather than like the 'enemies' they have been asked to be.

With reference to poor people and blacks, Americans are finally learning that it is more difficult to subjugate a wise and politically aware population than an ignorant one. We therefore should not be surprised at the inability of a reactive and repressive system of justice, based on the assumption that criminals are so ignorant they will be detected, to deal with wise criminals who are learning to utilize in crime the organizational forms which have brought commercial success to landlords, shopkeepers, industrialists, corporation executives, bankers, politicians, university administrators, and a host of others.

The message is becoming loud and clear: criminal organizations should be dealt with as organizations, not merely as collections of individual criminals, and any 'attack' on them must deal with organizational structures and the social contexts in which the structures thrive. It seems rather obvious, for example, that the activities of task forces of lorry hijackers would be greatly curtailed if only one organizational position, the fence, were eliminated. This position, which can be described as a 'place' within an organization is often occupied by seemingly legitimate businessmen who insert stolen merchandise into the legitimate streams of commerce. The position itself, not the person occupying it, exists because some members of the society are willing to purchase merchandise at bargain prices without asking too many questions. In making a similar point, a noted economist has said:

> At the level of national policy, if not of local practice, the dominant approach to organized crime is through indictment and conviction, not through regulation, accommodation, or the restructuring of

markets and business conditions. This is in striking contrast to the enforcement of antitrust or food and drug laws, or the regulation of industries affecting the public interest.[11]

There are, then, alternatives to asking the police to 'attack' Cosa Nostra and other forms of criminal organization or even to asking the police to defend us from them.[12] Robert F. Kennedy, when he was United States Attorney General, frequently suggested that the economic base of the Cosa Nostra organization would be damaged if people stopped purchasing the illegal goods and services it has for sale, and he ran an unsuccessful campaign to educate the public on this matter. Attorney General John Mitchell and Senator John F. McClellan have both proposed, alternatively, that the economic base of the organization be damaged by passing and then enforcing new laws, similar to antitrust laws, which would divest criminal organizations of their profits.[13] Consistently, many of us have proposed that the Cosa Nostra organization would suffer if additional forms of gambling were legalized, thus puting gambling money into the public treasury rather than into the pockets of organized criminals.[14]

By the same token, tolerance of political corruption establishes a place in criminal organizations for corrupter and corruptee positions, and eliminating that tolerance will eliminate the place, thus curtailing the activities of the organizations. Similarly, the profits going to organized criminals from usury would be greatly decreased if a governmental agency went into competition with usurers, providing short-term loans for desperate persons who have no collateral except their bodies. Universities and government agencies already provide such loans to needy students.

Strategic, long-range programmes for reducing the crimes of working groups of criminals who commit project crimes are more difficult to propose. The range of the behaviour is broad. In general, however, we should build on the principle implicit in the statement of American bank robber Willie Sutton who replied, when asked why he robbed banks, 'Because that's where the money is.' It is not impossible that we will before long see the day when computerized credit systems eliminate money from banks, thus eliminating bank robbers. This method of banking will be a welcome relief from the inconsistency of California bank officials, who, in an attempt to show that they had the common touch, invented the slogan: 'Come in and ask for it by name—MONEY.' They broadcast it, televised it, and advertised it. And then, when the Willie Suttons from all over the state came into banks and asked for MONEY the bankers and the companies insuring them cried for 'law and order' in California.

A few years ago I held a minor position on a research team of engineers and social scientists. By means of an elegantly stated research proposal and dozens of federal forms, the team applied for a government grant for study of systems which might be used to reduce the high frequency at which bus drivers were then being robbed. While the application forms were still being processed, the team solved the problem by changing the system in which the robberies were taking place. It invented the 'ready fare' or 'exact fare' procedure of payment which effectively removes cash from the buses. Within a few months, the procedure was widely adopted by transit companies, and bus robberies decreased dramatically. A more radical solution would have involved socializing and subsidizing bus services so that all passengers could ride free of charge; after all, vertical transportation (on lifts and escalators) is not paid for by the ride, and it could logically be argued that horizontal transportation should be free also.

I do not pretend that the so-called 'crime problem' or even the 'organized crime problem' can be immediately solved by such systems approaches. The systems are too unmanageable. The competitive development of technology by police and criminals has given first one side and then the other the advantage. When the police and safe manufacturers were ahead, some safe-burglars went into other types of crime; as the criminals learned to utilize modern technology, other criminals followed suit and the number of safe-burglars increased. I expect that competitive development of 'organizational techniques' produces similar patterns. Even the simple solution to bus robbery might merely have driven robbers off buses and into taxis, lunch stands, and petrol stations. Similarly, if a system of computerized credit transfers eventually foils bank robbers, it might nevertheless merely direct robbers to other establishments. Alternatively, invention of such a computerized system surely would make an illegitimate opportunity structure available only to criminals possessing the skills of sophisticated electronics technicians and engineers.

But in coping with organized crime we must constantly keep in mind the fact that, in the long run, social problems disappear only when their place in a social system disappears. Piracy was not eliminated by strict police action; it was eliminated when the advent of the steamship made piracy unprofitable. American Cosa Nostra bosses did not get out of the prostitution business because of police crackdowns; they got out because, due to changes in immigration, a decrease in the number of unattached men, and an increase in the number of willing women in large cities the demand for prostitutes was reduced. Organized crime of other varieties will not disappear until similar structural changes modify the systemic places we have created for them. Sutherland, a pioneer in this area of deviancy, recognized that 'adequate control of professional crime cannot be attained by proceeding against thieves one at a time either by punitive or reformative policies. Control calls, in addition, for modifications in the general social order out of which professional theft grows.' [15]

Thus, we must defend ourselves against crime by locating its place in social systems—including the small systems called criminal organizations—and then eliminating that place. This seems a reasonable supplement, or even alternative, to the current criminal-law approach which, when the layers of rhetoric are peeled away, lies exposed as a procedure for punishing individual criminals and not for understanding crime or for reducing its incidence.

NOTES

1. U.S. President's Commission on Law Enforcement and Administration of Justice, *Task Force Report: The Courts* (Washington, D.C.: U.S. Government Printing Office, 1967), pp. 99–100.

2. U.S. President's Commission, *Task Force Report: Organized Crime, op. cit.,* p. 19.

3. *Lanzetta v. New Jersey,* 306 U.S. 451 (1939).

4. U.S. President's Commission on Law Enforcement and Administration of Justice, *Task Force Report: Science and Technology* (Washington, D.C.: U.S. Government Printing Office, 1967).

5. For a list of the many proposals, see U.S. President's Commission, *Task Force Report: Organized Crime, op. cit.,* pp. 16–24.

6. George Rusche and Otto Kirchheimer, *Punishment and Social Structure* (New York: Columbia University Press, 1939), p. 201.

7. William J. Keating with Richard Carter, *The Man Who Rocked the Boat* (New York: Harper and Row, 1965), pp. 87–88.

8. Mary McIntosh, "Changes in the Organization of Thieving," in Stanley Cohen (Editor), *Images of Deviance* (London, 1971), pp. 98–133. At p. 128.

9. Leon Radzinowicz, "The Dangerous Offender" (The Fourth Frank Newsam Memorial Lecture, Police College, Bramshill), *The Police Journal,* 41 (1968), pp. 411–447.

10. Robert T. Anderson, "From Mafia to Costa Nostra," *American Journal of Sociology,* 71 (1965), pp. 302–310.

11. Thomas C. Schelling, "Economic Analysis and Organized Crime," in U.S. President's Commission, *Task Force Report: Organized Crime, op. cit.,* Appendix D, pp. 114–126. At p. 114.

12. See Harold W. Kelton, Jr. and Charles M. Unkovic, "Charac-

teristics of Organized Criminal Groups," *Canadian Journal of Criminology and Corrections,* 13 (1971), pp. 68–78.

13. John N. Mitchell, "Address," Antitrust Section of the American Bar Association, 27 March 1969, p. 11; John L. McClellan, "The Corrupt Organizations Act of 1969," *Congressional Record,* 115, pp. S279–S281.

14. Schelling, "Economic Analysis and Organized Crime," *op. cit.,* p. 124. See also Ralph Salerno and John S. Tompkins, *The Crime Confederation: Cosa Nostra and Allied Operations in Organized Crime* (Garden City, New York, 1969), pp. 354–362; and Donald R. Cressey, "Bet taking, Costa Nostra, and Negotiated Social Order," *Journal of Public Law,* 19 (1970), pp. 13–22.

15. Edwin H. Sutherland, *The Professional Thief* (Chicago: University of Chicago Press, 1937), p. 229.

Chapter Nine

White-Collar Criminal: The Offender in Business and the Professions

Gilbert Geis

A sense of injustice, provoked by examples of inequities in the legal treatment of the powerful and the weak, has often led to imprecations against the crimes and sins of members of the upper classes—persons in government, business, and the professions. Often, those in power and those with professional training and social position are held to higher standards than their less fortunate brethren, on the ground that their background demands added social responsibility. It is these ideas, coupled with the view that no behavior is beyond scrutiny and appraisal, that have provided much of the impetus for the study of acts now grouped as "white-collar crime," "occupational crime," and "economic crime."

It is an intriguing enterprise to attempt to locate in different historical periods the sources of the most powerful forms of social criticism directed against the entrenched classes. Nay-saying prophets, as well as disenchanted members of the ruling classes and free-swinging muckrakers, have at various times led crusades against those they believed were deviating from acceptable standards of conduct.

In the United States social censure and caricature have long

Reprinted by permission of the author from "White–Collar Criminal," Atherton Press, 1968.

been the territory of novelists. If, for instance, Mark Schorer's biography of Sinclair Lewis is an accurate appraisal, some of these writers, exiles from a world to which they longed to belong, stood outside, jeering and casting diabolically well-aimed brickbats. Others, undoubtedly motivated by a sincere desire for social reform, found the literary license of fictional creation the most hospitable milieu for the advocacy of their ideals.

Rather subtly, however, the function performed by novelists in the United States began to be assumed by sociologists, members of a newly emergent academic discipline. Writers of fiction then turned more toward clinical dissection of individual motivation and toward portraiture of their protagonists—people responding to given social conditions which, however deplorable they might be, nonetheless demanded their due and, failing to exact it, took their reasonable psychic and social toll.

The early sociological scholars came together from a wide diversity of sources, but few would miss the strong ministerial tone that pervaded their ranks. They were persons of evangelical bent who believed that they had found the resolution of man's difficulties in a moral fervor buttressed by the dictates and metaphors of science. They were marked by a distaste of fuzzy speculation, a devotion to principles that can best be called "quasi-empirical," and by an insistent thrust to the roots of society where they intended to work their will, fortified by the tools of their trade and the trappings of their academic positions.

In 1896, when sociology was barely out of swaddling clothes, Edward A. Ross, author of the first significant sociological statement made in the United States about white-collar crime, could condescendingly describe sociology before his time as "a turgid mass of stale metaphysics, dark sayings, random historical illusions, and mawkish ethical raptures." [1] Ross' intense interest in social reform is clearly evident in his tribute to Lester F. Ward, his uncle by marriage, and the first president (1906–1907) of the American Sociological Society. "Suckled on the practicalism of Ward," wrote Ross, "I wouldn't give a snap of my fingers for the 'pussyfooting' sociologists." [2]

Sociology was a field, Ross noted, that "does not meekly sidle in among the established sciences dealing with the various aspects of social life"; it "aspires to nothing less than suzerainty." [3] In his turn, Ward told how the new science would operate: Society, he wrote, "should not drift aimlessly to and fro, backwards and forwards, without guidance. Rather, the group should carefully study its situations, comprehend the aims it desires to accomplish, study scientifically the best methods for attainment of these, and then concentrate social energy to the task set before it." [4] In these terms, Ward found agencies such as legislatures well on their way toward senescence. Perhaps they would have to be maintained, he noted, "but more and more they will become a merely formal way of putting the final sanction of society on decisions that have been worked out in the . . . sociological laboratory." [5] For Albion W. Small, a third pioneering sociologist, even the question of social values was readily susceptible to resolution by means of science. "The most reliable criterion of human values which science can propose," Small wrote, "would be the consensus of councils of scientists representing the largest possible variety of human interest, and cooperating to reduce their special judgments to a scale which would render their due to each of the interests of the total calculation." [6]

It is from this heritage that the present-day study of white-collar crime emerged. Edwin H. Sutherland, who in 1940 gave white-collar crime its label and a set of postulates, reflects both the early traditions of sociology and its subsequent development. . . . Sutherland's approach was clearly one of scientific muckraking. Though he eschewed melioristic statements and stressed that his interest lay not in the reform of society but merely in reform of criminological theory, no contemporary reader is apt to regard this as anything other than a patent disingenuousness very similar to the disclaimers of eighteenth-century satirists faced with ostracism or excommunication were their professional heresies to become manifest.

. . .

The early rationale of sociology, arising from "that general groping for social betterment produced by the misery that came in the wake of the industrial revolution and the factory system," was to be ridiculed by later sociologists as a preoccupation with "sex, sin, and sewage."

. . .

The polemical and theoretical return of American sociologists to matters of immediate social concern coincided with the conclusion of World War II; this approach has gained considerable momentum in the 1960s. . . .

Explanations for the shift in stress may be found in changes in the surrounding political and social atmosphere, conditions which inevitably influence what subjects are studied and how they are approached. Matters of personnel recruitment, availability of funds for certain kinds of research, and differentiated rewards from colleagues and others—all play into the formation of a pattern of work in an academic discipline. For sociology, its chronological position vis-à-vis other defined areas of study and its own movement from infancy through adolescence may have aided in eliminating some self-consciousness and contributed to a breakdown of occupational immurement.

These items must be taken into account, at least partially, in reviewing the development and present position of studies of white-collar crime. There are also matters of personal influence, items generally difficult to assess and weigh properly. Much work regarding white-collar crime was clearly generated from a pattern of respect and discipleship accorded to Sutherland. . . .

Personal influences and cross-disciplinary roots have undoubtedly provided studies of white-collar crime with direction and sophistication. The impact of secularization on an intellectual endeavor is like the impact of foreigners on a previously isolated geographical area —a seaport city, for instance, almost invariably becomes more cosmopolitan than its hinterland neighbors. Sociologists have responded to charges of "fatuous liberalism" raised from legal circles by attempting to buttress their conclusions and recommendations with sounder data. Reisman observed that "When a law professor comes to a sociologist because he is worried about the unequal distribution of justice, and regards legal aid work as a drop in the bucket, the latter's preoccupation with methodology and lack of reformist concern may surprise him and send him back to his own devices"; [7] barbs like that exert real suasion on sociological thought. On the other hand, the sociologist's scorn for legal conclusions that appear to be jerry-built on untested and unwarranted assumptions about human behavior and social activity provide pressure for experimental materials and for the acquisition of the complex and delicate skills essential for the collection of impregnable data.

It is developments such as these that have placed the study of white-collar crime in the position it occupies today and which portend the direction in which such studies are apt to move. Many gaps remain to be filled of course. . . . Moreover, articulation between inquiries into organization structures and studies of white-collar crime has only barely gotten under way. Finally, the necessity to relate white-collar crime to theories of deviance and to general theories of human behavior has persistently challenged scholars and remains a major issue which must be carefully addressed.

. . . The consequences of white-collar crime for the integrity of a society and the commission of "ordinary" kinds of crime, the importance of distinguishing between illegal and other kinds of meretricious behavior, the historical emergence of conditions that gave rise to laws defining white-collar crime, the need for typologies of such crime, and a summary review of general merits and shortcomings of Sutherland's pioneering position provide substance for the remaining introductory remarks.

It is important, initially, to realize that Sutherland, by virtue of his position in American sociology, the attractiveness of his terminology, and the illustrations he used to support his views, broadened the horizons of criminological research well beyond their traditional limits. The tendency to generalize about crime and criminals on the basis of the more readily visible forms of criminal activity, such as murder, assault, and robbery, was irreversibly affected by Sutherland's analysis that the propensity to violate the law is not confined to the stereotyped "criminal." That differential opportunities to commit different kinds of crime must be included in criminological analysis represents a major contribution of the Sutherland focus on white-collar offenses and should not be undervalued. In his foreword to the 1961 edition of *White Collar Crime,* Donald R. Cressey also observes that "the lasting merit of this book . . . is its demonstration that a pattern of crime can be found to exist outside both the focus of popular preoccupation with crime and the focus of scientific investigation of crime and criminality." [8] For Cressey, a paramount problem is the determination of why white-collar crime was able to remain beyond popular and criminological purview for so long.

Justice Oliver Wendell Holmes provided an approach to this issue when he pointed out that matters which a society chooses to study and acts which it decides to proscribe are telling indications of fundamental values. "It is perfectly proper to regard and study law simply as a great anthropological document," Holmes noted, continuing:

> It is proper to resort to [law] to discover what ideals of society have been strong enough to reach that final form of expression, or what have been the changes in dominant ideas from century to century. It is proper to study it as an exercise in the morphology and transformation of human ideas. The study pursued for such ends becomes science in its strictest sense.[9]

The same idea has been stated in the metaphorical language of Justice Cardozo: "Life casts the molds of conduct, which will some day become fixed as law," Cardozo wrote. "Law preserves the molds, which have taken form and shape from life." [10]

Few scholars have directed their attention to the charting of circumstances giving rise to statutes designed to discourage and to punish certain derelictions by members of the more powerful and entrenched segments of the society, though many have noted the striking increase in such rules and have marked signposts along the way. Holmes, for instance, has observed:

> When we read in the old books that it is the duty of one exercising a common calling to do his work upon demand and do it with reasonable skill, we shall see that the gentleman is in the saddle, and means to have the common people kept up to the mark for his convenience. We recognize the imperative tone which in our day has changed sides, and is oftener to be heard from the hotel clerk than from the guest.[11]

The growing concentration of statutory law on principles such as *caveat vendor*—"let the seller beware"—undoubtedly represents a function of, among other things, population growth, the development of cities, greater life expectancy, and enhanced technology, the last rich in its potential and awesome in its threat. As Pound has noted "The points at which the claims and desires of each individual and those of his fellows conflict or overlap have increased enormously. Likewise, new agencies of menace to the general security have developed in profusion."[12]

Two dominant motifs mark the history of response to acts now considered white-collar crime. On the one hand, throughout time there has been a broad sweep of denunciation based almost exclusively on moral principles, usually deemed as self-evident and part of a natural, immutable code. Witness, for example, the diatribes of the Biblical prophets, such as Micah, the yeoman farmer of the eighth century before Christ who bespoke the doom of Judah because of its low ethical level;[13] note, too, the uncompromising verdict of the Book of Ecclesiastes regarding commercial activities:

> A merchant shall hardly keep himself from doing wrong, and a huckster shall not be freed from sin. . . . As a nail sticketh fast between the joining of the stones, so doth sin stick close to buying and selling.[14]

On the other hand, there has been a rambling and variegated response in the law to conditions such as those denounced in Biblical writings. Part of the explanation for the discrepancy between moral and legal codes can be found in the nature and the function of law. Law, for instance, may be employed to maintain the status quo as well as to establish new ground rules. The latter situation, as de Tocqueville has pointed out, is not likely to occur when conditions are at their worst, but rather when they are in the process of change to the better.[15] It is then that people come to taste potential gains and to stir restively about the rate of change. Through most of history, with highly segmented and compartmentalized class patterns and strong authoritarian rule, those on the lower rungs of the social order were not likely to insist that they be treated fairly or decently or that their resources not be unreasonably exploited.

The reading of the legal record, however, is not merely a question of rote perusal of provisions with the assumption that absence equals indifference. Failure to outlaw certain behavior may represent espousal of goals likely to be compromised if lesser aims are accentuated. Legal statements may also stand for quite fanciful positions, and the discrepancy between the law on the books and the law in fact may be substantial. In addition, the oft-repeated dictum that law tends to be a reflection, however belated, of customary conditions fails to do justice to the basic question of *whose* customary ways will prevail and for what reason they will do so.

In such terms, a major thesis regarding white-collar crime is that the legal delineation of such offenses can be said to represent, though not in a direct or simple manner, social views that, for complex reasons, have come to be embodied in official codes. One facet of this development may be briefly summarized by reference to extension of the law of theft into white-collar realms.

Anthropological evidence makes clear that a sense of rightful possession of private property is far from an innate human characteristic. Sociologists have suggested that for Western civilization the doctrine of predestination, arising with notable intensity in countries persuaded to Calvinistic dogma, became translated into a belief that material possessions indicated divine approval, manifest in their bestowal.[16] Extratheological precepts also obviously contributed to a belief in the sovereignty of ownership. In the United States, the early entrenchment of this thesis is marked in the ringing words of John Adams, the country's second President:

> Property is surely a right of mankind as really as liberty. . . . The moment the idea is admitted into society, that property is not as sacred as the laws of God, and that there is not a force of law and public justice to protect it, anarchy and tyranny commence.[17]

It was from such an ideological perspective that the law of fraud, fundamental in white-collar crime, emerged. In his meticulous tracing of this development in *Theft, Law, and Society,* Jerome Hall concentrates initially upon the decision in the Carrier's Case in 1473, a decision which for the first time included within the definition of theft the appropriation of goods by a middleman. Prior to 1473, virtually all theft invólved cattle, and the law covered only direct acts. By the time of the Carrier's Case, however, manufacturing had begun to replace the feudal system. The new middle class had started to take shape, and its trade interests coincided with those of the Crown. In addition, the Carrier's Case involved wool and textile products, and these goods had recently become England's most significant exports. It was these conditions which coalesced in 1473 to change the Anglo-Saxon definition of theft.[18]

The slow, erratic, but nonetheless inexorable expansion of the concept of commercial fraud during the almost half-millenium since the Carrier's Case provides fascinating material on the interplay between those in possession of goods seeking to protect them and place themselves in a position to acquire more and other groups seeking their own advantage—with the state in the middle attempting to set rules by which the game will be played.

A few landmarks along the way may be noted briefly.[19] The thirteenth-century English courts, for instance, provided that there was to be "no remedy for the man who to his damage had trusted the word of a liar." [20] Even in the eighteenth century, a British Chief Justice could rhetorically ask: "When A got money from B by pretending that C had sent for it, shall we indict one man for making a fool of another?" [21] It was only in 1757 that a statutory provision for the punishment of "mere private cheating" was placed into English law. It was such judicial sentiments that led Jonathan Swift to locate an ancient Hebrew tradition in a land visited by Gulliver:

> [The Lilliputians] look upon fraud as a greater crime than theft, and
> therefore seldom fail to punish it with death; for they allege that care
> and vigilance, with a very common understanding, may preserve a
> man's goods from theft, but honesty has no defense against superior
> cunning.[22]

In the United States, the law of fraud developed too, and was fought each step of the way by those who held the view, expressed in the words of Chief Justice Stone, that "any interference with the operation of the natural laws of greed" was "subversive of liberty." [23]

The present state of this movement—a movement that demands concentrated attention from students interested in understanding the roots of white-collar crime—is epitomized by a recent popular panegyric on the relationship between the activities of federal regulatory agencies and the better life that we presumably all live: "You may never meet an investigator for the United States Government," it begins, "but you are safer, more comfortable, and more secure because thousands of Federal agents labor unceasingly in the background of American life." It proceeds to praise "kilocycle cops" who patrol radio and television airwaves, guardians of drug and advertising standards, enforcers of wage-and-hour laws, and similar federal agents.[24] It requires only a comparison between such sentiments and John Adams' equally self-righteous view on private property and its divine attributes to appreciate the extraordinary social revolution that provides the historical background of acts now designated as white-collar crime.

Use of white-collar crime statistics and case studies to take the moral temperature of the nation is a tempting enterprise. *Life* magazine, for instance, declared that white-collar crime represents a "moral lightheadedness" that "whatever its cause, is potentially far more dangerous than any number of juvenile 'rumbles.' " [25] C. Wright Mills also thought he discerned great social malaise in reactions to announcements of white-collar crimes. "As news of higher immoralities breaks," Mills wrote, "people often say, 'Well, another one got caught today,' thereby implying that the cases disclosed are not odd events involving occasional characters but symptoms of widespread conditions." [26]

The accuracy of such statements and their basic meaning is not readily apparent. Note, for instance, a Biblical commentator's summary of conditions at the time that Micah was inveighing against the scandals he saw in Hebrew life:

> Morals were appallingly low. Government officials were dishonest. A low ethical level prevailed in most areas of life. Because the nation had lost her moral integrity, she had become sinful, soft, and ripe for conquest.[27]

The tone has not changed in almost three thousand years, and the following observations can be made about contemporary American society:

> There is much evidence of a widespread apathy toward the traditional values of American life. The ideas of strict honesty have become out of date in many fields of endeavor, public as well as private. The fall of certain television quiz heroes led to a widespread suspicion that a sick industry built them up, and that the commercialism

which underwrites its programs is cynical and defiant. The crass disregard of the elemental essentials of straightforward dealing has invaded many areas of our society. One investigation after another reveals blunted moral sensibilities on the part of certain public officials and some of the agents of private enterprise who deal with them. Furthermore, the accused seem genuinely to feel justified in their actions, proclaiming one after another that no wrongdoing was involved nor intended. The victims of the deception, while diverse in their reactions, show surprisingly little moral indignation.[28]

In the same vein, early Greece, we are told, had its predators who in violation of its codes bought up land that they had learned would subsequently be acquired by the government; the Alcmaenoids, a leading Greek family, are reported to have contracted to build a solid marble temple, but instead to have employed concrete, veneering it with marble.[29] It is a rather long step, however, to maintain that ancient precursors of present-day white-collar crime underlay the demise of the Greek state, unless one employs such data to fill out Durant's skeletal commentary, built on an analysis of the bones of departed civilizations, that "a nation is born stoic and dies epicurean," [30]—which, if translated into white-collar crime terms, indicates that self-indulgent, exploitative, and unprincipled behavior ultimately dooms a society. The paradox implicit in Durant's observation is that stable, stoic societes, while they may persist longer than their epicurean counterparts, often do so at the expense of items such as vitality and enterprise, freedom and opportunity for self-determination. On the other hand, societies providing scope for such values, all of which in some measure are considered fundamental in American life, also appear to encourage deviation, variation, and innovation among some persons often at the expense of others.

The necessity for historical and comparative cross-cultural studies of white-collar crime, relating its forms and its intensity to measures of social vitality, is clearly indicated before a better evaluation can be made of the meaning of such crime for a nation's survival or demise.

The relationship between white-collar crime and "ordinary" or "traditional" kinds of crime seems somewhat better established than that between white-collar crime and cultural well-being. Perceptions regarding the ubiquitous nature of white-collar crime are said to have consequences for other kinds of crime, particularly in terms of permitting an individual to "rationalize" or "neutralize" his behavior; that is, to provide an explanation for his offense satisfactory to himself and to his presumed or real accusers. Lacking such an explanation, the offender may be forced to regard himself as an alien and abject creature, unable to control his behavior and incapable of acting in a manner which he has introjected as desirable.

Perhaps the best-known piece of research on this subject is by Sykes and Matza; they categorized the rationalizations of delinquents into several types, including an "appeal to higher loyalties" (loyalty to gang friends, for instance, is considered a more important moral obligation than respect for private property) and "condemnation of the condemners." [31] It is with this latter explanation, insisting that the delinquent is but one among many predators in the society, that the issue of white-collar crime comes into focus. Well-versed in newspaper reports of chicanery in high places, the juvenile may maintain that he is no worse and in some respects much better, than so-called "respectable" citizens, who not only commit crimes but also compound their offenses by being hypocritical about them.

This point is made more formally by Sheldon and Eleanor Glueck, noted investigators of juvenile delinquency, who point out that "the demands made upon the growing boy by every vehicle of modern life are numerous, involved, often subtle, sometimes inconsistent." The Gluecks draw the following implications from this situation:

> The child is told that he must be honest, non-aggressive, self-controlled, but on every hand he runs into vivid contradictory attitudes, values, and behavior in an environment that—both in and out of politics—seemingly rewards selfishness, aggression, a predatory attitude, and success by any means. It does not require the wisdom of a Seneca to convince the child, as it convinced that wise statesman, that "successful and fortunate crime is called virtue." [32]

Research probes into the less favored economic segments of the society reinforce the suggestion that in such groups individuals tend to regard others as exploitative and hostile, and to take comfort in such perceptions as justification for their own behavior. Cohen and Hodges, for example, found the ideas that "people are no good" and that the world "resembles a jungle" pervading responses to a questionnaire given persons in the "lower-blue-collar" class. Particularly notable was the cynicism concerning merchandising and service occupations:

> Economic and occupational success, they most often agreed, is accomplished by "friends or connections," "luck or chance," "pull or manipulating," or "cheating or underhanded dealing" (in contrast to

"daring and taking risks," "education," or "hard, day-by-day work").
[In contrast to members of other classes] they most often agree that
television repairmen, politicians, doctors, auto mechanics, butchers,
union officials, and businessmen are not trustworthy.[33]

Lower-blue-collar class members were found to be the most
credulous members of the society regarding the accuracy of the written
or printed word. Cohen and Hodges believe that limited experience,
both direct and vicarious, makes such individuals particularly vulnerable to messages seeming to emanate from trustworthy sources. The
researchers suggest that there is no conflict between their findings of
credulity and misanthropy. "It is one thing to feel a generalized distrust of human beings, their motives and their claims," they write. "It
is another to form an attitude on a specific claim or message where one
has few independent criteria for evaluating the content of the message,
little awareness of specific alternatives and little disposition to weigh
evidence." [34]

The data necessary to refine the observations presented by
Gibbons are as yet not available. It would be informative to learn
about the perceptions regarding the prevalence of white-collar crime
that are held by different kinds of traditional offenders and to determine the views on white-collar crime among individuals raised
in social strata which produce a disproportionately high percentage of
traditional offenders—and to do so *before* such individuals separate
into essentially law-abiding or criminal categories. An informal California survey suggests the possibility that prison inmates in that state
usually do not have recourse to white-collar crime as justification for
their own offenses.[35] Persistent demands by the state parole board
that offenders accept categorically their own guilt and personal responsibility for their acts—a thesis based upon Freudian principles
of therapeutic grace—may condition verbal responses by prisoners.
Group therapy, widely practiced in California correctional institutions, tends to divert attention from expressions of social cynicism
and concentrate it upon psychic inadequacies. The California study,
for instance, found expressions such as "I do my own number" and
"I have myself to worry about" the most common answers to questions
regarding the influence of knowledge and beliefs concerning white-
collar crime upon the individual's own violation.

Most causal explanations of white-collar crime derive from
an "evil causes evil" view based on the belief that only deplorable
conditions of person or place can give rise to criminal behavior. There
is neglect of the fact that perfectly adequate human beings and perfectly adequate social situations, judged by reasonable criteria, may

produce untoward consequences, in the manner that both kindness and murder kill.

One of the earliest and hardiest explanations of white-collar crime is suggested by Aristotle in *Politics*. "Men may desire super-fluities in order to enjoy pleasure unaccompanied with pain, and therefore they commit crimes," he noted. "The greatest crimes are caused by excess and not by necessity." [36] Sutherland, however, in perhaps the most telling of his observations on crime causation, laid to rest the Aristotelian postulate and its contemporary kin. "Though criminal behavior is an expression of general needs and values," Sutherland emphasized, "it is not explained by those general needs and values, since non-criminal behavior is an expression of the same needs and values." [37] The financially pressed corporate executive, Sutherland's view points out, may embezzle or he may move to a cheaper house, send his wife to work, himself take a weekend job, or borrow money from an uncle. Each of these alternatives may be able to satisfy his necessity adequately. The need alone, shared by untold numbers of other individuals who resolve it both legally and illegally, offers little clue to the precise method that will be selected for its satisfaction.

Sutherland's focus was on the enunciation of a theory to ex-plain all crime. In an article on corporate violations, for instance, he noted mockingly that General Motors does not have an inferiority complex, United States Steel does not suffer from an unresolved Oedipus problem, and the DuPonts do not desire to return to the womb. It was a clever piece of invective, designed to decimate the position of clinical theorists in criminology. "The assumption that an offender may have some such pathological distortion of the intellect seems to me absurd," Sutherland wrote, "and if it is absurd regarding the crimes of businessmen, it is equally absurd regarding the crimes of persons in the lower economic classes." [38]

To substitute for partial explanations and for psychological theses regarding criminal behavior, Sutherland advanced his own hypothesis which, "for reasons of economy, simplicity, and logic," was to be used to explain both white-collar criminality and lower-class criminality. This was his theory of differential association. "Crim-inality is learned," it stated in part, "in direct or indirect association with those who already practice the behavior." Since criminality is so learned, Sutherland observed, it can be and is learned at all social levels. [39]

It appears likely that Sutherland was led by his theoretical preconceptions into a number of intellectual traps which rendered the concept of white-collar crime of dubious utility for theoretical purposes. Having at hand an explanatory scheme which could embrace virtually the entire range of human conduct, Sutherland felt no need to differentiate carefully among an extraordinarily wide range of offenses—criminal, ethical, and moral—engaged in by persons who were "respected" and "socially accepted and approved." All would fit neatly into his interpretative scheme for white-collar crime in the same manner that professional crime, aggressive crime following encephalitis, and a host of other highly divergent forms of behavior could be "explained" by differential association.

It is important to realize that no one, of course, had ever maintained that General Motors or its management personnel suffered from an inferiority complex, any more than any serious scholar would have taken the position that all criminals, of either the lower or upper class, are driven by an unrequited yearning to return to the womb. Sutherland was obviously flailing a theoretical nonesuch, and it was, in fact, Sutherland himself who, in one vital respect, came nearest to the theories he was belaboring, with his insistence that all criminals could, and should, be analyzed in terms of a single theoretical interpretation.

It was this commitment that inevitably tended to blur action distinctions for Sutherland. As Merton has noted, "the decision to encompass a great variety of behaviors under one heading naturally leads us to look for an all-encompassing set of propositions which will account for the entire range of behavior." "This is not too remote," Merton points out, "from the assumption of a John Brown or a Benjamin Rush that there must be *a* theory of disease, rather than distinct theories of disease—of tuberculosis and of arthritis, of typhoid and syphilis—theories which are diverse rather than single." [40]

A present need in regard to the concept of white-collar crime appears to be to separate those types of activity that fall within the range of criminal statutes and then to gather together into less ubiquitous groupings those forms of behavior which analytically resemble one another, both in their manifestations and in the ingredients that enter into their origin. As a starting point, it might be desirable to separate white-collar crimes committed (1) by individuals as individuals (for example, lawyers or doctors), (2) by employees against a corporation or business (embezzlers), and (3) by policy-making officials for the firm (for example, in antitrust cases).

It would seem desirable that studies of embezzlers, for instance, should at first be evaluated on their own merits (as Cressey did [41]) rather than as investigations into a type of behavior similar to the crimes of corporate officials. Sutherland himself pointed out that "the ordinary case of embezzlement is a crime by a single individual in a subordinate position against a strong corporation," [42] and Daniel Bell, after declaring that Sutherland's *White Collar Crime* is "misleadingly entitled," goes on to remark that bank embezzlers, as a group, are not upper-class individuals, but members of the middle class.[43] Embezzlers, to carry the point somewhat further, usually work alone, while antitrust violators must work in compact with others. The embezzler benefits himself directly, and harms his employer. On the other hand, offenders such as antitrust violators. though they undoubtedly most often operate in terms of personal advantage, can rationalize their offense as contributing to the fiscal health of their employer. These may not be crucial variations, but it would seem preferable to examine offenses such as embezzling, tax evasion, corporate violations, and fee splitting as distinct forms of crime which may be related to each other in some ways and to other offenses in different ways. It would also appear reasonable to concentrate initially on the elements of the criminal act for purposes of grouping it rather than upon the social characteristics of the perpetrators of the acts, and to group behavior in terms of the latter item only for the most compelling pragmatic or interpretative reasons. The crimes of medical doctors, for instance, would appear to be susceptible to differentiation on more meaningful terms than the professional status of their perpetrators. The offenses of fee splitting and abortion, both committed by doctors, seem about as related in most essential respects as the offenses of infanticide and adultery, both of which may be committed by mothers.

Until this analytical impasse is more fully resolved, the concept of white-collar crime may stand indicted on Tappan's charge that it soars "into vacuity, wide and handsome," [44] and on Vold's allegation that it is at the moment "ambiguous, uncertain, and controversial." [45]

It may be noted in conclusion that the need for white-collar crime to be studied in terms of more homogeneous units reprents a requirement common to the field of criminology.

NOTES

1. Edward A. Ross, Review of Giddings, "Principles of Sociology," *Educational Review*, 12 (June, 1896), p. 92.

2. Edward A. Ross, *Seventy Years of It* (New York, 1936), p. 180.

3. Edward A. Ross, *Foundations of Sociology*, 5th ed. (New York, 1926), p. 8.

4. James Quayle Dealey, "Lester Frank Ward," in Howard W. Odum, ed., *American Masters of Social Science* (New York, 1927), p. 82.

5. Lester F. Ward, *Applied Sociology* (Boston, 1906), pp. 338–339.

6. Albion W. Small, *The Meaning of Social Science* (Chicago, 1910), p. 242.

7. David Riesman, "Law and Sociology," in William M. Evan, ed., *Law and Sociology* (New York, 1962), pp. 30–31.

8. Donald R. Cressey, "Foreword," *White Collar Crime* (New York, 1961), p. xii.

9. Oliver Wendell Holmes, "Law in Science and Science in Law," in *Collected Legal Papers* (New York, 1921), p. 212.

10. Benjamin N. Cardozo, *The Nature of the Judicial Process* (New Haven, Conn., 1921), p. 64.

11. Holmes, *op. cit.*, pp. 213–214.

12. Roscoe Pound, *Criminal Justice in America* (New York, 1930), p. 12.

13. Micah 1:1–16 and 2:1–12.

14. Ecclesiastes 27:2.

15. Alexis de Tocqueville, *The Old Regime and the French Revolution,* trans. by Stuart Gilbert (Garden City, N.Y., 1955), pp. 176–177.

16. Max Weber, *The Protestant Ethic and the Spirit of Capitalism,* trans. by Talcott Parsons (London, 1930).

17. John Adams, *Works,* vol. 6 (Boston, 1853), pp. 8–9.

18. Jerome Hall, *Theft, Law and Society,* 2d ed. (Indianapolis, 1952), pp. 1–33.

19. Much of this material is drawn from Hermann Mannheim, *Criminal Justice and Social Reconstruction* (London, 1946), sect. 3; and Hermann Mannheim, *Comparative Criminology* (Boston, 1967), chap. 21.

20. Frederick Pollock and Frederic William Maitland, *History of English Law,* vol. 2 (Boston, 1909), p. 535.

21. Quoted by Hermann Mannheim, *Criminal Justice and Social Reconstruction, op. cit.,* p. 121.

22. Jonathan Swift, "A Voyage to Lilliput," in *Gulliver's Travels,* pt. 1, chap. 6 (1735).

23. Alpheus T. Mason, *Harlan Fiske Stone: Pillar of the Law* (New York, 1956), p. 380.

24. Miriam Ottenberg, *The Federal Investigators* (Englewood Cliffs, N.J., 1962), pp. xi–xii.

25. Frank Gibney, "The Crooks in White Collars," *Life,* 43 (October 14, 1957), p. 176.

26. C. Wright Mills, *The Power Elite* (New York, 1956), pp. 343–344.

27. Rolland W. Wolfe, "The Book of Micah," in *The Interpreter's Bible,* vol. 6 (Nashville, Tenn., 1951), pp. 898–899.

28. Leroy Bowman, *Youth and Delinquency in an Inadequate Society* (New York, League for Industrial Democracy, 1960), p. 21.

29. John McConaughy, *From Cain to Capone: Racketeering down the Ages* (New York, 1931), p. 24.

30. Will Durant, *Our Oriental Heritage* (New York, 1954), p. 259.

31. Gresham M. Sykes and David Matza, "Techniques of Neutralization: A Theory of Delinquency," *American Sociological Review*, 22 (December, 1967), pp. 664–670.

32. Sheldon Glueck and Eleanor Glueck, *Ventures in Criminology* (Cambridge, 1965), p. 20.

33. Albert K. Cohen and Harold M. Hodges, Jr., "Characteristics of the Lower Blue-Collar-Class," *Social Problems*, 10 (Spring, 1963), p. 323.

34. *Ibid.*, 325.

35. The conclusions were reached by James H. Cosby in 1966 after more than a dozen discussions of the subject with groups of inmates of a California prison.

36. Aristotle, *Politics*, trans. by J. E. C. Welldon (London, 1932), Book II, chap. 7, p. 65.

37. Edwin H. Sutherland and Donald R. Cressey, *Principles of Criminology*, 7th ed. (Philadelphia, 1966), p. 82.

38. Edwin H. Sutherland, "Crimes of Corporations," in Albert Cohen, Alfred Lindesmith, and Karl Schuessler, eds., *The Sutherland Papers* (Bloomington, Ind., 1956), p. 96.

39. See Sutherland and Cressey, *op. cit.*, chap. 4.

40. Robert K. Merton, in Helen L. Witmer and Ruth Kotinsky, eds., *New Perspctives for Research on Juvenile Delinquency*, Washington, D.C., Children's Bureau Publication No. 356, 1956, p. 27.

41. Donald R. Cressey, *Other People's Money: The Social Psychology of Embezzlement* (New York, 1953).

42. Edwin H. Sutherland, *White Collar Crime* (New York, 1949), p. 231.

43. Daniel Bell, "Crime As an American Way of Life," in *End of Ideology* (New York, 1960), p. 382.

44. Paul W. Tappan, "Who Is the Criminal?" *American Sociological Review*, 12 February, 1947), p. 98.

45. George B. Vold, *Theoretical Criminology* (New York, 1958), p. 253.

Chapter Ten

The Nature, Impact and Prosecution of White-Collar Crime

Herbert Edelhertz

The term "white-collar crime" is not subject to any one clear definition. Everyone believes he knows what the term means, but when definitions are compared there are usually sharp divergences as to whether one crime or another comes within the definition. . . .

For the purpose of this paper, the term will be defined as *an illegal act or series of illegal acts committed by nonphysical means and by concealment or guile, to obtain money or property, to avoid the payment or loss of money or property, or to obtain business or personal advantage.*

The definition, in that it hinges on the modifying words "an illegal act or series of illegal acts," does not go to the question whether particular activities should be the subject of criminal proscriptions.

It is a definition which differs markedly from that advanced by Edwin H. Sutherland, who said that "*** white-collar crime may be defined approximately as a crime committed by a person of respectability and high social status in the course of his occupation." Sutherland[1] introduced this definition with the comment that these

Reprinted by permission of the National Institute of Mental Health, U.S. Dept. of Health, Education and Welfare, 1970.

white-collar crimes are violations of law by persons in the "upper socio-economic class."

Sutherland's definition is far too restrictive. His view provided a rational basis for the economic determinism which was the underlying theme of his analysis, but did not comprehend the many crimes committed outside one's occupation. Ready examples of crimes falling outside one's occupation would be personal and nonbusiness false income tax returns, fraudulent claims for social security benefits, concealing assets in a personal bankruptcy, and use of large-scale buying on credit with no intention or capability to ever pay for purchases. His definition does not take into account crime as a business, such as a planned bankruptcy, or an old fashioned "con game" operated in a business milieu. Though these crimes fall outside Sutherland's definition, they were considered and discussed by him.

Sutherland made a valuable contribution. He illuminated the double standard built into our law enforcement structure, and contrasted society's treatment of abusive acts by the well-to-do with law enforcement and penal provisions applicable to abusive acts by those less fortunate or well placed. He forcefully pointed out that our legislation had established a unique legal structure with a complex of administrative proceedings, injunctions, and cease and desist orders, to meet common law fraud if committed in a business context, thus largely preempting the field of enforcement and making criminal proceedings unlikely or seemingly inappropriate. He showed how fraudulent sales practices, or sale of drugs by misrepresentations, or patent abuses, can continue through years of administrative and judicial proceedings to a determination which is no more than a slap on the wrist, whereas the less sophisticated thief must face additional criminal charges if he commits further and similar acts in the course of his much briefer and less lucrative activity.

Sutherland was basically concerned with society's disparate approach to the crimes of the respectable and well-to-do on the one hand, and those of the poor and disadvantaged on the other. His definition of white-collar crime concentrated, therefore, on characterizing violators rather than violations. The definition on which this paper is based is, hopefully, a more inclusive one.

White-collar crime is democratic. It can be committed by a bank teller or the head of his institution. The offender can be a high government official with a conflict of interest. He can be the destitute beneficiary of a poverty program who is told to hire a work group and puts fictional workers on the payroll so that he can appropriate their wages. The character of white-collar crime must be found in its modi operandi and its objectives rather in the nature of the offenders.

It is important that in our definitions of crime we concentrate on the nature of the crime rather than on the personal characteristics or status of the criminal. The latter analysis may be relevant and even of primary utility in the design and implementation of specific law enforcement programs, or to rehabilitation of offenders. Confusion and discriminatory application of penal sanctions must necessarily flow, however, from personalizing our conceptions of the nature of any one crime or group of crimes.

The above definition is the cornerstone of the following conceptualizations of various aspects of white-collar crime. It is crucial to this discussion of deterrence, investigation, evaluation, prosecution, and sentencing.

The Impact of White-Collar Crime

Sutherland published his "White Collar Crime" in 1949, a year already in the buried past. The complexity of our society in the intervening fifth of a century has increased so rapidly that it is difficult to do more than recognize resemblances between the problem he described and that which we face today. He saw the problem as one of victimization and discrimination, valid today as then. More important now, however, is our expanded vulnerability to white-collar crime because of changes in our economic and social environment.

We should not fall into the trap of idealizing the past . . . but we can recognize that progress has its harmful side effects. In the white-collar field the basic side effect is the weakening of certain safeguards which were built into the marketing and distribution patterns of an earlier age, and which retained much of their vitality only 20 years ago.

Most purchases were once made in stores which were managed and serviced by their individual owners. Owners either lived in the communities which they serviced, or had close ties to these communities. They were known to their customers and had to face them after a purchase as well as before. These proprietors competed on the basis of service and reliability and, even though products might be presold by advertising, they would bear the brunt of customer dissatisfaction. Today most consumer goods—food, drugs, appliances— are sold by chains or similar large organizations, and the mobility of their personnel is matched, in part at least, by the mobility of their customers. On the retail level there has developed an essentially faceless transactional environment.

Today transactions are executed or moved by nonpersonal or credit instrumentalities. Retail credit is no longer carried on the books of the retailer, to be financed by retailer bank loans, but is now the subject of highly sophisticated and costly credit transactions involving bank and non-bank credit cards, revolving credit, credit life insurance—all substituting the credit granting and administering entities for the retailer after the sale is made.

The genesis of transactions between businesses, and within businesses, is less the subject of individual decisions and more the result of programmed procedures. Thus we now have electronic links, managed by computers. A perpetual inventory system may trigger a purchase order which in turn galvanizes a series of computer-induced stages culminating in an automatically written and signed check to pay for the purchase.

Conflicting objectives internal to business operations multiply exposure to white-collar crimes. Thus manufacturing and sales departments within a company will seek to override the restraints imposed by a credit department with consequent vulnerability to bankruptcy fraud operations. Sales departments will deliberately court risks, as by mailing of unsolicited credit cards, relegating possible fraud losses to the status of costs of doing business as if mere rent or utility charges. This may be an acceptable price to pay for economic growth, but it does invite white-collar crime.

Business planning is more and more keyed to the creation of needs, rather than to discovering or satisfying needs. Thus we have patterns of built-in style obsolescence, in hard goods and soft, and products may also be manufactured with a limited useful life.

Our economy has passed the point where it is geared to meet only the basic and elemental needs of the greater part of our population. The number of "haves" is very high, and large numbers of "have-nots" possess items which generate the desire for similar items on the part of their neighbors. Television exposes even the poorest to an incessant barrage of incitation to consumption of nonnecessities and to the titillation of desires based on nothing more than the exploitation of longing for status, beauty, or virility. The juxtaposition of these desires with our credit economy intensifies the incentive and opportunity for fraud in the marketing of consumer goods and services.

Our social and economic organization exposes us to new species of white-collar crime, having different or mixed objectives. In an earlier age the unlawful or ethically questionable amassing of wealth was characteristically accomplished by bald plunder or seizure of the public domain. "Teapot Dome" was a classic case, as was the land-grant device which provided the capital for building much of this Nation's railroad grid. Today such blatant power and property grabs are avoided. The new avenues for creation of wealth often involve tax avoidance (or evasion, which is criminal) to facilitate the accumulation of capital on which further acquisitions of wealth may be based. Tax avoidance or evasion are advantages to be wielded as is the ability to obtain favored treatment by zoning commissions, or special favors in connection with public guarantees of real property loans, or to be free from regulation in the operation of quasi-public utilities. The boundaries of the permissible and the impermissible are not drawn with precision, and perhaps they should not be. But as a consequence substantial loopholes persist, permitting the commission of crimes or acts inconsistent with policy limits set by our society.

The affluence of our society heightens exposure to criminal abuses by fiduciaries, an exposure which was once confined to the wealthy and the upper middle classes. More of us are now beneficiaries of trusts and quasi-trusts managed by the growing fiduciary industry. New targets for crime are the increasing proportion of trusts and estates of middle-class decedents, interests in union and company pension, welfare, and profit-sharing funds, and the broad panoply of mutual funds, investment trusts, credit unions, and investment clubs.

. . .

As individuals we are more exposed to abuse. We are more likely to deal with strangers than with those we know (whose blemishes we can assess), and we are more vulnerable than we used to be because we tend to rely more on one another or on protection by Government. Those who buy securities are better protected than ever before because of the work of the Securities and Exchange Commission and comparable State agencies, yet are more exposed to the stock fraud artist who deceives the regulatory agency or totally circumvents its supervision. The buyer of food relies on weights and measures marked on prepackaged merchandise, since there is no occasion to look for the thumb on the seller's scale. We find it hard to believe that Government food inspectors would permit most unesthetic portions of animals to be ground into our hamburgers or sausages, and are therefore most shocked when sporadic inquiries disclose what we are eating. The physician relies on the vigilance of the Food and Drug Administration, and therefore accepts his education as to prescribable drugs from detail men sent to his office by pharmaceutical manufacturers. The certificates of guarantee which accompany our purchases of appliances and automobiles give us a false sense of security, no matter how often we have been burned in the past.[2] *Caveat emptor* loses meaning when we buy closed packages.

Technical developments increase our exposure to white-collar crime. A prime objective of computerization is the cutting of labor costs, which means substituting hardware and computer programs for expensive labor. Our experience has given us an extensive fund of knowledge (often imperfect) as to how we can control, audit, and monitor people, but we have only the most elementary knowledge of how to audit computers and those who have learned how to use them. Much thought is being given to methods of coping with computers from a management point of view, i.e., internal controls, but little to audit by outsiders such as regulatory or law enforcement agencies. The search for control procedures is complicated by the accelerating rate at which the computer art is developing, a rate which makes controls obsolete almost as quickly as they are developed. Existing control methodology is not adequate for internal control, or for investigation by investigating agencies, or for regulation by regulatory agencies.

White-collar crime is a low visibility, high impact factor in our society. Because of the changes in the nature of our economic organization, particularly new developments in marketing, distribution, and investment, it is a fair assumption that white-collar crime has increased at a rate which exceeds population growth. Its effects intersect with and interact with other problems of our society, such as poverty and discrimination. It also weighs heavily on the aged [3] who are, in our society, divorced from the homes and community of their children in contrast to most prior human social organization.

The increasing complexity of our society heightens vulnerability because it increases the difficulty of obtaining redress for losses suffered. Legal services are costly, prosecutors and investigators are overburdened, and court calendars are clogged. A victim must measure the time it takes to obtain redress and wonder whether he will not be the major sufferer, rather than the target of his complaint.

The prevention, deterrence, investigation, and prosecution of white-collar crime must compete with other interests for allocation of law enforcement dollars, in an atmosphere in which every other national problem is made more serious and more costly of solution by the increasing complexities of our society.

. . .

White-collar crime, like common crime, can have a serious influence on the social fabric, and on the freedom of commercial and interpersonal transactions. Every stock market fraud lessens confidence in the securities market. Every commercial bribe or kickback debases the level of business competition, often forcing other suppliers to join in the practice if they are to survive. The business which accumulates capital to finance expansion by tax evasion places at a disadvantage the competitor who pays his taxes and is compelled to turn to lenders (for operating and expansion capital). The pharmaceutical company which markets a new drug based on fraudulent test results undercuts its competitors who are still marketing the properly tested drugs, and may cause them to adopt similar methods. Competitors who join in a conspiracy to freeze out their competition, or to fix prices, may gravely influence the course of our economy, in addition to harming their competitors and customers. The tax evader adds to the ultimate burden of the man who pays his taxes.

We should take special note of the impact of white-collar crime on the elderly and the poor, especially ghetto residents. These groups are the victims of minor offenses, such as housing violations, and of what we conventionally refer to as "consumer frauds." The impact is self-evident, but there is little comprehension of the outward rippling from consumer frauds on the elderly and the poor.

. . .

Merchandising frauds may have severe impact. The typical case would involve an overpriced television set or furniture, with heavy finance charges. This kind of credit is extended only to those with jobs (to be endangered if wages are garnisheed) or to those whose obligations can be guaranteed by relatives or parents who have jobs or other assets. When installment payments are missed the entire obligation becomes immediately due and payable, and the victims are faced with the choice of refinancing and assuming even greater obligations, or becoming subject to garnishment procedures which could cost them their jobs.

While the contribution of consumer fraud to ghetto disturbances is not easily provable, it is clear that there is substantial hostility toward credit merchants by ghetto residents. This may be based on the use of fraudulent sales and credit practices by some merchants, and also on the frequent resort to such operations by direct or door-to-door sellers of expensive appliances, encyclopedias, self-improvement schools, etc. There is some reason to believe that resentments stirred by such tactics played a part in the Watts riot of July, 1966.

The social and economic costs of tax violations, self-dealing by corporate employees and bank officials, adulteration or watering of foods and drugs, charity frauds, insurance frauds, price fixing, frauds arising out of government procurement, and abuses of trust are clearly enormous even though not easily measured. If substantial progress can be made in the prevention, deterrence, and successful prosecution of these crimes we may reasonably anticipate substantial benefits to the material and qualitative aspects of our national life.

Common Elements of White-Collar Crimes

Basic to any determination of fruitful avenues of exploration with respect to the prevention, detection, and prosecution of white-collar crime, is an analysis of how it operates. What are its component parts? Where the spectrum of possible criminal acts is so broad and the perpetrators so different in character, status, and motivation, can there be identifiable elements of universal applicability? Can they apply to crimes so diverse as antitrust violations and bank embezzlement, or so diverse as tax fraud and the ordering of merchandise with no intention to pay?

Without implying that motivations are necessarily similar, and recognizing that the modi operandi may be as diverse as the activities of all mankind, it may be that there are common elements which may be basic to all white-collar crimes.

In any white-collar crime, we will find the following elements:

(*a*) Intent to commit a wrongful act or to achieve a purpose inconsistent with law or public policy.

(*b*) Disguise of purpose or intent.

(*c*) Reliance by perpetrator on ignorance or carelessness of victim.

(*d*) Acquiescence by victim in what he believes to be the true nature and content of the transaction.

(*e*) Concealment of crime by—

(1) Preventing the victim from realizing that he has been victimized, or

(2) Relying on the fact that only a small percentage of victims will react to what has happened, and making provisions for restitution to or other handling of the disgruntled victim, or

(3) Creation of a deceptive paper, organizational, or transactional facade to disguise the true nature of what has occurred.

If these are, in fact, common elements, or even elements which are present in the greater number of white-collar crimes, then awareness of this structure may help us in our search for preventive, deterrent, and prosecution measures.

(*a*) *Intent to commit a wrongful act or to achieve a purpose inconsistent with law or public policy*

The presence of this element is self-evident in the case of most white-collar crimes. It may be less easily seen in criminal cases in which prosecutors do not have the burden of showing that the defendant knew his act was unlawful or wrongful. Examples would be offenses of omission, such as failure to provide heat or proper repair, or failure to register securities for lack of awareness of the requirements of the Securities Act of 1933, or misinterpretation of such requirements. It is often difficult to prove such intent where the subject has been advised by counsel that his proposed course of conduct is legal, or where there has been a history of laxity with respect to such conduct by law enforcement authorities.

There is always an intent to commit a wrongful act or to achieve a purpose inconsistent with law or public policy where there is a white-collar crime or offense, even one not requiring proof of intent, notwithstanding the existence of advice of counsel, misinterpretations of law, omission rather than commission, or laxity by authorities. . . .

Some examples of complex problems of intent would be the following:

A landlord very rarely gets in trouble for failure to provide heat or maintenance, unless he skimps and tries to provide the minimum required by law, or sets out to provide less on the theory that the penalty will only be a minor fine and therefore a supportable cost of doing business. One who seeks advice of counsel in a borderline area is often seeking to establish a future defense in case his transaction is critically examined. A taxpayer plays the percentages when he takes an entertainment deduction which he knows will be disallowed if closely audited, suspecting that he risks only a 6 percent interest charge on the extra tax he should have paid. One who makes purchases on credit with no intent to pay, will use the defense that he was merely improvident, which may be a good defense, but most people know whether they have enough money to pay their bills. Even in the apparently innocuous situation where one writes a check today, knowing that by the time it clears he will have deposited a salary check to cover it, he is skirting the line in issuing a check, knowing there are no funds to cover it if immediately presented. In many instances in which check kites defraud banks of the principal amounts of large checks, the true intent of the defendant is to use the bank's capital without paying interest, or because his financial condition is not good enough to justify orthodox borrowing; he fully intends to ultimately cover his checks but "unforeseen" circumstances intervene. In a remarkably high proportion of white-collar crimes unforeseen circumstances do intervene. For example, money is embezzled to finance a profitable investment which will enable return of the funds prior to detection but the venture fails; or a furnace breaks down because maintenance did not anticipate a lengthy cold spell; or a shortcut in testing a drug could not be expected to result in such horrendous side effects as in the Thalidomide case.

(b) Disguise of purpose or intent

Once again, in the conventional situation this element is obviously present. It is to the unconventional situation that we must look in order to determine whether this is an element always, or almost always present in white-collar crimes.

Under discussion here is a basic misrepresentation as to the nature and purpose of the transaction which is at the heart of the violation.

In an antitrust case an agreement for reciprocal business dealings between supplier and purchaser conceals: (1) The absence of price, quality and service as elements inducing the transaction; and (2) the intent of the purchaser to foreclose supplier-competitors. In the SEC case the facade of a private offering to a purported limited number of offerees, or some other device, may conceal the effort to sell without a registration statement or offering circular which fully discloses the material facts which should influence investment decisions. In a commercial bribery or kickback case a buyer for a corporation is given an opportunity to buy something at far below cost, the purchase being subsidized by the corrupting supplier. An investment by a union officer in a business enterprise which employs his union members is in fact consideration for breach of his fiduciary duty to his membership. What looks like a simple purchase or sale of stock by a corporate insider, may in fact be a wrongful exploitation of inside information. The submission of an order for merchandise to a supplier may mask the intent or aim not to pay. A vanity publisher or correspondence school will attest to belief in the marketability of the victims' work or potential, concealing or failing to disclose its knowledge that the odds against any success or fulfillment are astronomical.

Disguise differs from intent. That they are distinct and separate elements can be seen if one compares a white-collar crime to a common crime. In a common crime the intent once formed is followed by the implementing act which is subject to no misinterpretation. The element of disguise in white-collar crime serves to blur intent to the point where it often can only be derived by interpretation.

(c) *Reliance by perpetrator on ignorance or carelessness of the victim*

The white-collar criminal must rely on the ignorance or carelessness of the victim and, in those areas in which regulatory agencies have a statutory mandate to protect the public, the ignorance of the public must be maintained by misleading the agency or circumventing its disclosure requirements.

One example would be the looting of an automobile liability insurance carrier. In a typical situation such a carrier will be purchased by a group which will promptly sell off good assets in its portfolios and replace these with worthless or overvalued assets. The policy holders are ignorant of these manipulations. The State insurance department either accepts these new assets at their represented value, or does no more than look at over-the-counter stock quotations which may have been manipulated for this purpose. Since the State insurance department is ignorant (possibly because of less than adequate audit procedures) of the hollowness of the assets in the portfolio, it permits the company to continue in business, collecting premiums, and holding off settlement of claims against its insureds. When the collapse comes, claimants cannot collect on their claims or judgments and policy holders are helplessly exposed to the very liabilities they paid premiums to avoid.

Ignorance or carelessness of the victim is crucial to the success of the white-collar criminal, and is the objective sought by the disguise of purpose or intent referred to above. In a home improvement scheme the victim is ignorant of the work history of the company which solicits him, and does not take the precaution of requiring or checking on references. The victim is customarily unaware of the contents of the documents he signs, generally having no idea of the true price and the credit terms, and few victims have ever even suspected that they were placing mortgages on their homes as part of the deal.

. . .

In some instances ignorance of the victim is almost a certainty because of the context in which the wrongful actions arise. In one case (not resulting in prosecution) a department manager in a defense industry deliberately shifted labor costs from a fixed price contract to the performance of a cost reimbursable contract. He did this without the knowledge of his employer, the sole motive being to make his department more profitable and thus enhance his career and promotion prospects. This was a case where the direct financial reward from the scheme came to an innocent, albeit ignorant party (the employer), whose ignorance promoted the ignorance of the Government which was the ultimate victim of the scheme.

Ignorance of the true facts is sometimes inevitable in the face of a calculated effort to deceive, but the perpetrator's efforts to deceive and mislead are only too often matched by the carelessness, self-deception, or cupidity of victims. It does little good to require a prospectus to be issued in connection with the sale of stock if the purchaser of stock will not read it. This raises the central question of what measures can be taken to strike at the ignorance of victims or abate their cupidity.

(d) Acquiescence by victim in what he believes to be the true nature and content of the transaction

White-collar crimes are unique. They generally require the victim to acquiesce in being victimized. In the great majority of cases we are confronted with crimes which require affirmative acts of co-operation by victims before the fraud can be completed. Put another way, victims must help to "dig their own graves."

In considering this element the term "victim" must be broadly construed. For a white-collar crime to succeed someone with an interest, either as a direct victim or as a protector of potential victims, must affirmatively cooperate or passively acquiesce in the crime.

. . .

With respect to many *malum prohibitum* offenses acquiescence is negative rather than affirmative. The tenement dweller acquiesces in being deprived of heat or repairs because he does not fully comprehend that this deprivation is a transaction different from that mandated by law. Collusive pricing succeeds because purchasers believe the prices quoted have been individually arrived at and do not know that the bidders have conspired. The Food and Drug Administration acquiesces in the marketing of a drug because it believes the tests are as represented, and physicians affirmatively prescribe such drugs for their patients in reliance on drug company salesmen, drug advertising, and the presumed vigilance of the Food and Drug Administration.

Since someone's acquiescence is needed for a white-collar crime to be committed (in contrast to murder, robbery, assault or rape), a central question is how to prevent acquiescence, affirmative or negative.

(e) Concealment of crime

When a murder, robbery, burglary, assault, or rape has been committed, it is clear there has been a violation, though there may be some question as to the identity of the perpetrator or his legal or mental capacity to form the requisite criminal intent. This is not the case with white-collar crimes, where victims almost never know they have been victimized until well after the executing transactions or occurrences and, in fact, may never know they have been victimized.

The ideal scheme or plan, from the point of view of the perpetrator, is one in which the victim never learns the true nature of the blow struck. Charity frauds classically illustrate such a scheme. The takings are small for éach individual no matter how large cumulatively, and few victims have sufficient personal interest in their contributions to attempt to follow up. As a result charity frauds almost always are exposed through the curiosity of news media or the vigilance of public officials, rather than as the result of investigations following victims' complaints. If prepackaged goods are marked with short weights it is highly unlikely that any customer will weigh his purchase to check the labeled weight. If the grade or quality of food is mismarked, we have the victim eating the evidence.

. . .

Since it is not always possible to anticipate an uninterrupted series of complacent victims, standby tactics are often employed. Thus some schemes will contemplate making immediate restitution to any victim who complains, to make the victim feel that the perpetrators acted in good faith or to ensure the victim's silence.

The most usual form of concealment is the lulling tactic, followed by silence and the collapse of a corporate entity. This works best when the scheme involves a continuity of performance. In an advance fee swindle a businessman seeking a loan will agree to pay $2,000 to a loan broker for securing a $75,000 loan. The loan broker will ask for $500 or $750 initially, graciously offering to waive the balance until he has delivered the promised financing. The loan broker has no intention of ever earning the balance. His objective is the initial retainer. A series of lulling letters is then used to keep the victim quiet while others are being victimized, and to tire the victim out. Finally, the loan brokerage firm collapses and the grifter who closed the deal (and who was working on a commission basis) drifts on to other schemes. A year may elapse while pre-programmed lulling letters continue, with the victim sinking into bankruptcy or incapacitating despondency. If the victim still is afloat after all this, the wind is usually taken out of his sails when he learns that the loan brokerage company is no longer in existence.

Concealment is achieved by design of an organizational structure to frustrate and discourage complaint or pursuit by victims. A typical example would be a home improvement fraud in which a faceless corporation is set up, hires itinerant salesman, and promptly negotiates its paper to so-called holders in due course. The victims are so tied in legal knots that they find it hard to even consider complaining to enforcement authorities—since they do not believe this will protect them against the "holders in due course." Attorneys will rarely take these as charity cases, and if the victim does obtain legal assistance his attorneys will usually concentrate on trying to settle obligations for less than the face amount of the paper. All cooperate in muffling the outcry.

. . .

It is not uncommon for a prosecutor to face the most difficult evaluation problem where he has what amounts to a stipulated set of facts before him. One example would be the case of the "vanity publisher" who signs a contract with a would-be author to publish his book, send copies to reviewers, advertise the book in respectable publications, and provide editing services. The publisher receives many thousands of dollars for this service and, in fact, he does provide editing service, does provide a number of hard cover copies, does advertise, and does send copies to reviewers. The victim, in such cases, is led to hope that his book is being promoted and handled as it would be by a legitimate publisher, though he has nothing in writing. Is there a fraud when the publisher knows that the reviewers throw all his books in the trash can, that the advertisement in a reputable newspaper's book section is almost a classified ad in format, and that of the multitude of books published by vanity presses in recent years only a miniscule number have recovered as much as the victim's own cash outlay?

Categories of White-Collar Crimes (Excluding Organized Crime)

A. *Crimes by persons operating on an individual, ad hoc basis*

1. Purchases on credit with no intention to pay, or purchases by mail in the name of another.
2. Individual income tax violations.
3. Credit card frauds.
4. Bankruptcy frauds.
5. Title II home improvement loan frauds.
6. Frauds with respect to social security, unemployment insurance, or welfare.
7. Unorganized or occasional frauds on insurance companies (theft, casualty, health, etc.).

8. Violations of Federal Reserve regulations by pledging stock for further purchases, flouting margin requirements.
9. Unorganized "lonely hearts" appeal by mail.

B. *Crimes in the course of their occupations by those operating inside business, Government, or other establishments, in violation of their duty of loyalty and fidelity to employer or client*

1. Commercial bribery and kickbacks, i.e., by and to buyers, insurance adjusters, contracting officers, quality inspectors, government inspectors and auditors, etc.
2. Bank violations by bank officers, employees, and directors.
3. Embezzlement or self-dealing by business or union officers and employees.
4. Securities fraud by insiders trading to their advantage by the use of special knowledge, or causing their firms to take positions in the market to benefit themselves.
5. Employee petty larceny and expense account frauds.
6. Frauds by computer, causing unauthorized payouts.
7. "Sweetheart contracts" entered into by union officers.
8. Embezzlement or self-dealing by attorneys, trustees, and fiduciaries.
9. Fraud against the Government.
   (a) Padding of payrolls.
   (b) Conflicts of interest.
   (c) False travel, expense, or per diem claims.

C. *Crimes incidental to and in furtherance of business operations, but not the central purpose of the business*

1. Tax violations.
2. Antitrust violations.
3. Commercial bribery of another's employee, officer or fiduciary (including union officers).
4. Food and drug violations.
5. False weights and measures by retailers.
6. Violations of Truth-in-Lending Act by misrepresentation of credit terms and prices.
7. Submission or publication of false financial statements to obtain credit.

8. Use of fictitious or over-valued collateral.
9. Check-kiting to obtain operating capital on short term financing.
10. Securities Act violations, i.e., sale of non-registered securities, to obtain operating capital, false proxy statements, manipulation of market to support corporate credit or access to capital markets, etc.
11. Collusion between physicians and pharmacists to cause the writing of unnecessary prescriptions.
12. Dispensing by pharmacists in violation of law, excluding narcotics traffic.
13. Immigration fraud in support of employment agency operations to provide domestics.
14. Housing code violations by landlords.
15. Deceptive advertising.
16. Fraud against the Government:
    (*a*) False claims.
    (*b*) False statements:
        (1) to induce contracts
        (2) AID frauds
        (3) Housing frauds
        (4) SBA frauds, such as SBIC bootstrapping, self-dealing, cross-dealing, etc., or obtaining direct loans by use of false financial statements.
    (*c*) Moving contracts in urban renewal.
17. Labor violations (Davis-Bacon Act).
18. Commercial espionage.

D. *White-collar crime as a business, or as the central activity*

1. Medical or health frauds.
2. Advance fee swindles.
3. Phony contests.
4. Bankruptcy fraud, including schemes devised as salvage operation after insolvency of otherwise legitimate businesses.
5. Securities fraud and commodities fraud.
6. Chain referral schemes.
7. Home improvement schemes.
8. Debt consolidation schemes.
9. Mortgage milking.

10. Merchandise swindles:
    (*a*) Gun and coin swindles.
    (*b*) General merchandise.
    (*c*) Buying or pyramid clubs.
11. Land frauds.
12. Directory advertising schemes.
13. Charity and religious frauds.
14. Personal improvement schemes:
    (*a*) Diploma Mills.
    (*b*) Correspondence Schools.
    (*c*) Modeling Schools.
15. Fraudulent application for, use and/or sale of credit cards, airline tickets, etc.
16. Insurance frauds:
    (*a*) Phony accident rings.
    (*b*) Looting of companies by purchase of over-valued assets, phony management contracts, self-dealing with agents, inter-company transfers, etc.
    (*c*) Frauds by agents writing false policies to obtain advance commissions.
    (*d*) Issuance of annuities or paidup life insurance, with no consideration, so that they can be used as collateral for loans.
    (*e*) Sales by misrepresentations to military personnel or those otherwise uninsurable.
17. Vanity and song publishing schemes.
18. Ponzi schemes.
19. False security frauds, i.e., Billy Sol Estes or De Angelis type schemes.
20. Purchase of banks, or control thereof, with deliberate intention to loot them.
21. Fraudulent establishing and operation of banks or savings and loan associations.
22. Fraud against the Government:
    (*a*) Organized income tax refund swindles, sometimes operated by income tax "counselors."
    (*b*) AID frauds, i.e., where totally worthless goods shipped.
    (*c*) F.H.A. frauds:
        (1) Obtaining guarantees of mortgages on multiple family housing far in excess of value of property with foreseeable inevitable foreclosure.
        (2) Home improvement frauds.

23. Executive placement and employment agency frauds.

24. Coupon redemption frauds.

25. Money order swindles.

NOTES

1. Edwin H. Sutherland, *White Collar Crime* (City Publisher, 1949), p. 9.

2. Guarantees are drafted more to limit liability than to assure the purchaser's satisfaction, since in the absence of guarantees the manufacturer might be held to a far broader standard of liability. The requirement that items be packaged and returned to the maker, with a handling fee, insures minimal accountability.

3. U.S. Congress, Senate, Special Committee on Aging, Subcommittee on Frauds and Misrepresentations Affecting the Elderly; hearings, January 15–17, 1963. Washington, D.C., 1963.

Chapter Eleven

Burglary in a Suburb

John E. Conklin
Egon Bittner

In recent years American society has experienced a "crime wave." As the public has grown more fearful of "crime in the streets," politicians and law enforcement officials have fed the hysteria with promises to reduce the increasing threat to law-abiding citizens. Some students of crime have questioned the reality of the rise in crime rates, arguing that the increase is due to better reporting and better record-keeping by the police. Others have argued that the rise is real, but can be attributed to such changes as the urbanization of the nation or the rising proportion of the population in the high crime rate age group under 25.[1] While one may question the reality or the causes of the recent rise in crime rates, it is nonetheless a social fact that public concern about crime has increased in the last few years.

There has been considerable research in recent years on the nature of the public's reaction to the crime problem, some studies finding response to crime to be most intense in high crime rate areas,[2] others finding that suburban residents express greater concern with crime.[3] One point on which this research appears to agree is that one

"Burglary in a Suburb," by John E. Conklin and Egon Bittner is reprinted from *Criminology*, Vol. 11, No. 2 (Aug., 1973), pp. 206–231, by permission of the Publishers, Sage Publications, Inc.

of the crimes that is most resented and that evokes bitter denunciation of existing crime control methods is burglary. According to definitions contained in the penal law and according to common belief, burglary consists of illegal—for the most part forced—entry into a building with the intention of committing a felony, usually theft. Though clearly a breach of the peace, burglary is generally perceived to be a "peaceful" crime, and burglars are thought to try to avoid violence. Nevertheless, the possible confrontation of a burglar with his victim contains an appreciable risk of violence. Accordingly, burglaries committed at night, when victims are most likely to be home, are perceived to be an aggravated form of the crime. Moreover, and probably because of deeply ingrained notions of what constitutes a sporting chance, nighttime burglaries gain in gravity because darkness gives the thief undue advantage.

Whether done by day or by night, burglary is "a significant . . . reason for America's alarm about crime." [4] Why does burglary cause such concern? No doubt the material loss involved in the crime is an important source of it. How large is this loss? Judged by cumulative national estimates the amount of money involved is of the same order as the amount involved in loan sharking operations. To use another comparison, the loss is estimated to be less than a third of the loss due to unreported commercial thefts. Burglary has also been estimated to account for approximately 15% of the total loss due to all crimes against property.[5] However, overall figures of this kind are not really very helpful. It might be maintained that even comparatively small losses are still compatible with a very high level of concern. For example, indignation could derive from the fact that burglaries commonly entail losses of personal property such as the contents of households, rather than property associated with the conduct of business or some official function. As is well known, Americans tend to be more forgiving in cases involving thefts of property that is held somewhat anonymously than they are when the victims are identifiable individuals.[6]

In addition to questions about the meaning of the loss due to burglary, there is another consideration that must be taken into account. It appears that the concern about burglary is heavily concentrated in the suburbs. Here the feeling of anger and resentment may result from the more or less explicit realization that the rise in reported burglary rates might be connected with the ascendance of suburban life as such. It does not take very great powers of discernment to see that burglars capitalize on low population density, the absence of street traffic, the privacy of single family dwellings, the extensive inventory of portable wealth which suburban homes typically contain, and the frequent need for both spouses to work to finance such luxuries. Add to this a life-style in which this sheltered, free and well-appointed family home is the center of people's existence, and it becomes easy to appreciate that burglaries jeopardize much more than mere possessions. That is, the alarm is probably rooted in the feeling that what is at stake is the continued availability and stability of those conditions that make life meaningful and satisfying for people who struggled for a place in the suburbs, namely, the exclusive access to a private life space contained in the family home.

Even if one were to accept the plausibility of this interpretation, we lack the kinds of information about burglary which are required for responsible conjecturing. That is, while we have data of the kind published by the Federal Bureau of Investigation, and while we have some very fine accounts of the activities of individual burglars,[7] virtually nothing is known about burglary at an intermediate level. We have no detailed information about the experience of a community with burglary. In an effort to begin to remedy this shortcoming, we have undertaken a modest study of burglary in a suburb located in a large metropolitan area in the Northeast. Our efforts were directed towards the assembly of a relatively detailed cumulative picture of the crime over a significant period of time in a fairly typical suburban community.

The data describe the experience with burglary of an incorporated suburb of approximately 100,000 inhabitants. We coded all the information about burglaries, attempted burglaries, and suspected burglaries contained in the records of the local police department, for the period from July 1, 1968, to June 30, 1969. This coding resulted in a tally of 945 cases. We took the entire tally rather than sampling it, because we did not find the task of coding too burdensome and because we hoped to be able to make statements about certain matters in which we expected to have relatively few cases. We knew, for example, that we could not expect a very high clearance rate and that we had better not cut any corners if we wanted to fill the relevant cells of our tables at all. Moreover, we coded virtually all the information contained in the records, even though we did not expect to find all of it useful. In a few cases where we found the records ambiguous or unclear, we sought and obtained the help of the officer in charge of the records or other officers who had the information we needed. On the basis of these contacts and on the basis of a number of additional informal conversations with members of the police department, we have concluded that the records give a fairly adequate representation of what is known by the police about burglary in the town. To be sure, there are some cases in which officers indicated that they did not believe that what the record contained was complete or trustworthy. For example, in some cases the magnitude of the loss reported by the victim led certain officers to suspect that the offense had been committed by a known thief, though the record did not contain such a conjecture. However, the vast majority of the cases, at least nine of every ten, were straightforward and without qualifications; that is, the record was scant and almost certainly no more was ever known by any officer. In addition to our finding information in the police records, we were afforded an opportunity to accompany detectives on about a dozen field investigations of reported burglaries. We used these observations less for purposes of learning about burglaries or burglary investigations than to gain a grasp of the correspondence between what victims reported and what official records contained. The only lesson we learned from the fieldwork was that things are often written in the record with a greater sense of certainty than they are talked about in the investigation. Certainty aside, however, we found that the record contained a terse but reasonably adequate account of all that was known and relevant.

RECENT TRENDS IN BURGLARY
IN THE SUBURB

The suburb experienced a rapid and substantial increase in the number of reported burglaries in the 1960s, despite the fact that the total population actually declined slightly during the decade. Although the actual numbers in the time series in Table 1 were probably not well known to most citizens, the people were generally aware of the trend. Certainly the town government was aware of the facts and public concern was frequently expressed about them. Aside from the increases in the incidence of burglary, the police and community leaders also knew that burglary was by far the most serious law enforcement problem in the town, representing approximately one half of all the Uniform Crime Reports Index Offenses. These facts acquired added importance in a community whose residents are known to be strongly upwardly mobile, acquisitive, and very property conscious. Finally, the view was sometimes expressed that by being attractive to burglars, most of whom were assumed to come from the outside, especially from the adjoining metropolis, the town was laying itself open to other sorts of depredations. That is, the increase in

TABLE 1
INCIDENCE OF BURGLARIES
IN THE SUBURB, 1960–1969

Year	Number of Burglaries
1960	Incomplete data
1961	431
1962	437
1963	445
1964	546
1965	726
1966	751
1967	664
1968	864
1969	888

burglary tended to be seen as in some way presaging a breakdown of future crime control in general.

TYPES OF BURGLARY

The FBI distinguishes between residential burglaries and non-residential burglaries, the latter commonly involving commercial or industrial establishments. In 1968, the FBI reported that 54% of recorded burglaries and burglary attempts involved residences and 46% involved nonresidential buildings.[8] The corresponding figures for 1969 were 56% and 44%.[9] Although the FBI does not present data on types of burglaries in cities and suburbs separately, one study of burglary in Washington, D.C., found that from 1961 to 1965, 56% of all breaks were residential and the other 44% nonresidential, about the same proportions as exist nationally.

Table 2 shows the types of targets burglarized in the suburb. Understandably, a substantially larger proportion of burglaries in the town than in the nation as a whole were residential. Almost two-thirds (63.7%) of the offenses involved private homes, and only one-third involved nonresidential targets, a number involving illegal entry into schools or churches. Though Table 2 appears to indicate that residential burglaries constitute the major burglary problem, we must examine the figures in terms of the *risk* of burglary for residential and nonresidential buildings.

TABLE 2
TYPES OF BURGLARIES IN THE SUBURB

Type of Burglary	n	%
Private residence	602	63.7
Commercial establishment	239	25.3
School or church	63	6.7
Other targets	41	4.3
Total	945	100.0

In the one-year period under study during which 602 residential burglaries were recorded, there were about 27,000 private residences in the town, according to the town's Chamber of Commerce. The rate of burglaries per residence is thus 22 per 1,000. In other words, the chance of a house being burglarized is about one in 45. There were 239 commercial burglaries in the suburb during the year. According to the Chamber of Commerce estimate, there were 1,100 commercial establishments in the town at the time of the study, meaning that the rate of commercial burglaries was 217 per 1,000. On the average, more than one commercial establishment in five will be burglarized each year, a rate about ten times the rate for residences. Thus, while there were many more residential breaks than commercial breaks, this fact was largely because residences far outnumbered commercial establishments in the town. The rate of commercial burglaries, calculated with the number of opportunities rather than with the number of people in the town as a base, far exceeds the rate of residential burglaries.

TIME OF BURGLARY

It is rather easy to see that even under the very best conditions, the time of a burglary is difficult to determine. Under ordinary circumstances one can ascertain, with varying precision, the time the building was last seen intact and the time at which it was discovered that a burglary had taken place. For example, the record might contain information that a telephone call was received at 4:50 from a person reporting that he had just returned home and had found his place ransacked and that he had left the house at approximately 2:00. Taking the midpoint of this time interval as a reasonable guess of when the event took place, one would code it as having taken place at 3:25 plus or minus one and a half hours. Had the report indicated that the complainant had left the house at about 12:25 and had returned at 6:25, we would make the same guess, but the qualification would have been plus or minus three hours. Using this procedure, we were able to estimate the time of occurrence for 886 of the 945 cases. Of these, 37.8% were estimable within three-hour limits, 54.7% within six-hour limits, and 73.0% within 12-hour limits. The following analysis is based on cases in which time estimates were made within the three-hour limits. There were 298 such cases.

As Table 3 shows, almost two-thirds of these burglaries oc-

TABLE 3
ESTIMATED TIME OF OCCURRENCE
OF BURGLARIES

	Burglaries	
Time of Day	n	%
7 a.m. to 10 a.m.	17	5.7
11 a.m. to 2 p.m.	44	14.8
3 pm. to 6 p.m.	46	15.4
7 p.m. to 10 p.m.	119	39.9
11 p.m. to 2 a.m.	44	14.8
3 a.m. to 6 a.m.	28	9.4
Total	298	100.0

curred at night, between 7 p.m. and 6 a.m. Even more interesting is the observation that no less than two of every five offenses occurred between 6:31 p.m. and 10:30 p.m. In other words, 40% of the incidents were concentrated in 17% of the available time. The frequency of nighttime entries was somewhat lower for residential burglaries (61.4%) than for commercial burglaries (75.0%). This difference can probably be explained by the fact that except for holidays and Sundays, burglaries of commercial establishments are possible only at night when the business is closed, since this is the only time during which entry is illegal.

We have mentioned earlier that the distinction between nighttime and daytime burglary is based on the presumption of greater likelihood of confrontation at night. Evidence appears to confirm this surmise. Although the number of confrontations between burglar and occupant is small (25), the risk of confrontation is virtually the same in residential burglaries (2.8% of the cases) as in commercial burglaries (2.9% of the cases). Twenty-one of these 25 confrontations occurred between 7 p.m. and 6 a.m., the nighttime hours. While 84% of all confrontations occurred in this half of the day, there was no difference in the proportions of residential and commercial burglaries in the times of offenses which led to confrontations. Six of the 7 confrontations (85.2%) in commercial burglaries and 15 of the 18 (83.3%) residential burglary confrontations occurred in the nighttime. Although the sample of confrontation burglaries is small, there appears to be no difference in the times at which commercial or residential burglaries resulted in confrontations. Most of the confrontations did occur at night.[10]

Another dimension of the time of a burglary is the day of the week on which it occurs. Just as burglaries are more likely to be committed at night due to expected vacancy of buildings, so burglaries are also more apt to be committed on weekends, when the occupants of a home may be away and when the proprietor of a store may be home. If burglaries were evenly distributed over the days of the week, one would expect 43% of all offenses to occur on Friday, Saturday, and Sunday. In fact, 58.9% of the burglaries occurred on these days. Commercial burglaries were somewhat less likely to cluster on weekends than were residential burglaries, the former being relatively evenly spread throughout the days of the week, probably because vacancy of such buildings can be predicted at night. Because vacancy of residences is less predictable by hour of the day, although it is noticeable by the absence of lights in a home at night, burglaries of homes tend to be planned for times when vacancy can be predicted. One such time is weekends, especially weekends during the summer months, when people are likely to travel out of town.

Burglaries also tend to be concentrated in certain months of the year, namely those months when homes are most apt to be empty of occupants, the summer months.

Combining months roughly by season, the summer months of June, July, and August accounted for 27.7% of all burglaries; the winter months of December, January, and February accounted for 23.1%. Neither season deviated much from the expected proportion of 25% of the cases per season. Looking only at residential burglaries, the seasonal distribution still differs only slightly from the expected distribution, 30.5% of residential burglaries occuring in the summer and 23.3% occurring in the winter.

. . .

LOSS SUSTAINED IN BURGLARY

One of the most startling observations we made in the course of accompanying detectives in their investigations of burglary complaints concerned things that were *not* stolen. In burglarized homes we repeatedly encountered objects of considerable value, including jewelry, furs, art objects, watches, and television sets, which were in plain sight and would have been difficult to overlook even in darkness and haste. In fact, in most cases only a few things were stolen from places that undoubtedly contained many more pilferable items; in many instances the material loss was relatively negligible. Of course, some burglaries involved very substantial losses and were apparently thorough in execution, but their number was relatively small. Even in these instances the very large reported loss could usually be matched by what was left.

. . .

In the residential burglaries for which data were available, 51.8% involved the theft of such valuables as jewelry, furs, and silver; 34.9% involved the theft of money; 34.7% produced the theft of such instruments and appliances as television and stereo sets. Only 16.2% involved the loss of such personal use items as clothing and purses; and about the same proportion (16.3%) involved the loss of such miscellaneous items as pillowcases, revolvers, liquors, records, and brief cases. Although the evidence is only suggestive, the types of items taken by burglars suggest a relatively high degree of "professionalism." Most burglaries involved the loss of valuables and appliances that would primarily be fenced rather than used by burglars. Only a third of the cases involved the theft of cash. Young and inexperienced burglars are probably most interested in cash, for valuables and appliances would have to be converted into liquid assets (cash) through a fence. Lacking knowledge of how and where to find a fence, many inexperienced offenders probably prefer cash, though they may sometimes take liquor and cigarettes for personal use.

. . .

It must be emphasized that our data only support the inference that *when* the more expensive homes are "hit" they are more likely to be hit for "big scores" than are the less expensive homes. This point still leaves open the possibility that less expensive homes might be in the same, or perhaps even greater peril of being burglarized than the more expensive homes. To estimate the relative likelihood of these possibilities, we would have to compare our distribution of victimized homes with the overall distribution of homes in these value categories in the suburb. Such data were not available to us. Keeping this reservation in mind, however, we think it safe to say that expensive homes 'are probably more exposed to the depredations of "professional" thieves, while modest homes are more often the targets of "opportunistic" offenders who act in a "catch-as-catch-can" manner.

REPORTING OF BURGLARY

The time elapsed from the burglary to the reporting of the crime to the police may influence the likelihood of an arrest in the case, as well as the chance of recovering the lost money and goods. In fact, the possibility of investigating a case with a reasonable hope of getting useful information declines rather quickly with passing time.

In approximately one of every ten cases, the police were the first to learn that a burglary had taken place. Three of every four of these cases involved nonresidential buildings, the discovery of the offense usually being made during routine checks of commercial or industrial establishments. The few cases of police-discovered home burglaries involved cases in which residents asked the police to check their homes during periods of absence. Of the remaining burglaries, 60% were reported by victims. Employees of victims, most of which were business establishments, reported about 17% of the cases. Neighbors reported 6% and casual observers another 5%. Given the fact that the police are not in a good position to discover residential burglaries, partly because they are not informed of absences in most cases, the responsibility for the discovery and reporting falls on the shoulders of the homeowner. Quite apart from the fact that the homeowner cannot generally expect neighbors and others to protect his property from theft, he cannot even expect that the crime will be reported by them. From what we have found, this fact appears to be due less to people's refusal to "become involved" than to the fact that neighbors simply do not seem to be aware of what goes on in each other's homes.

Since burglars prefer to break into buildings that are relatively isolated from public view, it is uncommon for onlookers to report crimes to the police while they are in progress. However, it bears mentioning that information appearing on police records showed that the police questioned a total of 26 neighbors who had noticed something suspicious around the time of the burglary but had failed to report it to the police. Three-fifths of these neighbors noted the events between 7 a.m. and 7 p.m., meaning that the majority of the suspicious occurrences which they noticed were during daylight hours. Possibly they did not report these events to the police because they felt that people do not usually commit burglaries in the daytime. Looking at burglaries for which time of occurrence could be estimated within three hours, only 24.3% of those offenses actually reported by neighbors, passersby, and casual observers occurred between 7 a.m. and 7 p.m. Together, these data suggest that suspicious events may be less likely to be reported to the police if they occur in daylight hours than if they occur at night.

The National Crime Commission has shown that an inverse relationship exists between the time it takes for the police to respond to the scene of a crime and the likelihood of an arrest in the case.[11] In burglary cases, a significant amount of time often elapses from the time of the offense until the victim even learns of the crime, much less reports it to the police. The time it takes for the police to respond to the scene of the crime is often dwarfed by the time between the offense and its being reported to the police. Table 4 shows the time that elapsed from the estimated time of the break until the time the crime was reported to the police. Only one burglary in six (16.2%) was reported within an hour of its occurrence; only one-half (54.8%)

TABLE 4

**AMOUNT OF TIME FROM BURGLARY
TO POLICE REPORT**

	Burglaries	
Time Lag	n	%
In progress	69	7.8
Under 1 hour	74	8.4
1 to 3 hours	192	21.7
3 to 6 hours	150	16.9
6 to 12 hours	162	18.3
12 hours to 1 day	72	8.1
1 to 2 days	70	7.9
2 to 3 days	45	5.1
More than 3 days	52	5.9
Total	886	100.1

were reported within six hours. Quite clearly, for most burglaries it matters little whether the police take three minutes or half an hour in getting to the scene, since the crime is usually "cold" anyway.

. . .

POLICE RESPONSE TO BURGLARY

After a burglary is reported to the police, patrolmen and detectives go to the scene to investigate the crime. In two-thirds of our cases, both patrolmen and detectives responded to the scene, in one-tenth of the cases only a detective responded, and in a quarter of the cases only a patrolman investigated the case. When the time lag between burglary and report is small, it is usual for both patrolmen and detectives to be involved in the investigation. This greater investment of manpower is probably justified by a heightened expectation of success in "fresh" as opposed to "stale" cases.

One measure of police response to crime is the number of officers ever involved in the case, the assumption being that more work is done in the investigation of a crime when more officers are involved. The mean number of officers involved in a burglary case in the suburb was 3.8, with only a third of the cases involving five or more officers. In general, residential burglaries involve more officers than do commercial burglaries, 39.2% of the former and only 27.2% of the latter involving five or more officers. This difference may arise from the fact that residential burglaries lead to greater losses than commercial burglaries. Table 5 does demonstrate that burglaries involving greater losses elicit more police response in terms of number of personnel who work on the case. In cases in which the loss was more than $1,000, 45.5% of the cases involved five or more officers; while in cases involving a loss of less than $100, only 25.4% involved five or more officers.

Aside from the number of officers involved in a case, another measure of police response is the number of contacts the police have with the victim of the offense. Residential burglaries led to more police contacts than did commercial burglaries, half of the residential burglaries and only a fifth of the commercial offenses producing two or more contacts between the police and the victim. Again this fact is related to the difference in losses sustained in each type of burglary. Table 5 demonstrates that in cases involving greater losses, two or more contacts occur with greater frequency.

Because of the relationship between size of loss and assessed

TABLE 5
LOSS SUSTAINED AND POLICE RESPONSE TO ALL TYPES OF BURGLARIES (in percentages)

	Loss Sustained				
	No Loss	$1 to $99	$100 to $999	$1,000 to $9,999	$10,000 and over
Number of officers					
Zero, one, or two	43.4	45.3	25.7	14.1	5.9
Three or four	33.6	28.4	38.4	42.2	29.4
Five or more	23.1	26.4	35.8	43.8	64.6
Total number	265	95	229	192	17
Number of contacts of police with victims					
Zero or one	91.3	75.0	52.0	12.4	17.6
Two or more	8.7	25.0	48.0	87.6	82.4
Total number	265	96	229	193	17

value of a house, and because of the finding that large losses usually occur in residential burglaries, one might suggest that the greater police response is due more to the influence of the upper classes who own the highly assessed homes that suffer the larger losses, rather than that the police response is due to the size of the loss per se. Table 6 presents data to test this possibility. The first part of the table shows that if the loss is large, the same number of officers will respond regardless of the assessed value of the home. If the loss is small, there is a tendency for more officers to investigate cases involving highly assessed houses, although this tendency may be due to the officers' surmise that such expensive homes are more likely to suffer large losses than are less expensive homes. Looking at the second half of Table 6, we see that there appears to be even less differentiation in terms of police response for homes in the different assessment categories. Cases involving large losses are much more likely to involve multiple contacts than are cases involving small losses. Even more interestingly, there is no greater likelihood of a victim living in an expensive home having multiple contacts with the police than there is for a victim living in a more modest dwelling, if the amount of loss is held constant. In sum, the police seem to be responding to the amount of the loss in the burglary, not to the influence of those who own highly assessed houses.

TABLE 6
LOSS SUSTAINED AND POLICE RESPONSE BY ASSESSED VALUE OF HOME, RESIDENTIAL BURGLARIES
(in percentages)

| | Assessed Value of Home | | | | | |
| | Low, Lowest Value | | Middle Value | | High, Highest Value | |
	Loss under $1,000	Loss over $1,000	Loss under $1,000	Loss over $1,000	Loss under $1,000	Loss over $1,000
Number of officers						
Zero, one, or two	30.0	9.8	28.4	12.3	24.4	14.3
Three or four	39.3	45.1	36.5	45.6	28.0	40.0
Five or more	30.7	45.1	35.1	42.1	47.6	45.7
Total number	140	51	74	57	82	70
Number of contacts of police with victims						
Zero or one	65.7	7.8	66.2	7.0	64.6	10.0
Two or more	34.3	92.2	33.8	93.0	35.4	90.0
Total number	140	51	74	57	82	70

CLEARANCE OF BURGLARY CASES

The purpose of police-victim contacts is to develop information that might lead to the solution or clearance of the crime. In about a third of the burglaries in our sample some form of evidence was uncovered by the police, although in most instances the "evidence" consisted only of finding fingerprints at the scene of the offense. However, these prints were rarely good enough to provide any help to the police in their search for an offender.

The clearance rate for burglaries in the suburb was 4.55%. This rate is substantially lower than the rates reported for suburban areas in the rest of the nation—17.9% in 1968 and 18.2% in 1969. Unfortunately, we can only speculate about the reasons for this difference. Two considerations are especially relevant. First, in the suburb studied here every citizen complaint of a burglary was entered into the record. It is not unreasonable to suggest that a substantial proportion of the incidents reported as burglaries in our sample might be considered instances of trespass or mischief, or thought to be too trivial to record, in other jurisdictions. Second, and perhaps more important, though approximately half of the cleared cases represented multiple clearances, i.e., cases in which a suspect apprehended in connection with one burglary was also charged with having committed another, the police department does not engage in the widely prevalent practice of assigning dozens of unsolved cases to arrested suspects. In fact, we were told that it is not standard practice for detectives to press inquiries that might lead to such results. Given that arrested burglars are not induced to "confess" about their past activities, it is not farfetched to assume that the actual clearance rate might be higher than the reported one.

With these limitations mind, certain rate differentials might be worth reporting. In spite of the fact that the police paid somewhat more attention to residential burglaries, in terms of the number of officers who worked on the cases and the number of police contacts with victims, there was a slightly higher rate of clearance for commercial burglaries (7.1%) than for residential burglaries (3.7%). Even though more attention was paid to burglaries of highly assessed homes, the clearance rate for such burglaries was no higher than it was for burglaries of homes with lower assesment values, although the numbers of cases in each category were too small to be significant.

The shorter the time lag from incident to report, the greater the likelihood of clearance. Of the cases reported while in progress, 20.3% were cleared; of those reported within one hour, 4.1% were cleared; of those reported between one and three hours after the event, 5.2% were cleared; and of those reported more than three hours after the offense, only 2.4% were solved. Quick response, therefore, seems important, although there is probably little the police can do if the burglary is not reported in progress or very soon after its completion. If a home is burglarized while the residents are away, there may be a long lag from event to report. In such a case, quick police response *when the report is made* is probably worth nothing. What *is* important is *detection of the crime* soon after its occurrence, rather than quick response to the scene when the report is received. One way of bringing the police to the scene quickly is the use of alarms. There was about twice as much chance of a burglary producing an arrest if an alarm was present and sounded (clearance rate of 10.3%) as there was in other cases (clearance rate of 4.3%).

In spite of greater police response to cases involving large losses, there was no significant relationship between loss and clearance rate. However, there was a statistically significant relationship between number of police contacts with the victim and rate of clearance, with more clearances in those cases involving multiple contacts. Unfortunately, we were not able to determine whether more contacts led to more intensive investigations and consequently to better results, or whether once a case was cleared, it then produced additional contacts with victims.

CONCLUSIONS

Burglary in a large residential suburb was found to have increased substantially during the 1960s. All cases occurring in a one-year period of time were examined and coded. Though a ratio of three residential burglaries to one commercial burglary was found, the risk of a given residence being burglarized was only one-tenth of the risk for a given commercial establishment. In other words, there were more residential burglaries because there were more homes in the community.

Burglaries were more apt to occur in hours of darkness, this being especially true of commercial burglaries. On the other hand, residential burglaries were committed on weekends somewhat more often than one would expect by chance. There was only slight variation in the number of offenses committed by month of the year and by season of the year, with summer months having slightly more and winter months slightly less burglaries than would be expected by chance. Burglary incidents seemed to vary in time as a result of the predictability of the vacancy of buildings and the increased invisibility that offenders enjoy at certain times of the day.

Most burglaries were reported by private citizens, very few being discovered by the police themselves. If the police did discover a burglary, it usually involved a commercial establishment since they regularly check such buildings at night and on weekends. There was often a significant lag from time a burglary occurred until the police learned of it, and as a result the clearance rate was very low. More police officers were involved and more contacts with victims occurred in cases of residential burglaries than in cases in which commercial establishments were burglarized. Police response was also greater in those residential burglaries that involved large losses than in those that involved small losses.

About one burglary in four resulted in a loss of a thousand dollars or more, with residential burglaries involving such large losses more often than did commercial burglaries. This amount is clearly a very substantial loss; yet, it must not be forgotten that in about half of all the cases there was either no loss at all or a loss that would have been considered trivial even by persons of very modest means. How important is the material aspect of this crime? Our data are not reliable enough to permit an estimate of the overall loss with any confidence, but it is exceedingly unlikely that the total was more than one million dollars. What does this mean? No doubt this total is lower than the loss due to that species of depredations that patrons and employees visit on retail establishments that is euphemistically called "inventory shrinkage." We have also heard detectives remark that many victims "take" their insurance companies for twice what they have lost.

It would appear, therefore, that while there are many cases of burglary in which victims suffer financially, the widespread alarm about the crime is not justifiable solely in terms of the risks to property that the offense creates. It is not the consideration of what we stand to lose in a burglary which seems to matter but rather the fact that our homes are not secure from invasion by strangers.

NOTES

1. President's Commission on Law Enforcement and Administration of Justice, *The Challenge of Crime in a Free Society.* (Washington, D.C.: U.S. Government Printing Office, 1967), pp. 25–30.

2. J. E. Conklin, *Robbery and the Criminal Justice System* (Philadelphia: 1972).

3. See J. Rosenthal, "The Cage of Fear in Cities Beset by Crime," *Life Magazine,* July 11, 1967, p. 16. F. F. Furstenberg, Jr., "Public Reaction to Crime in the Streets," *American Scholar,* Vol. 40, p. 601.

4. President's Commission, *op. cit.,* p. 4.

5. *Statistical Abstracts of the United States* (Washington, D.C.: U.S. Government Printing Office, 1971), p. 147.

6. See E. O. Smigel, "Public Attitudes Towards Stealing as Related to the Size of the Victim Organization," *American Sociological Review,* Vol. 21, p. 320.

7. E. H. Sutherland, *The Professional Thief* (Chicago: 1937); F. J. Remington, D. J. Newman, E. L. Kimball, M. Melli, and H Goldstein, *Criminal Justice Administration* (Indianapolis: 1969), pp. 1305–1330; B. Jackson, *A Thief's Primer* (New York: 1969).

8. Federal Bureau of Investigation, *Uniform Crime Reports—1968* (Washington, D.C.: U.S. Government Printing Office, 1968), p. 17.

9. Federal Bureau of Investigation, *Uniform Crime Reports—1969* (Washington, D.C.: U.S. Government Printing Office, 1969), p 19.

10. Some of the burglaries in which there was a confrontation between victim and offender might have been classified by the police as a robbery, since the theft of property accompanied by the threat or use of force against the victim is a robbery rather than a burglary. However, there were only about a dozen robberies in the town during the time period we studied. Data from a study of robbery in Boston suggest that less than a tenth of all robberies take place inside residences. This fact would then suggest that there were probably only one or two burglaries in the town which turned into robberies when the victim confronted the burglar. We therefore lost little by limiting our analysis to those burglaries in which there was a confrontation without also examining the few robberies that occurred in the town during the one-year period we studied. See J. E. Conklin, supra note 2, p. 41.

11. President's Commission, *op. cit.,* p. 248.

Chapter Twelve

Deterrence

Certainty, Severity, and Skyjacking

Robert Chauncey

In the ongoing controversy surrounding the death penalty, several issues have been debated. They include the justification of the state to kill its members, the necessity of execution to prevent those convicted of particularly heinous crimes from ever committing them again, the cost of maintaining a life sentence versus the cost of the various legal maneuvers employed in the defense of those sentenced to death, the reluctance of juries to mete out capital punishment versus the inequities of mandatory sentencing, and so on. However, the key issue involves the question of deterrence. Does the threat of capital punishment provide a sufficient degree of marginal deterrence over the threat of life imprisonment to warrant its existence? [1]

Despite disclaimers from death penalty advocates ("This lack of evidence for deterrence [of the death penalty] means that deterrence has not been demonstrated statistically—not that non-deterrence has been." [2]) the overwhelming majority of evidence thus far compiled [3] points to the following conclusions:

"Deterrence: Certainty, Severity, and Skyjacking," by Robert Chauncey is reprinted from *Criminology*, Vol. 12, No. 4 (Feb. 1975), pp. 447–471 by permission of the Publisher, Sage Publications, Inc.

(1) Murder rates tend to remain constant despite the trend away from applying the death penalty.

(2) Murder rates within states are independent of the existence of the death penalty.

(3) Murderers rarely consider the consequences of their act prior to its commission.

. . .

Among those studies attempting to measure the effectiveness of legal threats, it appears that, in the areas of parking violations, white-collar crime, "amateur" shoplifting, abortion, and drunken driving, legal sanctions have a marginal deterrent effect. However, in other areas—morals offenses, "economic offenses," murder, and various property offenses—the existence of such a deterrent effect is clearly problematic. Therefore, the answer to the question: "Does punishment deter crime?" is, "It depends on the situation."

If we admit that, under certain conditions, punishment deters crime, one must inquire as to which element or elements of punishment are responsible for this effect in each offense or subgroup of offenders. Since the writings of Beccaria and Bentham, it has been concluded that deterrent effects of punishment involve one or a combination of severity, certainty, and celerity. However, celerity (quickness of punishment) has generally been omitted from detailed consideration for two reasons. First, long delays generally are not disadvantageous to the offender, as bail is usually available. Second, celerity tends to become intertwined with both certainty and severity, as long delays are associated with complex defense maneuvers, nonavailability of witnesses, and increased prosecution willingness to plea bargain. Thus, the major emphasis of the literature has centered on the attempt to distinguish the deterrent effects of severity from the effects of certainty.

The articles exploring this relationship, . . . aside from the inconsistency of their conclusions, these articles share a common shortcoming. They all measure severity and certainty according to the average length of sentence and the proportion of reported crimes cleared by conviction while assuming that these statistics are translated by the population in general when deciding whether or not to commit a crime. It is quite doubtful that a slim variation in the number of convictions has any effect on the decision-making processes of potential law-violators. The concept of marginal deterrence involves a widely publicized change in official policy—involving either a change in the degree of punishment associated with a violation of the law or a change in the criminal justice machinery designed to increase the likelihood of apprehension. In other words, the relationship between certainty and severity can only be deduced when a change in official policy serves to hold one constant while altering the other. Clearly then, one way to clarify the relationship between severity and certainty is to examine each offense in isolation, discover a series of "critical points" where either the severity or certainty of punishment was varied, and then compare the differential effects of these changes. Such an analysis will be carried out using the crime of skyjacking.

Skyjacking was selected for this effort for the following reasons:

(1) As skyjackings are relatively rare (347 attempts since 1961, when the first U.S. plane was diverted) and newsworthy occurrences, there are fewer problems with official statistics. However, with the recent advent of electronic detection systems at all airports, the problem of defining "attempted skyjackings" has arisen. For example, is an individual caught boarding a plane with a weapon considered a potential skyjacker, or does he have another purpose in mind? It is only in this area (largely since 1970) that this paper will have to depend on official definitions. Prior to the advent of airport security, it can be assumed that every attempted skyjacking was reported, since the perpetrator was able to initiate the skyjacking before the attempt became known.

(2) Related to the problem of official statistics, the study of skyjacking also avoids the problem of differential law enforcement. For example, the local police force may respond to political or popular pressure by sporadically concentrating their efforts toward the apprehension of certain types of crimes, resulting in an apparent increase in their commission. It is very difficult for similar "artificial" increases to occur in the rate of skyjacking.

(3) During the course of the skyjacking phenomenon, several different strategies were used to combat its occurrence. These strategies can be loosely defined as either increasing the severity of punishment (making skyjacking a capital offense, publicizing a lengthy prison term given in a widely read case), or the certainty of punishment (initiation of Cuban policy of returning foreign skyjackers to face criminal charges, sealing off ventral doors of Boeing 727 aircraft to prevent skyjacker-extortionists from parachuting to safety) without an accompanying change in the other. Interaction between certainty and severity generally occurs in various local anti-crime campaigns, where the addition

of new legislation is soon reflected in changes in police practices, or where public indignation may lead to increased police activity and, in turn, to more severe judicial sanctions.

(4) Although the total number of skyjackings is rather small, detailed descriptions of most of these events are easily accessible. Thus, theoretical clarity is gained, although at the expense of statistical power.

FINDINGS

In determining the differential deterrence of severity and certainty of punishment for skyjacking, the following strategy was undertaken. First, a list was made of all points in time where a rather abrupt change in either the severity or the certainty of punishment was publicized. Then the rates of skyjacking for three and six months prior and subsequent to each "critical point" were compiled to see if any significant change occurred which could be explained by a change in deterrence. Finally, the yearly rates of skyjackings were compiled to determine whether or not the general trend of skyjackings coincided with the advent of the critical points.

After a review of the literature, five events were categorized as critical points.

(1) On August 9, 1961, the first American commercial airliner was hijacked to Cuba. Soon after, Public Law 87–197 was signed by President Kennedy, which stated that sky piracy was punishable by a prison term of up to twenty years or death, if so determined by a jury. This event is viewed here as an increase in severity without an accompanying increase in certainty, as no additional security precautions were taken at this time.

(2) In response to a rash of unwanted skyjackers entering Cuba, and under increasing pressure from the State Department, Fidel Castro made a well-publicized effort of conciliation by returning six Americans to the United States on November 1, 1969, to face charges of air piracy. It is apparent that this event represents an increased increment of certainty of punishment, as it increased the likelihood of capture in spite of a successful diversion to Cuba (the prime destination of an overwhelming majority of skyjacking attempts

of that era) without any increase in the severity of punishment once caught.

(3) When the practice of limited screening of passengers based on a psychological profile failed to reduce the number of skyjackings, President Nixon authorized the organization of a force of skymarshals, which was implemented on October 7, 1970. The skymarshals represent an increase in both certainty of punishment, as they were an additional force which the hijacker had to neutralize if he were to be successful, and severity of punishment, since the marshals were armed and were given widely publicized orders to shoot to kill, if necessary. Obviously, the advent of skymarshals will not help to determine the differential influence of severity and certainty, but it will suggest the deterrent influence of the threat of force on the potential skyjacker.

(4) On June 30, 1972, R. F. McCoy was sentenced to 45 years in prison for hijacking a United Airlines plane on April 7, holding the plane and passengers hostage for $500,000 and then bailing out over Provo, Utah. This event was acclaimed by *Aviation Week and Space Technology* of July 17, 1972, as the first example of prominent press coverage given to the severe sentences which generally accompanied the conviction of skyjackers. This critical point is viewed as an increase in severity of punishment (without a concomitant increase in certainty) as it served to reinforce to the general public the potential costs involved in an attempted skyjacking.

(5) The final critical event occurred on January 5, 1973, when, in an emergency presidential directive, President Nixon required the nation's airlines to inspect all briefcases, purses, and other items carried aboard airliners, and to screen all passengers with metal detectors. This directive was a response both to the unwillingness of several airlines to adopt these costly screening practices and to the continuing rash of skyjackings victimizing some of these airlines.

In order to avoid the charge of investigator bias in the selection of these critical points, all other possible events and the reasons for their rejection will be briefly mentioned.

(1) The use of a psychological profile in selecting passengers for subsequent searches. Although this event was the first systematic effort to prevent skyjackings by searching selected passengers prior to boarding, it is not viewed as strongly influencing the certainty of punishment, as its use was limited to the major airports and applied to only a minimal number of passengers. As Arey points out, this precaution did little to deter a potential skyjacker: "Now the determined hijacker need only scout ahead for an unguarded boarding gate, buy a round-trip ticket, dress and act like a businessman on a routine business trip, and take one or two simple precautions (including a type of weapon) that we do not choose to describe." [4]

(2) In October of 1970, the Cuban government made skyjacking a crime against Cuban law. While this could be interpreted as increasing the degree of certainty, it is also true that, under the provisions of the law, the extradition of a foreign hijacker is not mandatory and is likely to be contingent on an exchange of prisoners or some other type of mutual agreement between nations. Thus, the reaction of the federal government and the media to this announcement was not as positive as the earlier reaction to the returning of the six American hijackers. This latter event was given broader press coverage and is therefore viewed here as a potentially more significant deterrent.

(3) During the first half of 1972, the major airlines agreed to seal the ventral doors of Boeing 727 aircraft to prevent the parachuting of skyjacker-extortionists. Although this effort was successful in reducing the rate of extortion attempts, it cannot be viewed as a critical event for the following reasons. First, the number of extortion attempts represents only a small percentage of skyjacking attempts. Thus, any rate reduction would be viewed as minimal. Second, the effect of this effort was not to *deter* extortions, but to *prevent* them. Deterrence involves the unwillingness to commit an act based on the threat of adverse consequences. Prevention involves the *inability* to commit the act. For example, an executed murderer is not *deterred* from committing future murders. Rather, he is *prevented* from doing so. Thus, future extortionists were prevented from hijacking 727s as there was no other way of escape. In only a limited sense can this event be viewed as a deterrent to

extortion, in that all future attempts would have to be made on other aircraft, where the difficulty of parachuting to safety is increased.

(4) In the Tokyo Convention of 1963, the Hague Convention of 1970, and the Montreal Convention of 1971, the United Nations attempted to deal with the problem of air piracy by adopting strong international punishments, forced extradition (a U.S. proposal), and sanctions against those countries that refused to cooperate. However, in typical UN fashion, these three conventions agreed upon little but the necessity of some action to curb the problem, although exactly what was to be done remained a question. Thus, none of these conferences was deemed a critical event.

Before examining the specific effects of the five chosen critical points, it will be useful to look at the annual skyjacking rates from 1961 (the first U.S. hijacking) to the present.

An examination of Table 1 reveals that the first critical event—

TABLE 1

	Total	Non-U.S.	U.S.
1961	10	5	5
1962	3	2	1
1963	3	1	2
1964	2	1	1
1965	4	2	2
1966	5	5	0
1967	6	5	1
1968	35	13[a]	22[a]
1969	89	47[a]	42[a]
1970	84	59	25[a]
1971	39	12[a]	27
1972	55	20	35
1973 (through June 30)	12	8	4[a]

SOURCES: Arey (1972: appdx. A) and the New York Times Index (1972–1973).

   a. This indicates a reversal in the trend of skyjackings or an increase/decrease within the same trend approaching a factor of 2.

the possible death penalty accompanying a conviction for air piracy (1961)—had an amorphous effect on the incidence of skyjackings. A closer examination shows the relationship given in Table 2.

TABLE 2
DEATH PENALTY FOR SKYJACKING—AUGUST, 1961

	U.S. Attempts		Non-U.S. Attempts	
6–3 mos. prior[a]	1		2	
3–0 mos. prior	4	5	2	4
0–3 mos. after	0		3	
3–6 mos. after	0	0	4	7

a. The three and six month intervals were used in an attempt to reduce the confusion of effects of the various critical points. Longer intervals would tend to involve a degree of overlap among contiguous points.

Although Table 2 reveals the possible existence of a short-term deterrent effect of an increase in severity of punishment, it is clear that evidence of a long-term effect is lacking as the annual rates show a minimal skyjacking rate from 1962–1967 for both U.S. and non-U.S. attempts, indicating the more likely conclusion that the era of the skyjacker was yet to come.

Table 1 also reveals a drastic rise in the number of hijackings during 1968 and 1969 in both U.S. and non-U.S. categories. Looking at the non-U.S. category first, there are two conceivable explanations for this increase. The first involves a dramatic increase in worldwide political tensions, with air piracy being used for extortion, propaganda, and escape from politically problematic countries. There were two major upheavals that took place during this era which could have contributed to the sudden change in the number of skyjackings—the Arab-Israeli war and the overthrow of the Greek monarchy. Yet, of the 60 non-U.S. hijackings which took place during 1968–1969, only eight in any way involved either of these two conflicts. However, of the remaining 52 non-U.S. skyjackings during the period, 41 of them involved North or South American aircraft being diverted to Cuba. Whereas the political atmosphere in Central and South American (only a few flights involved Canadian or Mexican aircraft) has traditionally been unstable, I can think of no reason or combination of reasons to explain the sudden increase in skyjackings to Cuba in political terms. One is left, therefore, with a second hypothesis that, due to the wide coverage of the earlier skyjacking attempts in the mid-sixties and the overwhelming probability of success, skyjacking became a *fad* to be used by those seeking personal acclaim, wealth, or a new life in another country.[5] The rash of skyjackings was not a direct result of the political atmosphere alone, but a combination of political dissent coupled with the glamorization of the skyjacker which attracted zealots and thrill-seekers alike.[6]

This conclusion is verified by an examination of U.S. skyjackings during the same period. From roughly 1964 through 1968, this country suffered the majority of its urban riots. During these years, black protest groups reached the zenith of their power and importance. However, with the loss of Eldridge Cleaver, Bobby Seale, Stokely Carmichael, and H. Rap Brown, the movement began sputtering, to be over-shadowed in the late sixties by the more amorphous peace movement. One would expect therefore that with dissonant blacks lacking an organization to popularize their views and with a growing number of predominantly white youth protesting against the war and being threatened by the draft, that the increase in skyjackings during the late sixties would reflect this political atmosphere. In other words, the political tensions hypothesis would predict that the majority of skyjackers during this period would be reflecting political attitudes rather than nonpolitical motivations. Although this hypothesis is most difficult to test, Table 3 may suggest a tentative conclusion.

TABLE 3
U.S. SKYJACKING ATTEMPTS

Year	Cubans Diverting to Cuba	Non-Cubans Diverting to Cuba	Unidentified to Cuba	Diverted Elsewhere
1967	0	1	0	0
1968	9	10	1	2
1969	11	24	3	4
1970	5	9	1	6
1971[a]	2	5	2	9

a. To July 24.

As demonstrated in Table 1, there was a sharp increase in U.S. skyjackings during 1968 and 1969, followed by a reduction in 1970 and a leveling off in 1971. This pattern is mirrored in Table 3 for both Cuban and non-Cuban skyjackers. Table 3 makes two assumptions. First, it assumes that the Cuban skyjackers were more likely to be motivated by personal reasons (a desire to return to Cuba) than by political reasons stemming from the political atmosphere in the late sixties, because the popular movements of that era were lacking in conspicuous Cuban or Latin American support. It is more likely that skyjackings representing political motivations would be committed by blacks or by the predominantly white peace-marchers. The second assumption of Table 3 is that all non-Cubans who diverted aircraft to Cuba were motivated by purely political reasons. Although this is an obviously untenable assumption, it will serve to overstate the importance of the political atmosphere as a skyjacking motivation. Thus, if it can be shown that, in spite of this bias, Table 3 seems to reflect the "fad" hypothesis rather than the political atmosphere hypothesis, the conclusion will have added significance.

To add further precision to Table 3, an attempt was made to categorize all "diverted elsewhere" attempts into politically or nonpolitically motivated. Of the 21 attempts in this category, 5 could be considered politically motivated attempts by U.S. citizens, with the remaining 16 attempts being categorized as politically motivated by foreigners (3), those wishing to return to their native country (3), those considered mentally deranged who apparently wished merely to hijack an aircraft (2), a suicide attempt, 3 extortion attempts, 3 individuals with unclear motives, and an unknown skyjacker. Thus Table 3 can be reduced to Table 4.

TABLE 4
U.S. SKYJACKING ATTEMPTS

Year	Non-politically Motivated (Including Cubans Diverting to Cuba)	Politically Motivated (Including non-Cubans Diverting to Cuba)	Others
1967	0	1	0
1968	9	11	2
1969	13	24	5
1970	7	9	10
1971	5	9	11

If one accepts the assumptions behind Tables 3 and 4, it appears that the "fad" hypothesis is more persuasive than the political atmosphere hypothesis in that the trend of nonpolitically motivated hijackings nearly matches the trend of politically motivated hijackings. Thus, the political scene in the United States cannot be held directly responsible for the rash of hijackings during the late sixties. If the political atmosphere had any influence at all, it was in popularizing skyjacking as a means of dissent, thus making others aware of its use for additional purposes.

As mentioned earlier, it is interesting to note that both politically motivated and non-politically motivated skyjackings declined after 1969. One possible explanation of this phenomenon is a continuation of the fad hypothesis. One could argue that skyjacking had become passé as a form of social protest, thus reducing the number of attempts. However, not only does this fail to explain the subsequent drop in the nonpolitically motivated attempts, but such an explanation would predict a gradual but steady decline in the rates, which does not agree with the rather stable rate of U.S. attempts from 1970 through 1972 (Table 1). A more persuasive hypothesis is based on the effect of the second "critical event"—the returning of six American skyjackers from Cuba on November 1, 1969, to face criminal prosecution.

Table 5 shows a decline in U.S. attempts from 19 during the

TABLE 5
RETURN OF SIX AMERICAN SKYJACKERS FROM CUBA

	U.S. Attempts		Non-U.S. Attempts	
6–3 mos. prior	9		12	
3–0 mos. prior	10	19	14	26
0–3 mos. after	6		18	
3–6 mos. after	4	10	14	32

six months prior to the second critical event to 10 during the six months after the event. The contention that this drop is due to the deterrent effect provided by the increase in the certainty of punishment is supported by two arguments. First, the decline in the U.S. rate is opposed by the increase in the non-U.S. rate, arguing against a general explanation as provided by the fad hypothesis or a general lessening of worldwide political tensions. Table 5 indicates that an explanation should come from a condition peculiar to the United States. That this condition is in fact the second critical point is supported by the finding that the entire drop in the U.S. rate is due to the reduction in flights diverted to Cuba, as shown in Table 6.

It would appear that certainty of punishment, as exemplified by the second critical event, acted as a deterrent to future efforts to divert aircraft to Cuba.

TABLE 6
U.S. FLIGHTS DIVERTED TO CUBA AND ELSEWHERE

	Diverted to Cuba	Diverted Elsewhere
6–0 mos. prior	16	3
0–6 mos. after	6	4

Approximately one year after the return of the six Americans, the third critical event occurred—the onset of the skymarshal program on October 7, 1970. Since it has already been noted that Table 1 shows a steady rate of U.S. skyjacking attempts from 1970 through 1972, it would appear that the skymarshals had little effect in deterring hijackers. This conclusion is borne out by Table 7.

TABLE 7
SKYMARSHAL PROGRAM—OCTOBER 7, 1970

	U.S. Attempts		Non-U.S. Attempts	
6–3 mos. prior	7		21	
3–0 mos. prior	8	15	19	40
0–3 mos. after	4		8	
3–6 mos. after	8	12	15	23

The reduction in the U.S. rate is clearly insignificant. Further, the more drastic reduction in the non-U.S. rate, as evidenced by Table 7, and the downturn in the long-term trend from 1969 through 1971, as shown in Table 1, indicates the possible presence of one or several alternative processes responsible for the general reduction of skyjacking attempts.[7]

For example, the decline in all categories shown in Table 8 suggests the operation of several processes working simultaneously. (The fad hypothesis can be ruled out as it is unlikely that the popularity of skyjacking could diminish so sharply and so suddenly.)

The decline in the rate of planes diverted to Cuba may be explained by official actions showing Castro's displeasure with the rash of unscheduled landings at Jose Marti Airport (as well as with the number of Cubans escaping to Miami by stealing a boat). The first sign of this change was the previously mentioned return of the six American skyjackers in November of 1969. In October of the following

TABLE 8

NON-U.S. SKYJACKINGS PLUS U.S. CRAFT DIVERTED BY
FOREIGN GUERRILLAS TO THE MID-EAST

	1970	1971[a]
Central and South America to Cuba	20	1
Communist to Non-Communist	13	2
Non-Communist to Communist	5	3
Craft Diverted to the Mid-East	17	2
Skyjackings Involving the Indo-Pakistani Conflict	0	1
Other	8	4
Total	63	13

a. To July 24.

year, skyjacking became a crime against Cuban law. In 1972, negotiations were initiated, through the Swedish embassy, between Cuba and the United States on ways to reduce the number of illegal entries made between the two countries. These negotiations resulted in the agreement of February 3, 1973, in which each country pledged to consider hijacking a plane or boat to escape to the other country as a criminal act, and promised to either return hijackers or to put them on trial. Although there is no evidence to measure the specific effect of these actions on the rate of hijacking, it can be hypothesized that the declining number of planes diverted to Cuba is at least partially a result of Cuba's attempts to increase the certainty of punishment for this act.

Table 8 also shows a large drop in the number of skyjackings initiated in Communist countries and diverted to non-Communist countries between 1970 and 1971. One possible reason for this drop can be found by examining the skyjacking rate of the Soviet Union. After suffering one unsuccessful attempt in 1964, another in 1965, and two in 1966, there were no further attempts made through the first six months of 1970. Throughout this period, the Russians refused to engage in international discussion on the skyjacking problem, claiming it to be a symptom of Western societal disruptions. However, from June through November of 1970, four separate hijacking attempts were made (two of them successful) involving a total of nineteen people. Russia responded to these events in three ways. First, they increased the number of security guards and ordered more thorough checks of passengers and baggage at Sheremetyevo Airport in Moscow. Prior to the latter two attempts, the New York *Times* of October 16, 1970, noted on page 1: "There are little if any, security measures to prevent hijacking at Soviet airports. Hand luggage is generally not checked, and personal searches are rare." Second, those captured in the first attempt (twelve Soviet Jews) were sentenced to death by the courts. Although these sentences were later commuted to long prison terms due to intense international pressure, the Soviet citizenry was made aware of the severity of punishment accompanying this offense. Third, the Soviet Union quickly joined the International Civil Aviation Organization in time to participate in the Hague Convention convened in December of 1970 (as did Czechoslovakia, Bulgaria, and Romania). During this conference, they took the position that skyjacking should be made a "serious crime" rather than a political crime, which would then allow mandatory extradition of all hijackers (as extradition of political criminals is frowned on by most nations in the United Nations).

As there have been no subsequent skyjackings of Soviet aircraft reported by the Soviets, one could make the tenable conclusion that this combination of events was responsible for the decrease in attempted skyjackings.

Table 8 also shows a drop in the number of aircraft diverted to the Middle East. One incident so predominated the issue of Middle East skyjackings during 1970 that it is the prime candidate to explain the sharp drop in the 1971 rate. On September 6, 1970, the Popular Front for the Liberation of Palestine (PFLP) engineered four hijackings (three of them successful) of major airliners on long-range international flights. Another successful skyjacking followed three days later. The result was the destruction of the four planes, and a total of 769 people held hostage on the Jordanian desert in exchange for the release of Palestinian guerrillas held captive throughout the world. Although this episode was meant to popularize the cause of the PFLP, it generally succeeded in gaining them international condemnation and an attempt by King Hussein to rid Jordan of PFLP members. To date, no further skyjackings have been attempted in their name.

This brief discussion of skyjacking with reference to Cuba, the Soviet Union, and the Middle East has reinforced the earlier assumption that the drop in the non-U.S. rate from 1970 to 1971 is due to a number of simultaneous events which were independent of any effort by the U.S. to curb their skyjacking rate.

The fourth event which has been considered a critical point is the sentencing of R. F. McCoy on June 30, 1972. Due to the nature of the crime—the first skyjacking-extortion attempt and the background of the defendant—a former Green Beret decorated for heroism, and ex-Sunday-school teacher and a student of police science at Brigham Young University—the conviction and sentencing were widely publicized. The length of the sentence (45 years) is viewed here as a perceptible increase in severity of punishmnt, as this was the first instance where the disposition of a skyjacker was given broad coverage. However, as Table 9 shows, the effect of this event was minimal at best.

TABLE 9

	U.S. Attempts		Non-U.S. Attempts	
6–3 mos. prior	8		5	
3–0 mos. prior	12	20	10	15
0–3 mos. after	9		5	
3–6 mos. after	8	17	8	13

The implications of Table 9 refute the assertions of death penalty advocates, whose position predicts that the publicity given to a severe sentence should deter crime. The charge that a greater deterrent effect would have resulted from a death sentence given to McCoy is refuted by Savitz [8] who found that several widely circulated instances of convicted murderers being sentenced to death failed to reduce the number of subsequent murders.

The first and last critical event occurred on January 5, 1973, when President Nixon issued an executive order requiring *all* airlines to inspect all carry-on luggage and to screen all passengers with metal detectors. The results of this event are capsulized in Table 10. The

TABLE 10

	U.S. Attempts		Non-U.S. Attempts	
6–3 mos. prior	12		5	
3–0 mos. prior	6	18	9	14
0–3 mos. after	4		2	
3–6 mos. after	0	4	6	8

drop in the U.S. rate is made even more dramatic by noting that two of the four attempts subsequent to January 5 occurred before February 16, the day that the program was fully implemented.

It can be argued that this drop in the U.S. rate is due not to the deterrent effects of the critical event, but to its preventive effects. That is, people are not being deterred from attmpting to hijack aircraft, they are merely being prevented from doing so. However, I propose that the January 5 event has had a deterrent effect as well, since, according to the FAA, as reported by the New York *Times* of April 8, 1973, an average of 415 persons were arrested monthly in searches made from September through December of 1972, while the average for January and February was only 175.

CONCLUSION

This paper has attempted to examine the differential deterrent effects of severity and certainty of punishment for the crime of skyjacking by focusing on changes in the rate of attempts which could be attributed to each of five "critical points"—of which two represent changes in severity, two represent changes in certainty, and one represents a combination of both. It was found that the two certainty events produced significant reductions in the rate of attempts, while the two severity events and the combination event yielded minimal or ambiguous results. The obvious conclusion is that, given the specific crime of skyjacking and the population of potential offenders, increasing the certainty of punishment acts as a better deterrent than increasing the severity of punishment. This conclusion is supported by the following arguments.

(1) There is no evidence available which shows that the threat of death is more feared than the threat of a life sentence. In fact, Hubbard argues that skyjackers in general are driven by a "clear suicidal intent," which hardly allows the death penalty to be a deterrent.[9] To the contrary, Hubbard finds that the inclusion of skyjacking as a capital offense made it even more attractive to many of his sample. . . .

(2) It is an obvious assertion that crime has proliferated throughout the history of mankind in spite of all efforts to eradicate it. Clearly, then, if one believes that severity of punishment is the basic deterrent, one is left with the predicament of choosing that punishment which combines a maximum of severity while not offending his or her sense of decency. In the Western world, we have decided that death, "humanely" applied, is the most severe punishment which we will allow ourselves to inflict upon each other. There is nothing sacred about the death penalty. It merely represents a compromise between our sensibilities and our efforts to deter. Implicit in this compromise is the notion that a more severe punishment (some form of mutilation, perhaps) would be a more successful deterrent,

while some less severe penalty (life imprisonment) would be less successful. However, were society to emphasize certainty of punishment, it would not have to make moral compromises with its desire to deter. There is no upper limit to the degree of torture which can be inflicted on an offender, nor is there any reasonable argument showing that partial mutilation resulting in death is a greater deterrent than total mutilation resulting in death. But one could reasonably argue that total certainty of punishment is likely to result in almost total deterrence, as only an irrational individual will attempt something which has no chance of success. It is not valid to argue that total certainty is impossible, for neither is total severity. But it is reasonable to argue that any increase in certainty is likely to yield an increase in deterrence, whereas Western society will not tolerate an increase in severity.

(3) Based on the above argument, advocates of the death penalty could conclude that deterrence could be maximized by maintaining the death penalty and then concentrating on improving the certainty of arrest, conviction, and execution. However, this position is untenable for the following reasons.

First, as previously mentioned, a plethora of studies has shown that the existence of the death penalty is independent of the rate of capital crimes, basically because, as Sellin notes, "The person who carefully plans his crime so as to avoid detection has no fear of consequences because he expects to escape them." [10] Second, judging from the Furman decision and the declining rate of executions prior to it, there is a growing proportion of our society unwilling to accept the moral compromise of the death penalty and in favor of exchanging the dubious increment of deterrence provided by the death penalty for the principle of the sanctity of life. Thus, an emphasis on severity leads to a moral dilemma and a lack of total deterrence when extended to its logical limits, whereas an emphasis on certainty results in deterrence approaching a maximum without regard for the morality of state executions.

Although the conclusion that severity is inferior to certainty as a deterrent to skyjackings is based on the empirical evidence supplied within this paper, it is open to criticism, as a definitive scientific study is an unreachable goal. Thus, several alternative explanations are available which must be refuted in order to add confidence in our conclusion.

(1) It is possible that some of the critical events influenced different segments of the population in different ways, thus clouding the results. For example, the death penalty (event 1) may have deterred fugitives from escaping to Cuba via skyjacking, but this same

event might have enticed those with suicidal tendencies to attempt such a crime. This argument is fallacious on two counts. First, the purpose of any deterrent is to inhibit a tendency to commit a given act for a major portion of the population. Therefore, those events which give mixed results are less effective, on the whole, than those events with more positive results. Second, the two pure certainty events showed a dramatic decrease among skyjackers with a variety of motives. Cuba's return of the six American skyjackers resulted in a decrease in diversion attempts to Cuba, regardless of motivation. Similarly, it can be argued that the drop in the U.S. rate from 1972 to the first six months of 1973 (35 to 4) most probably influenced the whole range of potential skyjackers as there was no clear pattern evidenced in the last four attempts.

(2) Van Den Haag argues that six months is an insufficient length of time to test the deterrent effect of any event.[11] However, it is rather unreasonable to asume that, in a society so deluged with media reporting as is this one, the significance of a particular event would become enhanced rather than overshadowed over time. Further, it is more sensible to assume that the decrease in the skyjacking rate from 1969 to 1970 was caused by an event in 1969 (return of hijackers) rather than by the sudden increased significance of an event in 1961 (death penalty), especially since one would be forced to further hypothesize that the 1961 event had limited significance through 1968 and 1969, as the skyjacking rate blossomed during this time.

Another objection to the six-month interval involves the effects of regression. Although there were rate reductions over a six-month period, a longer interval may have shown the gradual increase in the number of skyjackings approaching the pre-event mean rate. Although this is indeed a possibility, it is important to note that the regression effects cannot be calculated due to the lack of any long-term, predictable mean and the close proximity of several critical points. Yet it is useful to point out that certainty events were associated with a subsequent reduction in skyjackings, while the severity events were not.

(3) One could argue that, strictly speaking, this paper did not test the differential effects of severity and certainty, but merely the effects of five specific policies. This argument is basically true, in that I classified these events according to my own perspective rather than the perspective of the skyjackers. However, severity and certainty are ideals which must be translated into events, policies, or laws in order to be tested. If I am to be criticized on my typology rather than on the necessity of classification, so be it; but I feel I have already given sufficient rationale for the way in which each event was treated.

(4) The cell sizes of each table were insufficient to rigorously determine the deterrent effect on any event. While the cell sizes were rather small, I can see no way of avoiding this problem as the entire population was included in the analysis. Also, to rephrase an earlier statement, it is rather shallow to assume that coincidence was totally responsible for the ambiguous results of the severity events and the more dramatic results of the certainty events.

It would appear, then, that the balance of proof favors the assertion that certainty of punishment is a more effective deterrent than severity of punishment, at least for the crime of skyjacking. Clearly, the attempt must be made to examine the veracity of this conclusion as it pertains to other capital offenses so that the scientific community may prove useful in influencing the pending Constitutional fight initiated by the attempts of various state legislatures to circumvent the Furman decision.

NOTES

1. General deterrence (referred to here as deterrence) refers to the inhibition of the general population to commit an illegal act due to the threat of punishment associated with the act's commission. Marginal deterrence is the degree of *additional* deterrence provided by an increase in the certainty, severity, and/or celerity of punishment.

2. F. Van den Haag, "On Deterrence and the Death Penalty," *Journal of Criminal Law, Criminology, and Police Science* 60 (1969), p. 145.

3. See H. A. Bedau, *The Death Penalty in America* (Chicago, 1967). T. Sellin. *Capital Punishment* (New York, 1967).

4. J. Arey, *The Sky Pirates* (New York, 1972).

5. I define politically motivated skyjackings as those events committed by avowedly partisan individuals directly reflecting their country's political and social environment. Examples of politically motivated skyjackings include the activities of the Popular Front for the Liberation of Palestine (PFLP), self-avowed Black Panthers seeking political asylum, and Soviet Jews wishing to escape to the West. Nonpolitically motivated skyjackers include the several extortion attempts made by parachutists, various individuals of questionable rationality (Hubbard, 1971) seeking personal acclaim, and fugitives wishing to avoid prosecution.

While there is undoubtedly some ambiguity and overlap between these categories, I believe it to be of heuristic value to make the distinction between those whose actions are based on political allegiance and those acting on behalf of more personal motivations.

6. The distinction between the political tensions hypothesis involving a direct response to a perceived political or social inequity, and the fad hypothesis involving those with nebulous political or personal motivations, is

made by D. G. Hubbard in his characterization of skyjacking as a mass phenomenon. "[A] mood of national hysteria is involved, which sets loose a mob dynamic into which susceptible individuals are drawn. In many of these instances, both of these factors are involved; that is to say, certain sick people are swept up by the current mob psychology to perform this act which, in its own way, is a direct, symbolic dramatization of their own lunacy, as well as that of the community about them." *The Skyjacker: His Flights of Fantasy* (New York, 1971), pp. 17–18.

For example, several later skyjackings involved Blacks claiming to be Panthers in search of political asylum. However, unlike their predecessors, these men were generally not known to be members of the Black Panther Party prior to their commandeering the plane, and they tended to be fleeing from crimes not motivated by political concerns. Although one could look at these men as reacting to a political situation, I think it more proper to invoke the fad or mass phenomenon explanation.

7. This paper will clearly speculate on the reasons behind the drop in the non-U.S. skyjacking rate. Yet this effort is viewed as necessary in order to point out the presence of explanations perceived as more reasonable than the advent of skymarshals.

8. L. D. Savitz, "A Study in Capital Punishment," *Journal of Criminal Law: Criminology and Police Science*, 49 (1958), pp. 338–351.

9. D. G. Hubbard, *The Skyjacker: His Flights of Fantasy* (N.Y., 1971).

10. Sellin, *supra* note 3, p. 250.

11. Van den Haag, *supra* note 1, p. 146.

Chapter Thirteen

The Violent Offender

Daniel Glaser, Donald Kenefick,
and Vincent O'Leary

There are a variety of murderers and violent offenders. Each is a member of a subclass or category whose members are sufficiently similar (as to social class, psychic structure, biological nature, etc.) that his life history and reaction to specific situations probably can be predicted, within statistical limits. Some such classes are rather large (such as the "murderer from the culture of violence"); others (such as the "sexual murderer") are very rare. . . .

There appears to be several clusters of factors that are probably important in relation to the violent offender, in fact to all the conditions which are a concern to correction.[1] To oversimplify, these clusters are:

(1)*Biological,* both (a) the *general physical type* (for example, the more muscular the boy, the more apt is his assaultive behavior, if triggered off by *other* factors likely to be damaging enough to come to police attention), and (b) *physical* and, especially, *neurological defects.* For example, acting-out boys seem often to have had a protracted, nagging, minor illness in childhood—a common event in lower class milieu—such as otitis, mastoiditis, and so on.[2] These tend

---

Reprinted by permission of the National Institute of Mental Health, U.S. Dept. of Health, Education and Welfare, 1966.

to make life more painful than otherwise, to tax parental patience more, and to set up a situation where the parent, already over-whelmed with harsh reality, finds it easier to reject the child.

Also, we find a very high degree of what seems to be mild brain damage (indicated by diffuse electroencephalographic abnormalities and slight reflex deficits) in poorer children. This seems directly related to poor paranatal care.[3] The behavior it tends to perpetuate is probably more important than has been realized. First, mildly brain-damaged children may be more *impulsive* than others, quicker to respond to stimuli. Second, they may have greater difficulties in *learning*, especially the abstractions involved in reading. Boys who have either an acquired (i.e., brain damage from birth injury) or inherited (and these may number up to 10 percent of the population) difficulty in reading have a tremendous handicap, especially if they are lower class.

Better diagnostic and therapeutic facilities are available to middle class boys, and school authorities are somewhat more indulgent in their attitudes toward them. Lower class boys do not have these advantages. A lower class boy who cannot become a good student will usually get merely the opportunity to drop out of school.

Finally, we should mention mental deficiency. While this is too often exaggerated as a factor in criminality, our society may not provide enough noncriminal niches for the mildly deficient.

(2) Another cluster embraces *social* factors. Of particular interest here are the differential behavior preferences emphasized by the value systems of different classes and ethnic groups. These emphases are sometimes overt and conscious, but the most important are "automatic" and nonverbalized. A good example of differential emphasis is the "culture of violence" mentioned earlier.

To illustrate another facet, the general feeling of lower class society (or of certain ethnic groups at all class levels) that the rest of the world is against them and that they cannot be accepted into that world, is easily translatable into a value system (of contempt for the mark) that Tannenbaum has described for criminals[4] and Maurer specifically for con men.[5] An ambitious lower class boy, for example, who despairs of rising through the usual channels, may find it easy to obtain comfortable rationalizations for a life of predatory crime much easier than it would be for a middle or upper class boy.

(3) A variation of the above, important enough to isolate, are *familial* factors. It may help understanding to see the family as a device for socializing the child, i.e., for teaching him (directly, or by example, or by reacting to him when a parent may not even be aware

of so doing) how to be a human being, of a certain sex, in a given time and place. First, the nature of the parents is important. If there are certain gaps in their own ability to be social creatures, the same gaps will show up in their young, whether they intend it or not. A drunkard's child is either a drunk or a teetotaler; he is seldom a flexible realist in this area, at least. Further, if the parents are professional criminals and otherwise good parents, their admiring children may copy them. It often shocks the unsophisticated to find that many *professional* criminals (e.g., the Mafia) are graduates of loving homes, who are succesfully identifying with their fathers.

Next, both parents must be *there,* or their parental substitutes available, for adequate learning. Many lower class delinquents have been brought up by mothers alone; father is absent or distant, often admired unrealistically, yearned for but not available to copy. The compulsive masculinity, the high degree of homosexuality, the high rate of broken marriages in the lower class are all, in part, results of the absent father. Efficient learning takes place in an environment of consistent reward or consistent punishment, and consistency is usually a concomitant of tenderness toward the young. It is well to remember that the more difficult the environment, the harder it is to be a consistent parent. Finally, parents must have solved most of their own problems in regard to sexuality, aggression, and the like, and must have satisfactions in life *other* than their children, or the child becomes "the fall guy," the seduced, for parental needs.

The child is not, however, a passive piece of paper the parents write on. Some youngsters, especially active, muscular, curious, outgoing children, are harder to socialize.[6] The tremendous pressures and well-structured values of the middle class often just barely mold such children into acceptable citizens. When parents are generally cynical about the rewards of sobriety, politeness, and inhibition generally (often characteristic of lower class society) the results of their feebler attempts at socialization are about what would be expected. That is, the easily impressionable get moderately civilized, and can end up as reasonable facsimiles of people above them in the social scale; the hard cases remain at least moderately unsocialized by middle class standards.

(4) The last cluster of factors are those traditionally termed *psychodynamic.*[7] These are verbal or motoric responses of which the actor is largely or completely unaware, and which are more or less automatic. They have been learned, in early childhood, as a means of coping with difficult situations, usually those which threaten to arouse more direct and once unacceptable responses. A child whose sexuality or anger is aroused, in a situation when sexual excitement

or anger would be unacceptable (for example, to parents) is forced, on any repetition, to find ways of throttling, diverting, or disguising these feelings. One very important point of psychiatry deals with the whole issue of *recognizing* when a situation, such as those we mentioned, is in fact being repeated or not. The habit of human beings to "generalize," i.e., to see a given situation as actually something quite different from what it might seem to others, and to respond to the identified, not the real, situation, is a very important one.

Let us see if the factors listed . . . can be ordered so as to describe some of the varieties of violent offenders. We will direct most of our attention to the murderer. However, the discussion has applicability to a wide range of violent behavior. It is difficult to set out a highly valid typology of the murderer; that kind of classification waits for much more arduous and meticulous research. However, it is possible to describe a reasonable set of hypotheses derived from our present knowledge.[8]

First of all, murderers (and the "violent criminal") as has been implied, might be thought of as falling into two roughly defined groups. They either commit a crime that:

> (A) is understandable as being an appropriate reaction, under the given circumstances, to a specfic situation, and is so understood by most individuals of the same sex, ethnic group, social class, and age as the murderer;
> (B) or they do not.

This is not to say that a middle class businessman must consider that a rape or murder committed by an 18-year-old slum area youth is an appropriate reaction before it be placed in category (A). It is enough that a number of slum area teenagers think that the action is understandable. For example, a hysterical young woman who seems to advertise a sexual willingness, and then withdraws, usually produces merely irritation and anxiety in the well-trained middle class male; she may induce a rape in a lower class adolescent from certain groups. "Rape" under these circumstances may horrify middle class judges, but not the lower class males. The rape, however, of a virgin or anyone not giving sexual cues (or culturally not supposed to give any, like old people or children) arouses a good deal of resentment and anxiety in any class.

Conversely, category (B) is reserved for those whose crimes would not be, under the given circumstances, considered appropriate by anyone of the criminal's social class, age, and sex.

Very roughly, most murderers or violent criminals in category (A) are probably within the bounds of psychic function considered normal by their culture; psychiatrists who have had some experience with their particular social group would rate the majority as being no worse than neurotic (perhaps as "character neurotics" technically). Most murderers in category (B) would probably turn out to be a good deal more deviant than any social group tolerates and probably would be diagnosed as "psychopathic" or one or another kind of "psychotic."

Let us look at some of the murderers in category (A):

(1) *The "ordinary" murderer:* Most often, he is a good example of a product of the "culture of violence." The murderer frequently lives in a milieu where passionate assault, under certain circumstances, is not only excused but even expected. "Premeditation," when it exists, is usually some activity like staggering out of a barroom to find a convenient weapon. In a large number of cases, the person he murders on return is a friend. Both are drinking, both are trying to prove their masculinity, both know the survivor will not be severely condemned by the people that matter (their other friends) even if the police and the courts take a dim view of the outcome. The quick-triggered male who assaults (and kills, occasionally) is often responding to an affront to his maleness, doubly intolerable because it comes from another male.

A not uncommon subvariety of murderer is the "innocent bystander" (who may also end up as a victim), who is stimulated to intervene in another's quarrel, a kind of dangerous overidentification. Another is the boy who kills someone in a gang assault, carried away by the group spirit, as it were. Almost all of these are lower class males. They are often diagnosed as "psychopaths" by middle class psychiatrists, but they are actually not that deviant, compared to their milieu. They are trained in violence; they often have histories of being violently beaten in childhood by their mothers; they have had to prove themselves with their adolescent peers by their fists, and they constitute a "high risk" in certain situations: their closest and most vulnerable attachments are to other males, their social clubs, the corner bar, their basic attitude to the world above them an angry cynicism.

Kept away from alcohol and threats to their self-esteem, they are relatively nonassaultive people. They may be frightened enough of their own anger after one murder or violent assault to walk very circumspectly thereafter. The probability of their nonrecidivism is highest when they can be induced to accept more of the values of lower middle class citizens or when the situations likely to trigger assaultiveness are controlled.

(2) The *"cultural" murderer:* Another variety of the type (A)

murderer is the "cultural" murderer, i.e., a man who is compelled by social pressures to commit murder. An example is the Ku Kluxers in the Deep South, who are convinced they are preserving the fabric of a great society. Another is the occasional feuding seen among old American groups, usually of Scotch or North Irish descent. These murders are "premeditated," but are similar to those of the "ordinary murderer" in that the culture condones violence, in fact, insists on it, under the circumstances mentioned. They are individuals who possess, in exaggerated form, patterns of behavior condoned and supported by their environment. They are apt either to be normal or neurotic, seldom much worse.

Some, however, that seem at first to fit here, but really do not, have identified the situation as one in which they will *gain social esteem* by removing an *enemy of society* (and they may need such esteem more than most). A few others are quite disturbed and have misunderstood the subculture's attitude which does not tolerate murder under the given circumstances at all. For example, for a fervent Democrat to shoot a Republican governor would be unacceptable anywhere, for political assassination has never found a firm place in our political science. These will be discussed below under category (B).

(3) *The "professional" murderer:* Another variety, although relatively few in number, is the professional murderer. Of this type, there seem to be at least two subvarieties: The Mafia "soldier," who does the assigned task in line of duty, and the much rarer killer, of various ethnic groups, who is on call for anyone who can afford him. We know nothing scientifically about either, though we could hazard a guess that the first is not *necessarily* any more disturbed than many, and that the second *probably* is pretty disturbed, indeed. The first is apt to be a model prisoner unlikely to "reform"; the second is apt to be at the dead center of any riot and probably will not change either. There is a good chance that he resembles one or another of the subjects in the following section.

We come now to category (B), to those murderers and violent criminals whose acts are not condonable by their own milieu, may not even be understood by it. All of these taken together form probably a relatively small percentage of murderers. All are most probably psychiatrically disturbed. Their individual outlook for rehabilitation varies as their psychiatric condition, and since we do not know as much as we would like about the outcome of a given psychiatric conditon, prediction must be cautious.

(4) *The "inadequate" murderer:* When describing the cultural murderer, we noted that certain individuals take it upon themselves to avenge some social wrong. The less these individuals have

the official status to indulge in such behavior—that is, the more presumptuous is their wish to be the avenger—the more one is apt to find pathology. The murderer is often the never-quite-respected, never-quite-respectable fringe member of the group. The very instabilities and infantilities, that keep him peripheral, blind him to the fact that avenging the group will merely lay him open to greater hostility from it, since he is not even the official executioner.

It is one thing for a group to decide to take justice into its own hands; this may be deplorable, but it does not necessarily indicate the group is sick, simply that it is wrong. It is quite another for an *individual* to do so. This is apt to alienate him quite thoroughly even from the group he is trying to please. These individuals are not quite psychotic but their need for self-esteem is so pathetically great that they cannot be fed, as it were, by any action. They are bound to defeat themselves. Their outlook is poor, psychiatrically, since they usually have little insight and are frightened of getting more, since their fantasies of importance are all they have.

(5) *The "psychopathic" murderer:* There is no concept in psychiatry more abused than "psychopath." In Europe, the term is often used as we use "character neurosis" to designate a variety of common personality types, few of whom need be criminal. In this country, reviewing a series of cases diagnosed as "psychopath," it is hard to see any common denominators beyond lower class origin, a certain distrust of the original interviewer, and a characteristic way of *handling* some kinds of *stress*. Such cases seem to be a mixed bag, ranging from cases of minimal brain damage to ambulatory schizophrenia. The characteristic ways of handling some kinds of stress seemed to fall into one of two large areas (though normal, neurotic, and psychotic mechanisms are found in people so diagnosed):

(a) The person is stimulus-bound, i.e., he has to respond to certain stimuli. These people seem to be either compulsive neurotics or brain-damaged. A few violent crimes are certainly committed by the latter, but compulsive neurotics are generally excessively law-abiding.

A word might be in place here about "brain-damaged" criminals. After almost a half century of a relative neglect of the possibility of biologic defect being important in at least a few cases of criminality, we are probably ready to reassess the problem. For example, as Pasamanick [9] has shown, poor people are exposed to the possibility of brain damage around the time of birth to a much greater degree than middle class individuals. Also, as McDermott, et al.[10] have demonstrated, this is a good deal less likely to be diagnosed when the patient is poor. Most individuals with mild brain damage do not, of course, become criminals (they are much too restless, or inert, to become *professional* criminals, in any case). However, the combination of (i) lower class culture which tends to permit a certain impulsivity to normals and does not frown upon physical violence as much as middle class culture; (ii) muscularity, when present, and (iii) a tendency to labile responses, emotionally and physically, over and above those seen in normals—all this makes some brain-damaged youngsters likely perpetrators of "assault" and, under certain conditions, murder.

One rather mysterious condition, about which little is actually known, may fall into this group, the so-called 6/14 syndrome, from the characteristic pattern on the sleeping electroencephlogram.[11] The individuals showing this are usually children or adolescents, who very often are quiet, law-abiding "good" boys and girls. They may have had certain subtle organic symptoms: a tendency to stand heat or cold less well than others, recurrent abdominal pains, etc., all of which can theoretically be traced to some kind of imbalance in the autonomic nervous system, but they generally seem healthy and intelligent. Without much warning they commit a terrible crime: fire-setting, murder, etc., while in a dreamlike state (which they can remember, but usually without much emotion). Only when their brainwaves are recorded during sleep do their characteristic patterns appear.

(b) The second way of handling stress is more difficult to describe than is impulsivity. If there is any validity to the term "psychopath," it would hold for the individuals we are about to discuss. Basically, they show a complex *pattern* of response, which is still coherent enough to be recognizable.

First of all, these are people who seem "keyed up" most of the time, at least according to one intriguing investigation.[12] This is indicated by tests of blood pressure, pulse, skin-resistance, and the like—all of which rather crudely measure autonomic nervous system sensitivity. However—and this is the important point—somehow they have learned to deal with this constant jangling in a very pathologic way—they ignore it, are not really aware of it consciously at all. In other words, they are responding to stimuli more often and more vigorously than others, but are not really able to respond by appropriate means, using words and/or muscular action as "normals" do. Only one phase, the initial phase, of a response is operating. This surface inertia gives them that appearance of blandness, of not caring, that so irritates their fellows. One suspects that they have been brought up in an environment in which the infant and child were faced with bewildering cues —that is, by a parent who blew hot and cold toward them without discernible pattern. Psychoanalytic studies of the parents of children with behavior disorders tend to confirm this suspicion.[13, 14]

However, such a probable reaction to confused signals may

probably be found in other conditions also.[15] Why does this group, with its hypercontrol, actually break down suddenly, with eruptions of what others term "antisocial" behavior?

The answers are complex, and can only be indicated tentatively. First, such individuals need a constant series of stimuli to operate at all. They do rather well in a busy environment, respond to boredom poorly, often with attempts to create a synthetic busyness (and such busy-busy activity is often rather hard on innocent bystanders).

Second, they have been brought up, as noted, by inconstant parents. Trasler has pointed out that some restless, stimulus-seeking individuals need to be sat on firmly during the socializing process, and this is rarely a characteristic of the hit-or-miss socializing techniques of the lower class parent.[16] Moreover, the parents of the individuals we are discussing are themselves, as mentioned, highly ambivalent toward the child, uncertain how to deal with him, covertly hostile and seductive alternately, and so on. The child is often (a) not taught controls in certain areas, i.e., how to delay satisfaction, because the parent doesn't know how, either, or (b) may indeed be covertly taught to gratify "forbidden" needs, contrary to the standards of society, because the child's subsequent behavior *vicariously gratifies the parent.* The parent who gets a secret kick out of a child's delinquency is well known.[17]

One further note: These individuals seem to respond very poorly to punishment.[18] They do best when kept busy and positively rewarded, but very possibly the activity must be kept below a yet unknown threshold. Probably, if called upon to solve a complex problem that directly involves their self-esteem, they may overrespond and fall apart. Interestingly, such characteristics seem to disappear with increasing age. Why, we really do not know.

(6) *The "psychotic" murderer:* Most murderers kill one person only, usually in the heat of passion. The more people a person kills and the more occasions on which he kills, the more it can be taken as preliminary evidence that he will be found psychotic. Psychotics are, as a general rule, more law-abiding than the normal or neurotic, but when they do murder or assault, they do so with a certain exaggeration and bizarrie that is diagnostic. Looking at a bizarrie for a moment, one can generalize: Extending those murders which are committed incidentally, such as during a robbery, if a victim is either related by blood to the criminal, or is a total stranger, the more apt the criminal is to be psychotic. The "ordinary" murderer murders a friend or a spouse; the psychotic murders a parent or a casual stranger. This is why most murders are relatively easy for the police to solve

and why a "Jack-the-Ripper" or a "Boston Strangler" is an enigma, since this type murders strangers only.

One thing should be kept in mind: A psychotic is a person who habitually uses a distorted response to a situation. This does not mean that he habitually, at all times, must use distorted responses to *many* situations. Such individuals are easily recognized and usually end up in a State hospital, but there are much greater percentages of individuals who are utilizing distortion in a much less obvious way and maintain many adequate responses, especially in the social area. Such people are often called "borderlines"—they get by, sometimes rather creatively, and 99 percent are harmless, many very useful to society.

There are three main types of illness which may so alter the ordinary reactions of a person that a diagnosis of psychosis is warranted. One case is based on a wide variety of acute or chronic diseases of the brain. A hallmark, usually, of this kind of condition is confusion and disorientation or intellectual deficit or all of them together. These may be subtle or grossly evident. The condition, depending on its cause, is either over fairly quickly (like acute alcoholism) or may be permanent (like the results of severe encephalitis).

Most brain-damaged people are, of course, noncriminal. Their poor impulse control, their major difficulties in dealing with their guilt and inadequacy, and their need to feel useful—all, however, demand a realistically tolerant environment. Brain damage *per se,* is less likely to cause antisocial behavior than is the reaction of those around the sufferer to the fact of the damage.

A second type of psychotic reaction occasionally linked with murder or assault is moderately *severe depression,* not so severe that the sufferer is too depressed even to move, but severe enough to have the world around him pretty thoroughly colored blue. Depression intensifies our feelings of being abused, alone, and uncared for; some people use this mechanism more often than others. Depression seems more common in those classes (for example, our middle class) who tend to train their children to control aggression toward others and who tend to use punishments (like saying, "How can mother love a little boy who gets so dirty?") that threaten loss of love and arouse guilt. Suicide, for example, is far more common among the depressed (and middle and upper class individuals) than is murder or assault. One might almost say that, when a lower class person feels humiliated, he tends to strike out at the humiliators; when a middle or upper class person feels humiliated, he blames himself, feels guilty, and may get depressed and even suicidal.

But—the suicidal impulse is a thin disguise for a murderous

impulse. *Sometimes* the controls break down—rarely, but often enough to make the category significant. The prognosis for such cases, once removed from the stress that precipitated the depression, is good. Such offenders will generally murder only once. Paradoxically, however, they are often such timid and ineffective people that they rather like the ordered life of an institution.

The last category is the somewhat commoner, but still rare, *schizophrenic* murderer. There are at least two different illnesses, probably lumped together under this term. One is an acute reaction (most common in late adolescence) which has a good chance to resolve itself into a normal adjustment; the other is a slow sliding downhill (also first noticeable in late adolescence) into a kind of vegetative existence. Probably two-thirds of all individuals who show a schizophrenic reaction will either recover completely or will recover enough to get by in society.

Generally schizophrenics are more law abiding than the general population. They tend to have been "good" children and quiet, obedient adolescents prior to their breakdown. The breakdown comes at certain crucial developmental stages. Boys tend to show symptoms as they near the end of high school and are coming to the end of the period when they can function as "good" children. Girls may show a similar pattern but since schizophrenic girls are more apt to marry than schizophrenic boys, they may show it in the context of their first pregnancy or delivery.

Sometimes, a mild schizophrenic crisis goes almost unnoticed and may "harden," as it were, into a chronic distortion that often may escape notice for years. One result may be a kind of automatic going through the motions that often is socially viable, especially in lower class society. This pattern, rather common, is called "simple" schizophrenia when it comes to the attention of the diagnostician, though there are probably more such cases outside hospitals than inside. A more malignant variety is shown by the men or women who have solved their inner inadequacies by the simple device of blaming them on the world outside—the paranoid solution. The full-blown pattern takes about a decade to take shape, so that most victims are at least in their late twenties. Most paranoids are probably harmless, but some focus their hostility on a specific cause for their problems, such as a prominent man, and may cause considerable difficulty.

Schizophrenics, like most adolescents, are trying to sort out and deal with the problems arising from sexuality and self-assertion but lack the means that most youngsters have. The sudden and inexplicable murder and assault on a mother or an infant by a very few of the younger schizophrenics are often ways of dealing with, warding off, as it were, people they see as threatening to their shaky equilibrium. Sometimes, a person has sufficient strength to present a more or less normal front to society, a little studied variety often called "borderline," or "ambulatory" schizophrenics, rather more openly "normal" than the simple schizophrenics mentioned above. It is as if they have a "core" of psychotic thought and potential behavior, surrounded and hidden by acceptable social behaviors. Very, very rarely such a superficially intact person becomes a murderer, often, most likely, by stumbling accidentally on the fact that human beings can be killed rather easily and that total strangers can be murdered with relative impunity. Such men, to attempt to satisfy their sexual drives, may prey on the helpless, because of their fear of adult sexual objects. Since the most numerous category of the helpless (aged and children) may stand for some desirable but hated object in their past, more than sexuality may be triggered off by an encounter. Most bizarre, multiple "sexual" murders are in this group. They are seldom caught and even more rarely studied scientifically.[19]

The paranoids mentioned earlier also kill occasionally, usually an important person, or someone they fantasy has sexual or hurtful designs on them. Usually, this is a spectacular "execution" with enough of a crowd about to gratify their vanity.[20] Very rarely, they may go on a murderous spree, as if they are trying to get revenge on the universe.

The prognosis for them all is very guarded. The sexual and paranoid murderers usually do not show any signs of ameliorating their fierce and intractable sets. The remorse of the others, when they gain some insight into what they have done, often plunges them back into disorganization (or a paranoid set that retrospectively justified their action). Some workers have reported gains in intensive psychotherapy, but the sample of those treated is still very small.[21]

These listed cannot claim to have described types into which all murderers can be fitted. For example, the girl who kills her illegitimate baby; the heir who carefully kills off all rival claimants to the family fortune; and so on, have not been fully described. However, for practical purposes, the list substantially includes all those we are concerned about here. To briefly capitulate, a fairly well demarcated series of types emerge:

1. The "ordinary" murderer.
2. The "professional" murderer.
3. The "cultural" murderer.
4. The "inadequate" murderer.
5. The "brain-damaged" murderer.

6. The "psychopathic" murderer.

7. The "psychotic" murderer.

Surprisingly enough, not too many of these are calculatingly premeditated, in any usual sense of the term except, of course, those murders committed by type 2. Type 3 often plans, but in a sense he is under a social compulsion as great as any force a man has to deal with, and how psychologically free he is, is a question. Types 4 through 7 are all, in Durham jurisdictions, nonresponsible; in Mc-Naghten jurisdictions they usually, nowadays, end up in a hospital also. And type 1? Here the issue of responsibility is most debated. The general trend, even when responsibility is affirmed, is away from execution toward limited incarceration, which seems justified by the low violation rates of these individuals.

Persons in categories 4 through 7 are not at all like those in category 1. Sending them back into society without adequate and highly specialized treatment first (and a certain proportion remain untreatable) is quite dangerous.

What are the proportion of individuals in each category? We do not know. As an educated guess, probably all individuals in types 2 through 7 comprise a definite minority of the total of murderers.

NOTES

1. This discussion draws on some of the notions outlined in Eleanor and Sheldon Glueck, *Unravelling Juvenile Delinquency* (London, 1950).

2. Leslie Phillips, Clark University, Worcester, Mass., unpublished data.

3. B. Pasamanick and H. Knobloch, "Epidemiologic Studies on the Complications of Pregnancy and the Birth Process," in G. Caplan (ed.), *Prevention of Mental Disorders in Children* (New York, 1961).

4. F. Tannenbaum, *Crime and the Community* (New York, 1938).

5. D. W. Maurer, *The Big Con* (New York, 1940).

6. G. Trasler, *The Explanation of Criminality* (London, 1962).

7. Valuable sources of material on these and other classifications are P. Gebhard, et al., *Sex Offenders: An Analysis of Types* (New York, 1965); and J. W. Mohr, R. E. Turner, M. B. Jerry, *Pedophilia and Exhibitionism* (Toronto, 1964).

8. A substantial part of this section is derived from the work, as yet unpublished, of A. L. McGarry and D. Kenefick, Law-Medicine Institute, Boston University. See also M. S. Guttmacher, *The Mind of the Murderer* (New York, 1960).

9. B. Pasamanick and H. Knobloch, *op. cit.*

10. J. F. McDermott, *et al.,* "Social Class Factors in Diagnosis and Treatment," paper delivered at the March 1965 meeting of the American Orthopsychiatric Association.

11. See the following references, especially Woods, for bibliographies on this phenomenon: John F. Knott, "EEG and Behavior," *American Journal of Orthopsychiatry,* vol. 30 (1960), pp. 292–297; Earl A. Walker, "Murder or Epilepsy," *Journal of Nervous and Mental Diseases,* vol. 133 (1961), pp. 430–437; Sherwyn M. Woods, "Adolescent Violence and Suicide," *Archives of General Psychiatry,* vol. 5 (1961), pp. 528–534.

12. B. Lathane and S. Schachter, "Crime, Cognition and the Autonomic Nervous System," *Nebraska Symposium on Motivation* (University of Nebraska, 1964).

13. Ivy Bennet, *Delinquent and Neurotic Children* (New York, 1960).

14. Kate Friedlander, *The Psychoanalytical Approach to Juvenile Delinquency* (New York, 1960).

15. B. Goldstein, "The Relationship of Muscle Tension and Autonomic Activity to Psychiatric Disorders," *Psychosomatic Medicine,* vol. 27 (1965), pp. 39–52.

16. Trasler, *op. cit.*

17. M. E. Giffin, A. Johnson, and E. M. Litin, "Specific Factors Determining Anti-Social Acting Out," *American Journal of Orthopsychiatry,* vol. 24 (1954), pp. 668–684.

18. S. Schachter and B. Lathane, *op. cit.*

19. A. Hyatt Williams, "The Psychopathology and Treatment of Sexual Murderers," Rosen, I. (ed.), *The Pathology and Treatment of Sexual Deviation* (London, 1964).

20. D. A. Rothstein, "Presidential Assassination Syndrome," *Archives of General Psychiatry,* vol. 11 (1964), pp. 245–254.

21. A. Hyatt Williams, *op. cit.*

Part Four

Contemporary Approaches to Corrections

Introduction

Not only is the concept of crime not well understood, but also, and maybe even more importantly, we are not sure of how to correct the criminals. The history of penology evinces that many methods of punishing and rehabilitating the offenders have been attempted, but all have failed. Franklin E. Zimring analyzes one of these methods: deterrence. He discusses the perspectives of deterrence and concludes by contending that a gap exists between the information about the effects of legal threats and official beliefs. The other extreme on the line of treatment efforts, diversion from the justice system, is presented here by Nora Klapmuts who suggests that this focuses attention on the offender and his needs rather than on the inadequacies of intervention and control.

Behavior modification is again a contemporary problem of penology, Stephanie B. Stolz, Louis A. Wienckowski, and Bertram S. Brown discuss the critical issue that involves a rather forceful control of criminals. The incentives and use of prison labor, one of the most efficient and just rehabilitative instruments, poorly implemented for centuries, is the subject of Neil M. Singer's paper in which he points out how society could benefit from the work of the prisoners both economically and in some noneconomic ways.

Both D. Chapman and J. P. Martin write about the social

consequences of conviction, a kind of sentence meted out outside the courtroom which through stigmatization may destroy any beneficial outcome of treatment methods and could be a strong impedance in the way toward the rehabilitation of the criminal.

Finally, compensation to victims of crime is discussed by Stephen Schafer who proposes that we detach compensation from its charitable character and connect it with penology in order to make it one of the major instruments of corrections.

Chapter Fourteen

Perspectives
on Deterrence

Franklin E. Zimring

. . .

When discussing deterrence as a motive of crime-control policies, the proper focus of inquiry is on the attitudes and behavior of officials; when discussing the likelihood and magnitude of a deterrent effect, emphasis shifts to characteristics and reactions of potential criminals. . . . This section deals with the responses of threatened audiences, the major portion of the analysis being concerned with the *general* effects of threats: behavior that can be expected from people even if they are not caught and punished. Much of this discussion of general effects will be relevant as well to special deterrence, but the combination of actual punishment and further threats raises some special issues that are separately discussed in a brief concluding section.

SECTION 1. GENERAL DETERRENCE

The legal threat is both a distinctive class of phenomena, within which all members share certain similar characteristics, and a

Reprinted by permission of the National Institute of Mental Health, U.S. Dept. of Health, Education and Welfare, 1971.

composite grouping which includes communications that differ greatly in content and effectiveness. Exploring the concept of general deterrence thus becomes a two-pronged search: 1. for generalizations that apply to all threat situations, and 2. for explanations of the differences observable in the effectiveness of various legal threats.

Since threat responses are distributed over a spectrum that ranges from total lack of effect to almost full compliance, it appears at the outset that the differences between legal threats are more important than their similarities. But if present knowledge about threats in general is not sufficient to shed much light on the utility of particular legal threats, the initial consideration of a few generalizations about threats can still provide a framework for considering more important patterns of difference.

One common element of all threats (whose defining characteristic is the announcement that unpleasant consequences will be attached to particular behavior) is that they give their audience a new reason for avoiding the threatened behavior. The power of unpleasant consequences as a reason for avoiding behavior will vary, of course, but the existence of an additional barrier to commission of the threatened behavior is constant. Whether there are any other effects produced by all threats is debatable, but investigators have reported that with the creation of the new barrier, two further changes in outlook on the part of a threatened audience may be expected.

. . .

"Forbidden Fruit Is Always Sweeter"   According to some observers, existence of the threat as a barrier to committing a particular act causes members of a threatened audience to revise attitudes toward the desirability of the threatened behavior. People who felt that the threatened behavior was desirable in the absence of the threat will consider the behavior more desirable, even if they are persuaded by the prospect of consequences to heed the threat. To those who originally were neutral about the desirability of a threatened behavior, it will acquire some positive value, apart from the unpleasantness of threatened consequences.

It is probably unsafe to assume that an atmosphere of constraint and the "forbidden fruit" effect are inevitable products of threats. How a threat can produce feelings of constraint among those who were never tempted to engage in the threatened behavior is difficult to understand, unless the fact of the threat causes a significant reevaluation of the behavior. And where members of an audience have considered behavior to be highly undesirable in the absence of threat, it is not clear that the addition of a threat will make much difference in the way they view the behavior. Then, too, intervening variables would overwhelm any attempt to validate this prediction in many circumstances.

Even if constraint and reevaluation of the threatened behavior could be added to the creation of a new reason for avoiding it, the general model of the psychological dimensions of threats could not lead to predictions about behavior because the feelings toward the threatened behavior produced by threats lead in opposite directions, leaving the behavior more dangerous at the same time that it is more attractive, and no general statement can be made about which pull will be stronger.

At the same time, the "forbidden fruit" effect may exist in a wide variety of situations where members of an audience were not previously disinclined toward the behavior threatened, and the above psychological model of threat-effects can provide information about the emotional climate in which threats operate, even though it cannot predict the outcome of threats. For those who are tempted to commit threatened acts, threats produce reasons for avoiding them—reasons that compete with the attractiveness of the behavior, and with any new attraction that is added by threat. Where a legal threat is relevant to predicting behavior, it will produce conflicts. How such conflicts are resolved is a function of the differences between threats, but the existence of conflict is a common theme.

Still, the critical work in any discussion of the effectiveness of threats is the search for those variations in circumstance that account for the great differences noted in the results of threats. Toward this end, the following sections discuss (a) differences among men, (b) types of threatened behavior, (c) threat as communication, (d) applicability and credibility, (e) variations in threatened consequences, (f) variations in severity of consequences, (g) the moral quality of threatened behavior, and (h) the effects of group pressures.

A. Differences Among Men

One natural place to search for the explanation of different patterns of response to threats is within the great range of differences in psychology, sentiment, and status that set men apart from each other in a large and complex social order. Explanations of differential deterability that are based on differences among men—unlike hypotheses about differences in deterrence caused by variation in the nature of the threatened behavior—seek to establish general patterns of threat sensitivity that follow a particular person from one situation to another. Where it is known that Mr. Smith's relative immunity to the threat of sanctions while filling out his income tax is attributable to a personality characteristic, it is likely that the same characteristic will operate when he is exposed to the temptation to steal, or to speed. If differences among men were the only explanation of differential deterability, society could be neatly divided into deterable and non-deterable segments. But since differences among men can only be a part of the complex of factors conditioning the effectiveness of threats in different situations, general patterns of threat responsiveness based on personal differences will predict responses with only partial effectiveness. Knowing that Smith is relatively unconcerned about the threat of punishment for tax cheating, and that this lack of concern is related to a general tendency, will not tell us that he is more likely than not to be undeterred by the threat of punishment if confronted with the opportunity to commit armed robbery. Such information will, however, mean that Smith is more likely than others without this characteristic to be unimpressed with the threat of punishment for robbery. But the chances of deterrence in the second situation may still be overwhelmingly high.

Differences in Personality Type

A great number of different personality types coexist in the same social order. Various schools of thought in the psychic sciences use different schemes of classification to describe variations in personality type. Most of the personality differences that have been mentioned in connection with the effect of sanctions are based on simple distinctions not related to systematic explanations of human personality.

The Future vs. the Present   One such relatively simple distinction is between those individuals for whom the future is an important part of present thinking and those who are less "future-oriented." The future-oriented individual will be happy to forgo a large gain today in order to enjoy a larger one next week. The person without a significant sense of the importance of next week will accept a lesser but immediate reward. In the case of threat response, it is the converse of this effect that is significant: since the unpleasantness threatened will always come after the commission of the threatened act, and is often quite distant in both time and probability from the temptation to act, the future-oriented person will pay greater heed to the possibility of unpleasantness communicated by a threat, while the less future-oriented person will be more willing to place a heavy mortgage on events removed in time and space.

Group processes are of crucial importance even more directly in the large number of cases where decisions to obey or disobey the legal threat are made by small groups rather than individuals. Studies of juvenile offenders can be taken as evidence that much, perhaps even most, of juvenile crime is group activity. Offenses such as vandalism, gang-fighting, false fire alarm pulling, pack rape, and many of the property crimes committed by juveniles are typically committed by groups of youths. While group crime is less common among older offenders, it is far from unheard of, and mob violence is by definition a group phenomenon. When threat response is collective, individual members of a group may find themselves willing to risk unpleasantness that would be sufficient to deter them if each alone were responsible for the decision, because the significance and immediacy of group pressures toward participating in criminal activity overwhelm ordinary tendencies toward caution. Because the pressures generated by the group are powerful, it may be that legal threat must reach a particular proportion of the group, analogous to a critical mass, before any of the group members will be restrained by threat from engaging in criminal conduct. And deterring a large proportion of a group contemplating criminal activity may be difficult because fear of the law may not be considered a respectable emotion, and those who feel it may be unwilling to make their fears known. If these suppositions are correct, effective communication among group members will often be necessary if threats are to influence collective decisions.

SECTION 2. SPECIAL DETERRENCE

Most adults have been exposed to minor punishments for parking and traffic offenses; very few people have been subjected to major penalties. Those who have been subjected to legal consequences, large or small, may react differently to legal threats of all kinds, and particularly to legal threats concerning the behavior that led to previous punishment. For this reason, a separate discussion of some issues relating to special deterrence is appropriate.

Any difference in threat response between previously punished offenders and the rest of the members of a threatened audience could result from:

a. the fact that apprehended and punished offenders, particularly serious offenders, are a special high-risk group, independent of their experience with the legal system;

   b. changes in attitudes, expectations, or status that the experience of punishment brings about;
   c. a mixture of both.

The fact that apprehended offenders are a special group in the population, apart from whatever effects apprehension and punishment might have, is a necessary beginning to any discussion of special deterrence. When half of all those who have been convicted of larceny are arrested for larceny a second time, while less than one percent of all other members of a threatened audience are ever apprehended, some might be tempted to conclude that the apprehension and punishment of thieves does not deter them from further offenses. To the extent that this conclusion rests on a comparison with the criminality of the general population, it is, of course, faulty, because those punished for larceny are a specially selected group of property criminals, while the vast majority of the rest of the population never has and never will commit a serious property offense. If such a comparison is invalid, the only data available on the effect of conviction and punishment on larceny offenders are that half are subsequently reconvicted. It cannot be said that this percentage is just as high as it would have been if these violators had not been previously convicted, because they are part of a group that might otherwise have experienced 80 percent recidivism. It also cannot be said that this percentage is lower than it would otherwise be, since we cannot assume that all of those who commit larceny once will do so again, or that all of those who have been apprehended for larceny once will be caught in the future if they do repeat their crime.

The fact that those subjected to punishment are a special high-risk group of potential future offenders establishes the importance of studying the reactions of this group to punishment and the threat of punishment, because previously punished persons will be responsible for a far larger per capita amount of crime than the rest of the population. The share of crime that can be attributed to previously punished individuals will vary with the type of crime: previously convicted killers form a very small percentage of homicide arrests, but previously convicted robbers, narcotics sellers, and forgers are believed to be responsible for a large share of the total amount of these crimes. And those who have been convicted and punished for some major crime are much more likely than the rest of the population to become involved in other forms of serious crime later in their careers.

Understanding the responses of previously punished offenders to legal threats involves consideration of all the variables alluded to in the previous discussion of general deterrence, as well as recognition of the fact that apprehension and punishment will probably produce important changes in the attitudes and circumstances of offenders—changes that affect the propensity of such persons to commit crimes and their susceptibility to the influence of legal threats. Apprehension for committing a crime may cause offenders to revise upward their estimate of the probability of being apprehended again; it may also produce a public exposure of the individual's crime that can either sensitize him to the moral gravity of his act or harden his resistance to community judgments.

Punishment of offenders may cause a number of changes in attitude that affect their propensity to commit crimes in the future. Some of these changes are closely related to the effect of threats and others are not, but all are important to comprehending the role of special deterrence in crime prevention. Punishment effects that might condition future criminality include changes in:

    a. the offender's attitude toward threatened consequences;
    b. the offender's attitude toward the threatened behavior;
    c. the offender's attitude toward society;
    d. the offender's ability to live within the law.

Each of these facets can be affected by the nature, extent, timing, and social context of a particular punishment.

Changes in Offender's Attitude Toward Punishment

Commentators have suggested that experience with punishment may produce in its subjects changes in attitudes toward punishment that both increase and decrease the degree to which punishment is considered worth avoiding.

. . .

One reason for this effect is that punishment leads to an increase in the degree of reality of the punishment, by acquainting the subject with the sting of unpleasantness at first hand. This personal experience brings the unpleasantness of punishment much closer to the potential offender than threats which communicate a threat of unpleasantness that is "farther off" psychologically. . . .

In part, such an effect could be the result of the prospect of a particular punishment losing its uniqueness to the already punished subject. This would be particularly true when punishment assumes most of its negative value from censure, because once a person has lost a considerable amount of standing in the community, the threat of future censure conveys little by way of further deprivation. In some cases, exposure to censure will cause an individual to react defensively by rejecting the values of the group that rebukes him. . . . Thus, while punishment may operate both to increase and decrease the amount of anxiety its subjects experience about future punishment, it seems more likely that increased anxiety about future punishment would be dominant when highly socialized persons are subjected to minor punishments, and more likely that callousness to punishment would assume a major role in the punishment of less socialized persons and in the administration of penal measures that depend on feelings of strong social loyalties or fear of the unknown.

. . .

Changes in Attitude Toward the Threatened Behavior

When punishment is considered as a possibility by members of a threatened audience who have not experienced it, it is psychologically farther off than [the] desired goal attainable by committing the threatened offense. Once punishment is administered, the increased reality of the punishment experience may lead to changes in the subject's evaluation of the behavior that led to his discomfort. The experience of punishment may act, in Professor Andenaes' words, "as a moral eye-opener," bringing home to the offender the fact that his behavior is considered seriously wrong and thereby reducing the probability that the offense will be repeated. Failing moral revelation, the experience of punishment may make clearer to the offender the disadvantages that accompany the offense and by association give him more unpleasant feelings about the behavior, particularly if the punishment occurs soon after commission of the threatened behavior. On the other hand, the experience of punishment may cause offenders to experience conflict about the wisdom of their behavior and may lead the individual to rationalize that, after all, the opportunity to commit the threatened act was worth the punishment. In the process of such rationalization, the threatened behavior may acquire a value to subjects higher than it had prior to punishment.

This tendency to revalue behavior that has led to discomfort, in order to rationalize decisions, has been noted in laboratory experiments where the measure of sacrifice or discomfort was small: in one case, girls who were forced to undergo a protracted initiation in order to hear a dull sex lecture rated the lecture more interesting than girls who were subjected only to a mild "initiation." It is not clear whether more severe punishment would lead to a greater degree of the "it was worth it" effect or whether the whole process of rationalization would break down where the unpleasantness suffered is too great to permit a realistic judgment that the act could be worth the punishment. Moreover, because those caught and punished for committing offenses know that apprehension is uncertain, punished offenders can always find ways to rationalize without changing their opinion of the value of the threatened behavior: the offender can say to himself, "I shouldn't have been caught"—or, more ominously, "Next time I won't be caught"—and continue to see his initial offense as justified because the unpleasantness suffered was simply the result of bad luck.

In the criminal process, present penalty structures are high enough so that it would be difficult for most punished offenders to conclude that criminal conduct was worth the price they paid, and it seems reasonable to suppose that punishment will create negative associations with particular forms of threatened behavior, and with lawbreaking as a general concept, that outweigh any tendency to view the pleasures of criminal conduct through rose-colored glasses. However, it is not clear that punishment will lead to significant changes in attitude in all cases. The prospects for deflating the attractiveness of criminal alternatives are probably best when the consequences of apprehension activate latent moral judgments in the offender (as in the case of amateur shoplifters) and where drives toward the threatened behavior are initially weak. When the drive to commit an offense is strong and the reality of punishment does not bring the offender's moral sensibilities to bear on his criminal propensities, the likelihood of attitude-change is lessened.

Changes in Socialization

When the imposition of consequences for violation of a legal threat is an important event in a man's life, it may lead to changes in his attitudes toward society that influence his future behavior. This possibility is recognized by those who administer penal facilities and has led to the advocacy of rehabilitation as one goal of correctional administration. The theory of rehabilitation suggests that some forms of threatened consequences afford the opportunity to reorient the values of their subjects by discouraging commitment to antisocial values and encouraging loyalty to prevailing social norms.

The notion of rehabilitation as a result of punishment differs from narrower theories of punishment as a means of discouraging criminal conduct by associating unpleasantness with criminality in the mind of the offender, because rehabilitation also involves the transmission of positive social norms, which would tend to reduce criminality independent of the negative value of punishment.

It is also possible that the experience of punishment will lead to less favorable attitudes toward social norms on the part of punished offenders. The punishment process often generates hostility on the part of its subjects and creates some pressure to reject prevailing norms in order to protect self-esteem when punishment has conveyed a rejection of the offender by the social order. And since prison subjects the offender to constant association with others who have antisocial values and criminal skills, the net result of the punishment experience on an offender's attitudes may be an increased identification with deviant values. Isolating the factors that determine whether experience with punishment will produce greater or lesser loyalty toward prevailing social norms is a task beyond the scope of this discussion. It is sufficient for present purposes to note that either the rehabilitation or further alienation of punished offenders will have a significant impact on their future conduct.

. . .

One of many dangers in a survey treatment of a topic such as deterrence is the lack of focus that is likely to accompany the attempt to provide broad coverage. After touching on some of the many factors that condition the effectiveness of legal threats, it would perhaps be appropriate to search out basic themes which underlie the preceding analysis.

The first such theme is an overwhelming sense of the specificity of findings in research in deterrence. A particular legal threat involves a mix of factors—communication, enforcement, type and extent of threatened consequences, type of behavior, social attitudes—and the mix will be different for different threats. Since it is difficult to know precisely why a policy does or does not achieve results, it is dangerous to generalize from a particular finding to propositions about the marginal deterrent effects of other types of threat, or of the same threat with different levels of enforcement or communication. It will thus require a large number of studies of different types of threat before plausible generalizations about marginal deterrence emerge from research.

A second recurrent theme is the difference in texture between issues of absolute and marginal deterrence. The larger concept of deterrence encountered when discussing whether and how threatening behavior will reduce its rate is more complex and more difficult to study than the narrow issue of whether particular changes in the conditions of a legal threat produce results worth their cost. In the foreseeable future, research opportunities in deterrence will be spread unevenly over the range of issues—we will have ample opportunity to study the short-range marginal effects of modest changes in threat composition that normally take place in the process of administering the criminal law, but little opportunity to study large jumps, up and down the scale of punishment, or the results of decriminalizing behavior that society has regarded as dangerous. Since generalization is difficult, uneven research opportunities make for uneven progress in our understanding of deterrence. Future research will reveal more about marginal deterrent effects than about deterrence, more about small changes than large changes. We will be putting this knowledge to use long before basic issues about the effects of threat and punishment have approached a resolution.

A program of research in the coming years should include experiments in different methods of threat communication; the evaluation of procedures such as intensive police patrol and computer monitoring that increase probability of apprehension; the experimental reduction of penalties for major crime; and the experimental introduction of new ways of treating offenders in areas such as traffic crime, where the political climate permits changes in the kind as well as extent of threatened consequences. As more becomes known, experimental variations in the conditions of threat and punishment can be increased if advances in knowledge make public and official attitudes about crime control more flexible. But the relationship between increased knowledge and changes in official attitudes is by no means automatic. A communication gap already exists between the level of information available about the effects of legal threats and official beliefs. And any real progress in penal policy will depend as much on closing this gap as on our willingness and ability to increase knowledge.

Chapter Fifteen

Diversion from the Justice System

Nora Klapmuts

Diversion from the criminal justice system, which has achieved sudden prominence both in the literature and in the nomenclature of criminal justice practice in the last few years, has finally come into its own, not as a unique approach to the management of deviance but as an essential part of a much broader movement of social and criminal justice reform. It is part of the same evolutionary process that brought punishment of offenders into disrepute, substituting treatment and the provision of rehabilitative services for the punitive methods that have come to be viewed as counterproductive. It is associated with the movement away from incarceration of offenders in penal institutions and their ostracism upon release, receiving impetus from the same pressures that account for the immense popularity of alternatives to incarceration and community-based treatment. Parallels can also be found in efforts to involve the community in the reintegration of offenders, in removal of barriers to ex-offender employment, in reducing jail populations by means of pretrial release arrangements, in the extensive use of plea bargaining, and in efforts

Reprinted, with permission of the National Council on Crime and Delinquency, from *Crime and Delinquency Literature*, Vol. 6, No. 1, 1974, pp. 108–131.

to initiate legislation to decriminalize certain types of status offenses and victimless crimes. The central feature of all these interrelated developments is their emphasis on minimizing the involvement of the offender with traditional processes and practices on criminal justice and correction and returning to the community at least some of the responsibility for dealing with its antisocial or deviant members.

This broad movement to lighten the impact of criminal justice, which has been variously labeled "diversion," "minimizing penetration into the justice system," or utilizing the "least drastic alternative" satisfies both humanitarian and pragmatic concerns. . . .

The strategy is also pragmatic. Even the humane impulses to help the offender and avoid the debilitating impact of punitive measures are pragmatically oriented toward reducing recidivism and reclaiming the offender for society. Past efforts have not worked. Offenders are repeatedly processed through the criminal justice system, at great cost to the taxpayer, with no apparent effect on the crime problem. Minimizing penetration into the justice system is a pragmatic shift in stance, an attempt to achieve at least the same if not better results at considerably less cost to the public. It is also, and perhaps primarily, a practical response to what has become an unmanageable overload on the criminal courts and the correctional system, a choice between greatly expanding criminal justice system resources to deal with the huge volume of offenders drawn into it or drastically reducing the number of offenders subjected to the full criminal process. . . .

Restricting the use of the full process of criminal justice to deal only with serious crimes and dangerous offenders and minimizing its impact on the nondangerous or petty offender are designed to serve simultaneously the ends of humanitarianism, pragmatism, and social justice. As part of this trend in criminal justice and social reform, *diversion* as a concept and in practice both gains in strength and loses in clarity. The current popularity of diversion is attributable to the fact that it both meets the needs of administrative reform and is consistent with the ideology of a powerful movement in the direction of offender reintegration into the community. Unfortunately, the complexity of this trend has produced considerable confusion over the place of "diversion" within it, and discussions of the concept in the literature frequently begin by attempting to distinguish what is from what is not *true* diversion.

The confusion of diversion with community treatment, screening, decriminalization, crime prevention, or the provision of services to noncriminal or predelinquent persons and the lack of consensus on the goals of diversion are likely to result not only in the unsystematic development of programs with limited impact but also in a potential threat to individual rights.

. . .

WHAT IS DIVERSION?

The importance of establishing a widely accepted definition of diversion should not be dismissed as "merely a question of semantics." Although intricately related in practice, diversion must be conceptually distinguished from other approaches to criminal justice reform, since failure to do so will only further obscure the critical isues now facing the diversion effort. In the literature, diversion is sometimes loosely equated with the general policy of using the least restrictive alternative (e.g., "diversion" from incarceration to community-based correctional programs) or with referral to social services instead of criminal processing following decriminalization through legislative change (e.g., "diversion" of alcoholics from jail to detoxification centers). It is very often equated with pretrial release programs (e.g., "diversion" to employment or job-training programs of defendants who would otherwise be detained pending trial) or with referral of predelinquent juveniles to youth service bureaus.

Even when the concept is more narrowly defined to exclude prevention, decriminalization, and sentencing alternatives, diversion is commonly described as "the use of alternatives to the official processing of offenders into the criminal justice system," implying that persons are diverted *out of* the criminal justice system into nonjudicial community agencies or programs, whose services or treatment, it is frequently stressed, can be refused by those so diverted. While this description may appear adequate, any definition that relies on the idea of avoiding official action of the justice system or utilizing alternatives to criminal processing is likely to run into difficulties in implementation. Unless the present boundaries of the criminal justice system are accepted as fixed and alternatives to traditional processing are viewed as in no way an extension of the system, it will be difficult to know whether any alternative, short of simple screening and dismissal, is outside the realm of the criminal justice system. Moreover, as diversion programs become more formally established it will become increasingly difficult to label such dispositions alternatives to official action. From this perspective, diversion is a means of (1) reducing the volume of persons going through the entire process of arrest, arraignment, trial, conviction, and sentencing while at the same time (2) "doing something" to interrupt the cycle of recidivism among certain offenders without imposing the handicap of a criminal record. It is dealing with persons for whom conviction of an offense is otherwise likely without applying the stigma of prosecution and conviction. It is freeing the criminal justice system to concentrate most of its time and resources on more serious offenders. But whether it is removal from the justice system is at least debatable.

Cressey and McDermott, in a study of juvenile diversion, report that, if "true" diversion consists of removal of offenders from the purview of juvenile justice, then little true diversion exists. Most of the juvenile justice system representatives they interviewed tended to identify various action programs as "diversion" if they kept juveniles out of the official bureaucracy or reduced the stigma attached to traditional processing.[1] It is probably also true that most programs for adults diverted from criminal processing provide pretrial services for deferred prosecution cases rather than simple dismissal of charges and referral to voluntary social agencies.

"Diversion from the criminal justice system" is probably a misnomer. Most of the alternatives described as part of the "new" diversion (i.e., more than simple discretionary screening) are conditional and revocable, looking more like *delay* in criminal processing than diversion from it. Under most arrangements, the decision is taken in reference to a person who has, or probably has, committed an illegal act and who would not otherwise be screened out for lack of evidence or jurisdiction. In most instances the decision is contingent on the satisfactory resolution of the case by the offender's participation in a treatment or service program. Most commonly, if the conditions of diversion are not satisfied, the case can be plugged back into the system for further criminal processing. Diversion is thus concerned with persons who, under existing law, are properly within the criminal justice system, whose authority over these persons continues until satisfactory completion of the diversion conditions.

There are good reasons why those who develop standards for diversion efforts must cut through the euphemism and decide exactly what diversion is or should be and whether its operations are rightfully within or outside the criminal justice system before going on to determine who should be diverted under what conditions.

. . .

The National Advisory Commission on Criminal Justice Standards and Goals faced these issues squarely in its report on the courts. The term diversion, the Commission stated, "refers to halting or suspending before conviction formal criminal proceedings against a person on the condition or assumption that he will do something in return." This was distinguished from screening, which involves simply "the cessation of formal criminal proceedings and removal of the individual from the criminal justice system." About coercion the Commission was just as unflinching: "Diversion uses the threat or possibility of conviction of a criminal offiense to encourage an accused to do something. . . . This agreement may not be entirely voluntary as the accused often agrees to participate in a diversion program only because he fears formal criminal prosecution." Concerning jurisdiction, the Commission report states that diversion efforts "must be undertaken prior to adjudication and after a legally proscribed action has occurred. . . ." [2]

. . .

Currently, diversion from the criminal justice system has many different meanings, largely because the term does not accurately describe the different activities to which it is applied. The task of developing definitions and setting standards for the operation of diversion alternatives might be greatly simplified if the popularized notion of "diversion from the justice system" were discarded and replaced by terms descriptive of the various alternatives that may be invoked at each stage of traditional processing. Most of the programs that have been developed to reduce the number of offenders processed through the criminal or juvenile justice systems fall generally into three categories: community absorption, police alternatives to arrest or court referral, and pretrial intervention. The first is a decision by community residents to handle the problem without reporting it to police; the second is a decision by police not to arrest or not to refer to court; the third is a decision by the court or prosecutor's office not to proceed to trial.

COMMUNITY ABSORPTION

Community-level alternatives to criminal justice processing generally are directed toward those persons who it is believed do not belong in the justice system at all. While some communities have established privately run mental health services for the disturbed or retarded offender or detoxification facilities for the alcoholic offender, most community-level efforts have been directed toward the young.

For many years the whole range of youthful behavior problems, including those with no strictly illegal or criminal content at all, have been referred to the courts and the juvenile correctional system for resolution. Efforts to limit the very broad jurisdiction of the juvenile court, which in many states makes the juvenile who is runaway, truant, or disobedient to parents subject to delinquency adjudication, have generally failed to elicit any significant modification of delinquency laws. Diversion of such children, as well as some nonserious or first-time offenders, is frequently offered as an alternative means of achieving a similar end: avoiding processing by the justice system if not removal from its jurisdiction.

. . .

POLICE DIVERSION

Although the police are responsible for keeping a large proportion of potential defendants out of the official processes of justice through discretionary screening and informal resolution of complaints without arrest, the participation of police in formal diversion programs has, until fairly recently, been minimal. Studies of police discretion and arrest practices have indicated that rates of arrest (as distinct from informal measures) vary widely from one police department to another. In discussing the persuasive reasons for constructing diversion programs around law enforcement organization and operations, Lemert has pointed out that the police have the strategic power to determine what proportions and what kinds of problems become official and which ones are absorbed back into the community. The very broad discretionary power of police suggests the importance of developing diversion programs and policies that impact directly on law enforcement practices. Police departments currently are coming to recognize the crucial importance of individual police officer discretion, and some have begun to develop policies to guide and structure its use. Some departments have initiated formal diversion programs within the department, and others have participated in the design and operation of diversion programs administered by other agencies.

While some attention has been directed toward police diversion of persons with mental health problems, police diversion efforts are most often concentrated on youthful nonserious offenders. Other police diversion programs are concerned with the public drunkenness offender and with intervention in intrafamily disputes.

COURT-BASED DIVERSION

As with informal diversion at the police level, use of the opportunity to divert by court intake workers, prosecutors' staffs, and probation officials has generally been of such low visibility that its nature and extent are difficult to assess. Studies have shown dramatic variations in the use of screening and settlement procedures in different jurisdictions but such measures as unofficial probation, informal agreements between offender and prosecutor, and court-monitored settlements between offender and complainant appear to be in wide use throughout the country. Informal diversion procedures have been used most extensively for white-collar offenders, shoplifters, misdemeanants, and first offenders.

Various formal diversion programs have been initiated at the pretrial level in an attempt to structure decision-making and increase its visibility while retaining the flexibility of discretionary diversion. Recent efforts to formalize the diversion process at the post-arrest stage have ranged from the establishment of special diversion units in juvenile courts or probation departments to the enactment of statutes providing for restitution without prosecution; [3] but by far the most popular approach has been the development of pretrial release to supportive services—a program of conditional pretrial diversion that retains the option of prosecution in case of failure in treatment.

. . .

Conditional pretrial release to supportive services—employment, job training and placement, counseling, remedial education, and medical or other treatment—has developed into a rapidly growing criminal justice reform movement. In 1973 more than thirty such programs provided treatment or services to defendants before trial. Pretrial intervention is being incorporated into state and local criminal justice plans; enabling legislation has been enacted in some states and is pending in others; and legislation has been introduced that would incorporate pretrial services into the federal court system. Pretrial intervention leads to diversion only in cases in which "successful" participation produces a dismissal of charges. However, largely because this popular measure has been widely publicized and acclaimed, pretrial diversion is coming to be equated with conditional pretrial release.

. . .

DIVERSION: ISSUES AND PROBLEMS

The issues surrounding the diversion of persons from criminal or juvenile justice processing are highly complex and not amenable to simplistic analysis or resolution. At whatever level diversion occurs and whatever arrangements are made for the alternative handling of offenders and other deviant persons, the questions that arise involve broad public policy considerations of both a legal and a philosophical nature. Few general rules for diversion can be stated, first, because each of the variety of programs and procedures subsumed under the term is a unique problem requiring an individual solution and, second, because the law and underlying philosophies of criminal justice are already in a fluid state of evolution that greatly complicates the introduction of structural changes to allow for formalized diversion. The police role in diversion, for example, is more difficult to define because perceptions of the police role in society are undergoing change. The propriety of treating the alleged offender without proving him guilty is complicated by the fact that the effectiveness and appropriateness of treatment for offenders in general is currently being questioned. And the issue of who should be diverted is affected by the general uncertainty about the actual harmfulness of different kinds of socially undesirable behavior and the severity of sanctions necessary and sufficient to prevent or control different types of such behavior.

If diversion mechanisms are to be incorporated into the official apparatus of social control, further development and refinement of standards for their use will be necessary. A number of efforts have already been made to set down specific guides for the use of diversion at the community, police, and court levels. Diversion is treated by the National Advisory Commission on Criminal Justice Standards and Goals in its reports on the courts, correction, the police, and community crime prevention. The National Center for State Courts addresses the subjects of bail, pretrial release, and diversion in its guides for planning court improvement programs.[4] The American Bar Association's *Standards on the Urban Police Function* includes guides for police in the diversion of offenders.[5] The Police Foundation's Ad Hoc Diversion Committee has reported on police-based diversion programs.[6] And the ABA Commission on Correctional Facilities and Services is actively involved in developing standards for pretrial intervention services.[7]

Numerous questions, however, still have not been satisfactorily answered. The following are some of the issues and problems, briefly stated, that require attention wherever the establishment of a formal diversion alternative is envisioned:

1. *What is diversion?* Repeated attempts to pin down the term "diversion" have not produced a widely accepted and broadly applicable operational definition. It is likely that such a definition cannot be formulated and that different working definitions should be developed for "diversion" at different points in the decision-making process. The types of persons who should be diverted, the criteria for eligibility, the degree of voluntariness, and the extent of criminal justice involvement may differ according to the level at which the diversion alternative is made available. At this time diversion is most frequently an alterative to continued processing by the justice system that *delays* such processing while an effort is made to resolve the problem presented by the alleged offender and his behavior by other means.

2. *Who should be diverted?* There are two primary issues that must be addressed here—(1) the overall comprehensiveness of diversion and (2) the criteria for diversion in specific cases. Recommendations for the general use of diversion have ranged from limiting diversion to very minor offenders, such as juvenile or adult "status" offenders, to introducing its use for all *except* the very dangerous offender who requires incarceration or the offender whose behavior is so repulsive that society demands retribution. Most diversion programs currently in operation appear to be fairly restrictive, handling primarily those persons who have engaged in noncriminal or marginally criminal behavior, which largely accounts for the limited overall impact diversion has had on criminal justice workloads.

Informal or unofficial diversion, as part of the process of selection for criminal processing, has generally worked to the disadvantage of certain social groups and contributed to inequalities in criminal justice. Attempts to overcome these inequalities by developing explicit criteria for diversion have not, and probably cannot, eliminate discriminatory decision-making from the selection process, but written standards are at least accessible to review. Currently, some old biases are being written into eligibility guidelines (including the "character" of the offender) and some newly articulated standards are formalizing opportunities for discriminatory application (e.g., the ambiguous stipulation that the "needs and interests of the victim and society" be better served by diversion).

3. *What arrangements should be made for funding, administering, and monitoring diversion programs? Who should set policy?*

Who defines "failure" in programs? These and related questions having to do with the development and implementation of diversion programs will be answered in time, as Zaloom points out, "through a normal process of development." [8] In other words, diversion programs and procedures are likely to "just grow." Some general recommendations are found in recent standards, suggesting, for example, that policy should be set by those responsible for administering the program in cooperation with other agencies, but much more attention is needed in these vital areas to ensure the effective and fair operation of diversion alternatives.

4. *What are the rights of diverted persons?* Inherent in the diversion process are a number of potential violations of individual rights. Some of the questions that must be answered are these: How shall the diverted person waive his right to speedy trial? How can due process and equal protection best be guaranteed in selection for diversion or in termination of unsuccessful participants? Can a formal guilty plea be required before a defendant is eligible for diversion? Does an individual have the right to confidentiality of program records? Is the protection against double jeopardy violated in any way by court processing subsequent to diversion programing? How long can prosecution be suspended, or how long can a person be retained under program control without trial? At what points does the diversion candidate or participant have the right to be represented by counsel? Some of these questions have been dealt with in recent standards and in existing program policy; others will probably have to be tested in the courts.

A primary issue, usually dealt with superficially in the literature on diversion, is the legal and moral correctness of subjecting a person to treatment or control without first finding him guilty of an offense. Most writers have maintained that participation should be "voluntary" while acknowledging that refusal of services may result in court referral. A possible approach might be to vary the conditions of voluntariness according to the nature of the offense, making referral to services completely voluntary for persons whose behavior should be decriminalized while retaining the threat of prosecution for more serious offenders?

5. *Is diversion effective? Will it change anything?* The effectiveness of diversion really has not been tested. Attempts to measure some aspect of effectiveness have generally been limited to a follow-up of recidivism among program clients. The need is for experimental studies comparing diversion alternatives with criminal justice processing, on the one hand, and with simple release or screening, on the other. There is no indication that persons subjected to diversion

programing could not have been just as safely released without supervision or treatment or voluntary services.

Another crucial question for research is whether the availability of diversion procedures and alternative treatment resources has any substantial impact on the operations of traditional criminal justice processes. How does diversion affect, for example, the plea bargaining process? To what extent are court workloads actually reduced by the availability of diversion before trial? Does the existence of nonjudicial alternatives in fact bring more persons under the jurisdiction of the justice system by reducing the number of potential defendants simply released? How is decision-making by various criminal justice officials influenced by the presence of diversion alternatives? Is discretion actually reduced or standardized by explicit policies for diversion? There is some evidence that the introduction of statutory change to permit diversion of petty offenders does not seriously inhibit discretionary decision-making by individual officials. One statutory effort to make shoplifting of less than $20 a divertible offense led officials to change the real or wholesale value of a $40 item to only $19 if the offender was a "typical" shoplifter (who merits diversion because she meets the preconceptions of officials), while less favored offenders were sometimes prosecuted for goods priced $21 in the store. In other words, the informal discretionary process operated to subvert the statutory intention.

6. *Is diversion the answer?* The "new" diversion has been hailed as a means of reducing workloads, compensating for overcriminalization, avoiding the stigmatizing effects of a criminal record, reducing the discrimination and inequalities of informal decision-making, and eliminating the gap between apprehension of offenders and their treatment. In actuality, the diversionary system now being created may simply shift responsibility for the problems of criminal justice rather than contribute to their solution. The availability of alternative intervention strategies may inhibit decriminalization by legislative change; the number of persons under some sort of coercive control is not likely to be reduced and may be increased; the stigmatization inherent in record-keeping by intervention agencies may become as onerous as that associated with arrest or conviction records; and the discriminatory application of diversion alternatives, for which there is considerable potential, may simply perpetuate the inequalities now so obvious in criminal justice.

Diversion programs and procedures may offer an interim solution to some of the more vexing problems of the criminal justice system until the statutory and judicial restructuring prerequisite to more permanent improvement can be achieved. Some good is undoubtedly accomplished by enabling selected offenders to avoid the harsh consequences of arrest, prosecution, and sentencing. But diversion is a compromise solution; if it is viewed as a panacea for the ills of a system in dire need of reform, then it may only impede real reform of the justice system by reducing the more immediate pressures for it.

The development of formal diversion opportunities has not yet radically altered the criminal justice system. Current concepts of diversion appear to be heavily entrenched in the dominant treatment ideology, which focuses attention on the offender and his needs rather than on the inadequacies of the official system of intervention and control. This orientation, unfortunately, only delays undertaking the more vital tasks of rewriting the law, streamlining the processes of criminal justice, and modifying official and public attitudes to achieve a more efficient and fair system of criminal and social justice.

NOTES

1. Donald R. Cressey and Robert A. McDermott, *Diversion from the Juvenile Justice System* (Ann Arbor, Mich., 1973), pp. 5–8.

2. U.S. National Advisory Commission on Criminal Justice Standards and Goals, *Courts* (Washington, D.C., U.S. Government Printing Office, 1973), pp. 27 ff.

3. Samuel J. Brakel, "Diversion from the Criminal Process: Informal Discretion, Motivation, and Formalization," *Denver Law Journal*, 48(2):211–238, 1971.

4. National Center for State Courts, *Court Improvement Programs: A Guidebook for Planners* (Washington, D.C., 1972).

5. American Bar Association, Advisory Committee on the Police Function, *Standards Relating to the Urban Police Function* (New York, 1972).

6. Police Foundation, *Police-Based Diversion: Status of Program Activity* (Washington, D.C., 1973).

7. ABA National Pretrial Intervention Service Center, *Diversion from the Criminal Justice System: Technical Assistance Handbook on Pretrial Intervention Techniques and Action Programs* (Washington, D.C., 1973).

8. J. Gordon Zaloom, "Viewpoint," *Criminal Justice Newsletter*, 4(20):4–5, 1973.

Chapter Sixteen

Behavior Modification
A Perspective on Critical Issues

Stephanie B. Stolz, Louis A. Wienckowski, and Bertram S. Brown

In the history of civilization, people have continuously tried to control their environment and find ways of teaching themselves and their children better means of acquiring new skills and capabilities. Commonsense notions of the ways in which reward and punishment can change behavior have existed since time immemorial. Thus, elements of what is now referred to as *behavior modification* were used long before psychologists and other behavioral scientists developed systematic principles of learning.

As behavior modification procedures are used ever more widely, many different concerns are being expressed. On the one hand, the public and mental health professionals are concerned about whether behavior modification procedures have been sufficiently well demonstrated through research to be generally recommended and widely disseminated. On the other hand, behavior modification has acted as a conceptual "lightning rod" in the midst of stormy controversies over ethical problems associated with attempts at social influence, drawing to it such highly charged issues as fear of "mind control" or concerns about the treatment of persons institutionalized

Reprinted by permission of the National Institute of Mental Health, U.S. Dept. of Health, Education and Welfare.

against their will. Apparent or actual infringements of rights, as well as some abuses of behavioral procedures, have led to litigation and calls for curbs on the use of behavior modification.

All of us try continually to influence our own and others' behavior, so that individuals using behavior modification procedures are distinctive only in that they attempt to influence behavior more systematically. Commenting on this issue, one attorney said that to be opposed to behavior modification is to be opposed to the law of gravity. Rather, the key issue is what sort of care, caution, and control should be exercised when behavioral principles are applied precisely and systematically.

. . .

To understand behavior modification, it is helpful first to clarify its relationship to a broader concept, behavior influence.

Behavior influence occurs whenever one person exerts some degree of control over another. This occurs constantly in such diverse situations as formal school education, advertising, child rearing, political campaigning, and other normal interpersonal interactions.

Behavior modification is a special form of behavior influence that involves primarily the application of principles derived from research in experimental psychology to alleviate human suffering and enhance human functioning. Behavior modification emphasizes systematic monitoring and evaluation of the effectiveness of these applications. The techniques of behavior modification are generally intended to facilitate improved self-control by expanding individuals' skills, abilities, and independence.

Most behavior modification procedures are based on the general principle that people are influenced by the consequences of their behavior. Behavior modification assumes that the current environment is more relevant in affecting an individual's behavior than most early life experiences, enduring intrapsychic conflicts, or personality structure. Insofar as possible, the behaviorally oriented mental health worker limits the conceptualization of the problem to observable behavior and its environmental context.

In the professional use of behavior modification, a contractual agreement may be negotiated, specifying mutually agreeable goals and procedures. When the clients are adults who have sought therapy, such a contract is made between them and the mental health worker. When the behavior modification program is to benefit a mentally disadvantaged group, such as the retarded, senile, or psychotic, the contract is often made between the individuals' guardians or other responsible persons and the mental health worker. Parents, who usually make decisions affecting their young children, generally are consulted by the mental health worker regarding treatment for their children.

Behavior therapy is a term that is sometimes used synonymously with behavior modification. In general, behavior modification is considered to be the broader term, while behavior therapy refers mainly to clinical interventions, usually applied in a one-to-one therapist-patient relationship. That is, behavior therapy is a special form of behavior modification.

In behavior modification, attempts to influence behavior are typically made by changing the environment and the way people interact, rather than by intervening directly through medical procedures (such as drugs) or surgical procedures (such as psychosurgery). Thus, behavior modification methods can be used in a broad range of situations, including the child-rearing efforts of parents and the instructional activities of teachers, as well as the therapeutic efforts of mental health workers in treating more serious psychological and behavioral problems. The effects of behavior modification, unlike the results of most surgical procedures, are relatively changeable and impermanent.

Behavior modification procedures require that the problem behavior be clearly specified. That is, the mental health worker must be able to define objectively the response that the service recipient wants to learn or to have reduced. Thus, certain kinds of problems treated by dynamic psychotherapy appear to be inappropriate candidates for behavior modification. In particular, the patient who seeks therapy primarily because of an existential crisis—"Who am I? Where am I going?"—is probably not an appropriate candidate for behavior modification. This quasi-philosophical problem does not lend itself to an approach dealing with specific identifiable behavior in particular environmental contexts. It is possible that a patient who describes his problem in this way actually has some specific behavioral deficits that may underlie his existential difficulties or occur alongside them. Whether a careful behavioral analysis of the patient's difficulties would reveal such deficits is not now known, however.

Although it is alleged that secret, powerful psychotechnological tools are being or could be used to control the masses, researchers in behavior modification point out that they have encouraged the dissemination of information about behavior processes. In fact, workers in this area believe that increased knowledge of behavior modification will help people understand social-influence processes in general and will actually enable them to counteract many attempts at control, should such attempts occur. Many persons using behavior modification methods not only evaluate the effectiveness of their procedures but also measure the consumers' satisfaction with the behavior modification program used.

. . .

Many persons who learn about the general procedures of behavior modification say that they seem to be nothing more than common sense. To some considerable extent, this is true. For example, parents use behavior modification techniques whenever they praise their children for good report cards in the hope of encouraging continued interest and application. In employment, promotions and incentive awards are universally accepted ways to encourage job performance. The very structure of our laws, which specifies fines and penalties for infractions, is intended to modify behavior through aversive control.

Behavior modification, however, like other scientific approaches, imposes an organization on its subject matter. While common sense often includes contradictory advice (both "out of sight, out of mind," and "absence makes the heart grow fonder"), the principles of behavior modification codify and organize common sense, showing under what conditions and in what circumstances each aspect of "common sense" should be applied. The parents and grandparents who use what can be described as behavior modification procedures may often do so inconsistently and then wonder why they fail.

. . .

As more publicity has been given to behavior modification, the term has come to be used loosely and imprecisely in the public media, often with a negative connotation. Thus, behavior modification has sometimes been said to include psychosurgery, electroconvulsive therapy, and the noncontingent administration of drugs, that is, the administration of drugs independent of any specific behavior by the person receiving the medication. However, even though procedures such as these do modify behavior, that does not make them *behavior modification techniques* in the sense in which most professionals in the field use the term. In this article, the use of the term *behavior modification* will be consistent with its professional use; that is, *behavior modification* will be used to refer to procedures based on the explicit and systematic application of principles and technology derived from research in experimental psychology, procedures that involve some change in the social or environmental context of a person's behavior. This use of the term specifically excludes psychosurgery, electroconvulsive therapy, and the administration of drugs independent of any specific behavior by the person receiving the medication.

. . .

Behavior modification is a family of techniques. The diverse methods included under the general label have in common the goal of enhancing persons' lives by altering specific aspects of their behavior. Ideally, the mental health worker and the service recipient should decide together on a mutually agreeable set of treatment goals and on the means for attaining these goals. The service recipient or his representative should be kept fully informed of the results of the treatment as it progresses and also participate in any modification of goals or techniques.

Initial analysis of the person's problem should typically begin with a detailed description of the behavior causing distress or interfering with optimal functioning of the individual in familial, social, vocational, or other important spheres of activity. The behavioral goals should be viewed in the context of everything the person is able to do and also in terms of what kinds of support his usual environment is capable of providing over the long term.

This description, whenever possible, should be based on observations of the individual in the setting in which he reports distress. These observations may be careful quantitative records, or they may be statements about the relative frequency of various behaviors. The person making the observations may be the therapist or his agent, a peer of the individual receiving the service, or the individual himself. For example, a parent might be trained to tally the frequency with which a child stutters; a teacher or hospital aide might keep a record of a child's aggressive outbursts; and a well-motivated individual could count the frequency of occurrence of an unacceptable habit such as nail biting.

In addition to obtaining this description of what the individual does and does not do, the behavioral mental health worker should try to find how the individual's behavior relates to various events and places in his current and past experiences. Events relevant to behavior modification are those that immediately precede and immediately follow the problem behavior. The goal should be to determine the circumstances under which the behavior seems to occur and the environmental consequences that might be maintaining it.

Behavior modification, then, involves the systematic variation of behavioral and environmental factors thought to be associated with an individual's difficulties, with the primary goal of modifying his behavior in the direction that, ideally, he himself (or his agent) has chosen.

. . .

Collecting evidence to show whether behavior modification is effective is not as easy as it may seem. Several conceptual issues first need to be resolved. In order to evaluate behavior modification, the types of problems for which it is appropriate must be delimited, suitable outcome measures must be selected, and appropriate comparison conditions must be chosen.

Although therapists who use behavior modification feel it is appropriate for a wide range of problems, other persons question the appropriateness of a behavioral approach to many mental health problems because they believe that therapy for a particular problem must direct itself to the root cause of the problem. According to this view, disorders of biological origin should be treated with biologically based principles, while those of psychological origin should be treated psychotherapeutically.

A substantial body of opinion insists there need not be a relationship between the etiology of a problem and the nature of the treatment that is effective in ameliorating it.

. . .

Recently, concerns have been widely expressed over the ethical and legal aspects of behavior modification techniques.

Some people fear behavior modification and control because of prevalent contemporary attitudes of distrust and skepticism of authority in general and of "mind control" in particular; others have more specific concerns related to the practice of behavior modification or, often, to myths and misconceptions about the practice of behavior modification.

Behavior modification is most often criticized when it is used to alter the behavior of persons who are involuntary participants in therapy. Involuntary patients or subjects include those who are disadvantaged, vulnerable, or powerless because of institutionalization, age, social position, or discrimination.

The most frequent complaints concern the treatment of hospitalized mental patients and institutionalized delinquents and criminals. There is growing sensitivity to the ambiguity that can underlie diagnosis and choice of treatment goals for these populations. According to one point of view, a thin line separates social deviance from a mental illness that requires hospitalization. Society may often find it more convenient to institutionalize the deviant individual than to deal with the problem he represents. Thus, hospitalization or incarceration may be more in the interest of social control than the deviant person's welfare.

Growing distrust about the exercise of control over the helpless and the disadvantaged is even challenging the legitimacy of the authority of those who attempt to treat these persons. The authority to treat the institutionalized mentally disordered, for example, has been eroded by the dissemination of the notion that mental "illness" is a myth. According to this view, people should accept responsibility for their own behavior, including behavior that might otherwise be termed "mentally ill." Furthermore, an emerging sociological model views the mentally disordered patient as a victim of stresses and strains residing primarily within the social structure rather than the individual.

Credence is increasingly being given to the picture of the mental patient as a victim who is hospitalized for the convenience of society. In this view, treatment is seen as either a form of punishment or a procedure designed to make the patient conform to the requirements of an oppressive society. The mental health worker who proposes to modify the patient's behavior thus can be seen as serving the interests of the oppressor, rather than favoring the right of the patient to express his individuality.

. . .

Behavior modification has become an increasingly controversial yet important law enforcement tool. Many people feel that the use of behavior modification in prisons conflicts with the values of individual privacy and dignity.

Persons using behavior modification procedures are being particularly criticized for their attempts to deal with the rebellious and nonconformist behavior of inmates in penal institutions. Because the behavioral professional is often in the position of assisting the management of prisoners whose rebelliousness and antagonism to authority are catalysts for conflict within the institution, the distinction among his multiple functions as therapist, manager, and rehabilitator can become blurred and his allegiance confused. Although the professional may quite accurately perceive his role as benefiting the individual, he may at the same time appear to have the institution, rather than the prisoner, as his primary client.

Frequently, the goal of effective behavior modification in penal institutions is the preservation of the institution's authoritarian control. Although some prison behavior modification programs are designed to educate the prisoners and benefit them in other ways, other programs are directed toward making the prisoners less troublesome and easier to handle, thus adjusting the inmates to the needs of the institution.

A related problem is that in prisons, as elsewhere, the term *behavior modification* is often misused as a label for any procedure that aims to alter behavior, including excessive isolation, sensory deprivation, and mere physical punishment. Behavior modification then becomes simply a new name for old and offensive techniques.

The question of voluntary consent is an especially difficult problem when those participating in a program are prison inmates (Shapiro, 1974). It is not clear whether there can ever be a real "volunteer" in a prison, because inmates generally believe they will improve their chances for early parole if they cooperate with prison officials' requests to participate in a special program. There are other pressures as well; for example, participation in a novel program may be a welcome relief from the monotony of prison life.

. . .

A major problem in using behavior modification in prisons is that positive programs begun with the best of intentions may become subverted to punitive ones by the oppressive prison atmosphere. Generally, behavior modification programs are intended to give prisoners the opportunity to learn behavior that will give them a chance to lead more successful lives in the world to which they will return, to enjoy some sense of achievement, and to understand and control their own behavior better. Unfortunately, in actual practice, the programs sometimes teach submission to authority instead.

Critical questions in the use of behavior modification in prisons are thus: How are the goals to be chosen for the program? How is continued adherence to those goals to be monitored? Behavior modification should not be used in an attempt to facilitate institutionalization of the inmate or to make him adjust to inhumane living conditions. Furthermore, no therapist should accept requests for treatment that take the form "make him *behave*," when the intent of the request is to make the person conform to oppressive conditions . . .

Behavior modification currently is the center of stormy controversy and debate.

. . .

Many years of laboratory research provide the basis or rationale for the development of behavior modification techniques and behavioral treatments. The behavior modification methods currently being used include procedures suitable for use in the clinic, such as desensitization, and in the mental institution, such as the token economy. The procedures can be used with normal adults and children and with the mentally disadvantaged, including the retarded, the senile, and the psychotic. Behavior modification methods have been used to ameliorate a wide range of problems, including mutism, self-destructive behavior, inappropriate fears, and nervous habits. Also, behavior modification methods have been used to teach a great variety of appropriate, normal behaviors, including normal speech, appropriate social behavior, and suitable classroom skills.

. . .

Concern has been expressed that behavior modification methods may be used by those in power to control and manipulate others. Some critics charge that the use of behavior modification methods is inconsistent with humanistic values. However, all kinds of therapies involve attempts to change the patient in some way. Behavior modification, like other therapeutic methods, requires a cooperative individual in order for it to be effective. Countercontrol, especially countercontrol based on knowledge of behavioral principles, is a major way in which individuals can respond to any attempted manipulation.

The concerns expressed about behavior modification have stimulated a reexamination of the assumptions and ethics of all psychosocial therapies. Ethical problems are particularly serious when therapies are used within institutions such as mental hospitals and prisons or with the institutionalized mentally retarded and senile. In these settings, mental health workers have to be sensitive to the implications of the imbalance in power between them and their clients.

Chapter Seventeen

Incentives and the
Use of Prison Labor

Neil M. Singer

. . .

The use of prison labor traditionally has represented a compromise between the desires of correctional officials and the conflicting preferences of society at large. Prison administrators have tried to teach inmates good work habits while employing them in maintenance activities and prison industries producing goods for government use. In contrast, both business and labor traditionally have feared and resisted the potential competition of efficient prison industries. The productive use of inmate labor is also limited by the attitude of the general public, which regards prison as a place whose primary purpose is punishment.

In view of these conflicting pressures, it is not surprising that the use of prison manpower has served the ends of none of these groups. In this paper we begin by examining the costs that the current system imposes on inmates, correctional officials, and society at large. Some constraints on the design of an efficient method of using inmate labor are then described. We conclude with an analysis of alternatives to current practice.

Reprinted, with permission of the National Council on Crime and Delinquency, from *Crime and Delinquency*, Vol. 19, No. 2, 1973, pp. 200–212.

INCENTIVES UNDER THE EXISTING SYSTEM

When we examine the willingness of a worker to supply labor, the first factor to consider is the wage he receives in return. The income that he can earn depends on his productivity, which in turn depends on his own aptitudes as well as the equipment available for him to work with. His choice of jobs, from a large number of equally rewarding options that we assume to be open to him, depends on his preferences for different kinds of work. Finally, we expect his motivation to have a time dimension: if the worker can look forward to rewards in the form of promotion and higher income or improved working conditions, we expect this willingness to work to increase. To summarize, work effort is positively related to (1) current income from work, (2) productivity derived from aptitude, (3) productivity derived from capital equipment, (4) preferences for particular kinds of work, and (5) the prospect of promotion and other rewards.

For Inmates

Work experiences in prison now offer inmates none of these incentives. Current income from work is either zero or absurdly low: inmates' wages typically are measured in cents per hour and may range as high as $1.50 *per day* in exceptional instances. The work that prisoners are offered (or required to perform) generally is not designed to take advantage of whatever aptitudes they may possess, and the capital equipment that they work with usually is technologically obsolete. Prison working environments are rarely conducive to productive effort. Finally, the unproductive nature of most prison work robs it of any value from the standpoint of postrelease employment.

These conditions deprive prisoners of any economic incentive to work. The incentives that do exist are the product of the peculiar environment of the correctional institution. One, coercion, has a dehumanizing effect that is itself detrimental to productivity. (The impact of depersonalization on productivity has been seen in the deterioration of product quality under assembly-line production conditions.) Another incentive for working is that it helps pass time. The principal incentive, however, is that by working and acting in other respects like a "model inmate," a prisoner can hope to increase his likelihood of parole. None of these incentives is related in any way to the efficient use of prison manpower, the use that takes greatest advantage of inmates' abilities and maximizes the value of the goods produced.

This incentive structure is applied also to the more general behavior of inmates in correctional institutions. Incentives for "good" behavior (that is, behavior compatible with the objectives of the institution) are negative rather than positive. Inmates work in order not to be punished (or bored) and to shorten their terms; they learn nothing about the rewards offered for work outside the narrow context of the institution. In other words, prison incentives do not help inmates learn anything to prevent them from becoming recidivists after release.

For Correctional Officials

The incentives that institutions offer prisoners stem directly from the perspective of correctional officials and thus, indirectly, from the way that society at large shapes its institutions. Prison administrators can be contrasted with producers, who, in economic theory, express rational demands for labor and other factors of production. The wage that a producer is willing to pay an employee depends on the latter's productivity, measured in units of product, and on the value of the goods produced. Entrepreneurs who have access to free markets decide what goods to produce on the basis of demand and production conditions. Thus, the wage rate that workers earn is affected by the value that consumers place upon the goods that producers sell.

This model does not describe the motivations of correctional administrators. Prison officials usually view inmate labor not as a valued resource but rather as a surplus commodity that must be disposed of without disturbing the other functions of the institution. The goods that prison labor can produce have no market value because society at large prevents prison-made goods from being sold in competition with the products of private industry. With no market for their potential output, administrators have no incentive to use labor in any way other than to minimize the costs that prisons impose on government budgets. Accordingly, inmate labor is used to provide goods and services related to the functioning of the prisons themselves rather than goods that are valued by society.

The budgetary costs of prisons that can be reduced by the use of inmate labor typically include various inmate and institutional maintenance services. Prisoners work as cooks and in laundries, repair prison equipment, and maintain the institution's physical facilities. What these activities have in common is their essentiality from the viewpoint of the institution, for if inmates did not perform these kinds of work the institution would have to contract with private firms to obtain the same services. The irrelevance of these jobs from the prisoners' standpoint has already been noted. But restricting inmates to these activities also poses problems for prison officials, since these manpower requirements typically fall far short of the supply of inmate labor.

When prison labor is used to produce goods for government use, no substantial modification occurs in this situation. Inmates recognize that their work does not train them for postrelease employment, and administrators continue to experience a superabundance of manpower. In addition to idleness, the extra labor manifests itself in "underemployment" or "disguised unemployment," in which workers are ostensibly occupied with tasks that actually require only a fraction of the time allowed to them. As a side effect, this underemployment reduces inmates' productivity because each worker has insufficient access to capital equipment.

For Society

Society at large countenances this allocation of prison manpower because of its traditional view of the function of incarceration. Despite the prevalent rhetoric of rehabilitation, imprisonment historically has been considered a form of punishment, and prison labor has often been used as a vehicle for punishment. Ironically, the elimination of "hard labor" resulted from the complaints of business and labor that, during periods of chronic depression, all jobs should be given to private industry. Even today, society continues to take the narrow view that the only benefit from prison labor is the extent to which it reduces the tax burden that society must bear for supporting penal institutions.

This view of prison manpower would not prevent economically rational use of it except for the general prohibition against prison industries' competing with private producers. While this prohibition precludes the efficient use of prison labor, it is ineffective in protecting private industry against prison competition. If prisoners were forbidden to perform maintenance services in prisons or to produce goods for the use of state and local governments, the same maintenance activities or government goods would have to be supplied by private firms.[1] But by foregoing a productive use of a resource (inmate manpower), society as a whole increases the burden it must bear in paying the costs of correctional institutions.

Current manpower use in prisons, therefore, is unsatisfactory from all viewpoints. Aside from the negative incentives present in any system of punishment, prisoners are given no incentive to perform productively or to contribute to their own rehabilitation. Prison administrators try to use the *maximum* amount of labor rather than the *most efficient* amount, and even so are faced with a chronic oversupply of labor. The lack of incentives for prisoners and the excess supply of manpower prevent officials from attaining their own limited goals—maintaining institutions at low budgetary costs and keeping inmates occupied. And society achieves neither of its objectives: to eliminate prison competition with private firms and to minimize the cost of correctional institutions.

CONSTRAINTS ON THE PRISON USE OF LABOR

Almost all prison inmates eventually are released from prison, either on parole or at the expiration of their sentences. The certainty of eventual release has important implications for the use of inmate manpower. Inmates are encouraged to view their sentences as only short-term disruptions of their "outside" mode of life. Accordingly, they have little incentive to participate in work programs that are useful only within correctional institutions.

The regulations and incentives that prison officials develop to govern the assignment of inmates to jobs in prison industries and institutional maintenance need not be punitive or inimical to inmate productivity. Instead, prison work programs often are intended to provide both productive employment while inmates are in prison and job training that will be useful to them upon release. The training content of these programs, however, is diminished because inmates are not taught the relationship between the "inside" work experience and the incentives that exist "outside." Prison cannot duplicate the "outside" incentives of current income, attractive working conditions, and the prospect of future income without opposing the administrators' goal of holding costs to the minimum. Thus, work programs acceptable to correctional officials can have only limited value in training inmates for productive postrelease employment. Programs that are successful from the administrators' standpoint are unlikely to contribute very much to the probability that inmates will not become recidivists after release from prison.

A second constraint on prisons' use of labor is related to length of sentence. Youthful offenders, for example, frequently serve terms of less than a year. A 1969-70 survey found that the average prison term of felons convicted of a variety of federal offenses was under twenty months.[2] These short terms offer prison officials little time to train inmates for jobs that they are not already able to perform. Inmates typically have low levels of achievement in both formal education and vocational training. Moreover, their motivation to learn within prison is limited by both the lack of proper incentives and the coercive aspect of prison life.

The likely effect of these factors can be seen by comparing prison training with other programs such as the Job Corps. Entering Jobs Corps trainees during the program's duration had levels of formal education somewhat higher than the norm among inmates and presumably were more highly motivated (as shown by their willingness to enroll in the Job Corps program). Both formal education and vocational training in the Job Corps were intensive, with modern equipment and highly motivated instructors. The average Job Corps trainee stayed in the program for about nine months and then was placed in a private-industry job. Most studies of the effectiveness of the program have concluded that the gains in skills (measured by the trainees' additional income) were marginal and that the trainees' employment experience was not very different from that of nontrainees. Applying this experience to prison training programs suggests that successful work programs will exist primarily for long-term inmates. Short-term inmates will have a low probability of benefiting from correctional work programs, even though they constitute by far the largest group in numbers as well as the group that should offer the greatest chance of successful re-integration into society (on the basis of the initial offense).

We can summarize the discussion up to this point by listing two groups of constraints imposed upon the use of prison labor. First are limitations on the demand for prisoners' output. Production for private markets is legally prohibited. Production for government markets is limited by both the kinds and the quantity of goods that governments use. Production for internal use is limited by the amount and type of goods and services that prisons need for their own operation. Thus, all categories of demand limit the variety of goods that prison manpower can be used to produce.

The second group of constraints relates to prisons' abilities to produce goods and services. Prison capital equipment usually is only marginally efficient at best. Prisoners typically have very low levels of both formal and vocational education, and the ability of institutions to upgrade prisoner capabilities is restricted by the short duration of most sentences, shortages of instructional personnel, and inadequate or outmoded capital equipment. Even if the legal and institutional limitations on the demand for prison-produced goods and services could be circumvented, therefore, prisons would find their productive ability stringently limited by their physical plants and inmates' characteristics.

ALTERNATIVES TO CURRENT PRACTICE

There are only two ways to improve the use of prison manpower: to upgrade prison industries or to offer inmates more extensive opportunities for "outside" work experience while in prison. The latter program, an expanded form of work-release programs now in use in many prison systems, will be discussed shortly. First, let us consider the possibility of introducing useful work experiences into the prison environment.

Expanding Prison Industries

In view of society's past objections, the only feasible route for expanding prison industries probably lies in inviting private businesses to establish branches within correctional institutions. These branch plants would be designed to produce the same goods that the firms produce in normal operation, and they would teach inmates the same skills that are useful "outside." The incentive for firms to participate in this program probably would be access to a cheap labor source. To allay the fears of labor unions, inmates might be allowed (or required) to become union members, in which event wages would be higher and prisons could recover some of their costs by charging inmates for maintenance and services. Even if inmate labor was not much cheaper than normal union labor, firms might be willing to establish prison factories in return for subsidies in the form of capital equipment or tax benefits.

. . .

Expanding Work Release

While few correctional systems or institutions have initiated programs to upgrade prison industries, many systems have adopted some form of work-release program in which jobs are obtained in private firms for inmates who then are permitted to leave the correctional institutions during working hours. Work release has not attained the status of a real alternative to traditional uses of prison labor. The percentage of inmates obtaining work release is rather small because of the shortage of jobs in many areas and the reluctance of prison officials to offer the program on a wholesale basis. Nonetheless, there has been extensive discussion of work release, with emphasis on its humanitarian benefits for prisoners as well as the additional risks that it may pose for the community. There seems, however, to have been no thorough economic appraisal of the program's effects on inmates, administrators, and society as a whole. Nor has there been a discussion of the opportunity that work release offers to reform the overall use of prison manpower.

Benefits for Inmates

The most direct economic benefit that work release offers an inmate is the immediate increase in his income over the negligible wages that he can earn in a prison industry.[3] If he has a family, this income may spare them the necessity of relying on welfare (and undergoing the destructive experiences that are a well-documented aspect of AFDC and other contemporary welfare programs). His dependents should have a higher standard of living than they would have under welfare, and the maintenance of family ties and stability may increase his chances of eventual successful release. If the inmate has no dependents, the additional income from work release may provide him with savings (against the date of release) or the purchase of personal items within the institution.

A second category of benefit for the inmate relates to his longrun (postrelease) employment experience. A major factor contributing to recidivism is the extremely limited availability of jobs for ex-prisoners, who are thus forced into crime as a means of support. Under certain conditions, work release may be seen by the inmate as a method of obtaining a postrelease job.

. . .

Benefits for Society

Finally, let us consider the impact of expanded work-release programs on society at large. Several kinds of economic benefits are apparent, and some noneconomic advantages seem likely. The most direct benefit stems from the additional income of inmates. Some of this income, used to support inmates' dependents, would reduce the tax costs imposed on the rest of society by welfare programs and other transfer payments. To the extent that inmates' income provided a source of revenue for correctional institutions, the tax costs imposed on the rest of society by correction would go down. A third kind of direct benefit would accrue to society at large in the form of the taxes that inmates would pay out of their increased incomes. These taxes would substitute for others now levied on the rest of society and thus would offer still another increase in the net incomes of other taxpayers.[4]

A second economic benefit for society relates to the changed functions of prisons that can be expected to develop if work-release programs are expanded. In discussing administrators' incentives, we saw that institutional space and resources that are now used for economically inefficient programs could be released to other uses. The ensuing reduction in the total costs of penal institutions would benefit society even if no charges were levied on inmates' additional incomes.

More generally, society would benefit from an overall improvement in the way its resources are used. The fact that capital equipment in prison industries is not used efficiently is only one aspect of the misuse of resources under the current treatment of inmate labor. Noninstitutional resources that now are used to produce equipment for prison industries could produce similar equipment for more productive use elsewhere in the economy. Prison manpower that now is used inefficiently, to produce goods either for institutions or for state and local governments, could be used in the production of the goods that society values most (based on preferences expressed through the market system). Economists recognize that when the cost of a good is artificially kept down through subsidies, more of the good will be produced than is economically efficient. By undervaluing inmate labor, corectional institutions hold down the price of prison-produced goods and thus encourage their overproduction, relative to the amount that society would demand if the goods' true resource cost were known. Work release offers a means of valuing inmate labor correctly and thus would result in an improvement of the overall allocation of society's resources.

Much of this improvement in resource allocation would accrue to inmates themselves in the form of their increases in income. But there are some reasons to believe that noninstitutional groups in society also would benefit. An increase in society's effective labor force through work release would increase the productivity of existing capital equipment, thus raising the incomes of owners of capital. In many instances, labor may experience "external economies" as a factor of production, meaning that when the use of labor increases, already employed workers' productivity rises. In any such case, the availability of inmate manpower would increase not only the incomes of inmates but also the incomes of non-inmate labor.

. . .

Work-release programs might have significant effects on labor markets in certain localities. This is an especially serious problem since most large penal institutions are not located near major employment centers. For an employer in a small labor market, employing inmates entails a constant turnover in his labor force since they are likely to leave the area when paroled or given outright release. The advantages (if any) that inmate labor offers are small compared to this cost, so the availability of inmate jobs in slack local labor markets is likely to be small compared to the number of inmates seeking work release. If a correctional system wants to expand its work-release program, it may have to shift those in its inmate population who are eligible for work release to urban institutions, either through the use of halfway houses or through cooperative arrangements with local custodial institutions. While the location of many institutions poses a problem for the expansion of work release, the problem is not one of disrupting local labor markets.

The social benefits discussed up to this point have been primarily economic in nature. There are other aspects of work release that might offer chiefly noneconomic benefits. In assessing the effect of work release upon inmates, we mentioned that the additional exposure to "outside" institutions and incentives might increase the probability of an inmate's eventual successful release. A lower chance of recidivism, however, is a benefit not only to the inmate, but also (and even predominantly) to society at large. Not only does society obtain a lower incidence of crime, but its future costs of incarcerating offenders and administering a system of justice are reduced. Though a lower crime rate cannot easily be reduced to economic terms, it may be a major element of the advantages of expanded work release.

Another benefit of work-release programs may be the change

that they produce in society's attitudes toward correction. Inmates and officials are aware that correctional experiences are almost transitory and that most inmates return to society affected little (if at all) by the programs of correctional institutions. Society at large, however, has tended to view correction as the "final solution" of the inmate problem, in the sense that once an inmate has entered an institution he is no longer of concern to the rest of the world. A corollary of treating correction as a final solution is to blame correctional officials for any perceived failings of correctional systems, such as high recidivism rates or offenses committed by inmates on temporary release or parole. Work-release programs counteract this social attitude in two ways. They show that many inmates respond to the same incentives as the rest of society (that is, an acceptable job with decent prospects for advancement and a living wage), and thus help to dispel the popular notion that offenders are a homogeneous deviant group for whom prisons must develop magical rehabilitation programs. Conversely, work release promotes the role of the prison as an institution *within* society rather than as an external Purgatory and thus may limit the license often given to correctional staffs to maltreat inmates.

CONCLUSION

In the long run, prisons must reflect social attitudes toward inmates and the process of correction. In this paper we have examined some of the shortcomings of the present system's use of inmate manpower and some constraints on improvements. Of two alternatives to the current system, expansion of prison industries seems less likely to benefit inmates, prison administrators, or society at large than would an expanded reliance on work release. This conclusion rests on a comparison of the primarily economic costs and benefits of the two programs. But the most significant effect of work release might be to create a sense of social accountability for prisons and the correctional process by exposing society to inmates and showing that inmates can respond to the same incentives as everyone else. Regardless of economic effects, this possibility provides a compelling argument for the expansion of work-release programs.

NOTES

1. Technically, this statement is true only if prisons and governments now demand the same goods that they would want if private firms were the suppliers; in practice, differences in prices probably would cause changes in demands. But the conclusion in the text, that prisons now compete with private firms, is clearly true if *any* of the goods now produced in prison would otherwise be demanded from private suppliers.

2. *Statistical Report, Fiscal Years 1969–1970* (Washington, D.C.: Bureau of Prisons, U.S. Dept. of Justice, undated), Table C–2, p. 40. Data on this point are scanty, but there are indications that average terms are falling. Statistics compiled from unpublished data for thirty-four states in 1964 yielded a median term of twenty-one months. In 1960, the average term for felons in state and federal institutions was about twenty-eight months. See *Prisoners Released from State and Federal Institutions, 1960* (Washington, D.C.: Bureau of Prisons, U.S. Dept. of Justice, 1963), Table B, p. 4.

3. Because of the barriers to the efficient use of resources in even upgraded prison industries, inmates' wages on work release are likely to be higher than what they could earn within prison.

4. This conclusion assumes that other governmental expenditures remain constant despite the increase in inmates' incomes. This is not usually a good assumption, but in the case of prison inmates it is hard to see how their demands for government goods and services could vary much with their incomes.

Chapter Eighteen

The Stereotype of the Criminal and the Social Consequences

D. Chapman

Criminology is a complex social phenomenon, studied by scholars, moralists, lawyers and administrators who are concerned with the ordering of society. Academic criminology has a traditional form with schools with identifiable characteristics and with an acceptance of scholarship, the reliance on authority and the demonstration of erudition rather than the application of the canons of scientific method. It may be noted in passing that the use of the scientific method in the social sciences is now under attack with the stigma of "Positivism" as a sufficient basis for its rejection.

The central body of criminology accepts that crime, behaviour defined by law, is a distiguishing characteristic of a class of persons. This may be all those who break the law, those who break a particular law or persons in a particular group—"white collar" people, women, immigrants, etc.—who break laws.

The literature contains information on the tattooing around the nipples of borstal girls in New Zealand and the chromosomes of Scottish prisoners convicted of assault and every other variable that could be associated with conviction in a court (except perhaps re-

Reprinted by permission of the *International Journal of Criminology and Penology*, Vol. 1, No. 1, 1973, pp. 15–30.

ligion). There is moreover a general tendency to concentrate interest on those offences which are punished with imprisonment, rather than a fine; those that concern individuals rather than corporate bodies and offences of physical assault and concerning "real" property.

It would not be unfair to say that both in the professional literature and public discussion crime is that behaviour which results in a person being punished by prison—and/or death. Conditioning is such that in my own experience I have been more disturbed by a trifling theft than by the loss of a large sum of money invested and lost in a company whose directors acquired my investment for themselves by "legal" means. There is a circular pattern in thinking: we are hostile to wicked people, wicked people are punished, punished people are wicked, we are hostile to punished people because they are wicked. The doubts which have been expressed about the validity of studies of convicted persons have led to an extension of the field of inquiry into wider areas. In Britain the term Delinquency was at one time popular, indeed the leading journal—the *British Journal of Criminology*—was originally the *British Journal of Delinquency,* evidence of the pressure of mainstream attitudes in the profession. Delinquency dealt with activities of an anti-social kind, not necessarily illegal, and activities which would be criminal if one or more variables like age were different. In order to take the study a stage further in the direction of science it is necessary to extend the field to Deviance. This assumes a distribution of behaviours around a norm with degrees of acceptability. Without empirical support the distribution has been assumed to be Gaussian. It is notable that the identification of deviants as being more than three standard deviations from the norm, with sinners on the right and saints on the left, has not resulted in a new science to study the characteristics of the virtuous although a study of the lives of saints would suggest a rich source of clinical material. In practice the study of Deviance is confined to the examination of behaviour which is disapproved and which tends to involve administrative action and includes behaviour problems in children, the field of the educational psychologist, alcoholism, begging, prostitution, etc. In Britain the subjects are generally the Poor and the administration and administrators derive from 19th-century Poor Law.

The extension of Criminology to include Deviance is not a development towards a scientific study of behaviour but an extension of the data to which the traditional approaches are applied.

The effect is therefore to increase the size and variety of the population subject to "Tagging," "Labelling" or "Stigmatising" according to which school one belongs.

It is important to consider the origin of the term "stigma" and to remember that it was a brand on a slave and on a criminal. An escaped slave was a criminal and the term "villain" derives from the Latin form *villanus*—a farm servant. All these identify the criminal with the poorest and most defenceless worker in a society. Moreover it is salutary to consider that although Christ and the two thieves bore stigmata, the marks left by the nails and spear at the Crucifixion, it is only those of the thief which command the attention of criminologists.

The concept of stigma is older than Christianity. The first criminal in the historical mythology of man, Cain, was thus marked and had personality qualities which distinguished him from his virtuous brother Abel.

Theories of criminality differ according to the degree of emphasis they place upon the characteristics of the individual and the extent to which they direct interest to social factors. A science which attempts to account for behaviour of a wide range is unlikely to find a generally agreed theory or group of theories.

My own theoretical position differs in one important respect from that of others. In my analysis a criminal is one who has been convicted of a crime, not one who has performed an action for which he has not been convicted of a crime, but including a person who has been convicted of a crime for one action which he has not performed. The processes which select a person for conviction and the consequences of conviction are crucial variables.

The Stigma theory, and the related theory of Primary and Secondary Deviation, is presented as a two or three stage theory and makes assumptions about the original nature of the subject leading to his stigmatisation and the changes in him resulting from his stigmatisation.[1] The theory of the stereotype which is derived from Communication theory, whilst not excluding this latter factor entirely, does not consider it to be of critical importance.

The Stigma theory assumes a predisposing configuration of behaviour, or in another form a predisposing attribute or attributes, which leads the subject to commit his first offence or a child to make his first steps towards delinquency. At this stage the subject is reproached, given a derogatory description, identified with a despised or rejected class of person, humiliated, discriminated against, rejected or expelled. His reaction to this treatment results in increasing alienation from the rejecting group and a search for security in a peer group.[2]

At this stage the stigmatised person accepts the description of himself, defines himself as a member of the outcast group, is no longer involved in the inner emotional conflict between ends and means and accepts their norms and values.[3]

A crucial problem for the theory arises when the reaction of the rejected subject is not to accept the definition placed on him. An equally interesting situation arises when the rejected person remains within the group and accepts and exploits the role. This is not the place to develop this discussion but it is observable that the "Favourite" and "Scapegoat" often exist with complementary roles in primary groups and that the roles are reversible. The fool or buffoon, sometimes a dwarf or cripple, played a highly complex role, including that of scapegoat, in medieval courts.

The second stage occurs after conviction and punishment. Punishment loses its deterrent value through familiarity. It now serves to integrate rather than separate (a comparison with traumatic initiation rituals is relevant here). He becomes socialised by his prison (or hospital) experience to accept the inmate value system, he rejects the goals of the larger society or becomes convinced that they are unattainable and finally reincorporation in the "normal" society becomes impossible in terms of the costs, time and effort involved.[4]

The theory of the stereotype does not depend on the assumption that the "victim" changes his value orientation or is recruited to a criminal group, society or sub-culture, but looks at the consequences of his imprisonment and recording.

The Stigma theory depends on the selection of types of crime, the nature of some of the evidence and it concentrates on a description, not of persons with behaviours, but convicted or hospitalised persons. Moreover it would be possible to extend the theory with little adaptation as a general theory of occupational choice and persistence. In these terms we should talk of skills and abilities, of goal setting by parents and other influential groups, of self-identification with approved roles and statutes, of experience of traditional examination techniques, of incorporation into professional, occupational and status groups, of inertia in the face of alienation and the difficulty of occupational change and the acquisition of new skills.

The first problem of the theory is that it must select certain types of crime or deviance. It is unlikely to be useful in relation to murder or in relation to offences which are not (as far as is known) repeated—the majority—nor in relation to persons whose offences are at rare intervals. It makes assumptions about the existence of groups, or in some cases subcultures, with little evidence and assumes that these exist in all places and all social classes.

· · ·

The theory of the Criminal or Delinquent sub-culture arises in the special circumstances of the United States where there have been successive waves of immigration from different cultures into dense urban areas with a particular political administrative system and a plural and, in some ways, naive legal system.[5]

A second difficulty of the theory is its dependence on subjective data. The generalisations which are made about self-definition, about rejection of values and acceptance of other values, etc., must derive from the answers given to criminologists, psychologists, sociologists, social workers, doctors and psychiatrists by convicted persons or persons in hospitals or institutions (with rare exceptions). There is in the interview a likelihood that the orientation of the questioner will be noticed by the respondent, that the question, even the rare, formal kind, will contain or imply the desired answer. The questioner will be a person of superior status, power and influence often with the capacity to reward the respondent. In these circumstances there is a probability that the subjective data obtained will fit the theory.[6]

The theory is, however, attractive in that it is compatible with other current theories. Thus it fits with the "Symbolic Interaction" theory and the "Differential Identification" theory which argues (on somewhat inaccessible data) that before a person commits an offence or embarks on a deviant course he changes his value system and selects a new role.

It is compatible with the sociological orientation of Merton and Cloward and Ohlin who draw attention to the pressures to seek goals, wealth, status, power and the limited opportunities available to certain groups and persons, leading them to choose disapproved or illegal means to approved or legitimate ends. In spite of the attention now being given to organised crime and criminal organisations little interest has been shown in the preoccupation of the legal departments of business in the search for legitimate means to illegitimate ends or to business as crime.[7]

Likewise it is compatible with Sutherland's theory of Differential Association, that initiation and confirmation in criminal activities or deviant behaviour come from association with deviant or criminal persons who are not randomly distributed in society.[8]

Finally, the theory is compatible with the traditional view and the traditional theoretical orientation that the criminal is different, different in the qualities that predispose him to certain behaviour and different in that he undergoes internal (permanent) changes in his attitudes, values, beliefs and orientation. All this produces an amplification of the response in society which confirms the attitudes and increases the tendency to criminal behaviour in the subject and his isolation from society. The analysis of Wilkins is relevant here.[9]

. . .

The theory implies also the acceptance of traditional forms of social change, parental education, charity, compassion, law reform, prison reform and aid to prisoners after discharge, etc. Social processes are adaptive in that they help the institutions to survive criticism.

The Stigma theory recognises that "society," by which is meant the administrative apparatus, the Press and in some cases religious organisations, identify and ostracise certain persons with certain behaviour but it fails to account for the acceptance by "society" of persons with identical behaviour. Social approval and disapproval is arbitrary but not random.

The Stigma theory does not deal with the social function of Stigmatisation (although the Structure-Function theory does) so that the problem of the *social* consequences of Destigmatisation receives little attention.

Finally, a weakness of the theory is that by concentrating attention on a relatively economically unimportant part of "criminal" or "deviant" behaviour, it distracts attention from organised crime and criminal organisation whose activities lead only to the stigmatisation of the operatives rather than the management of the organisation. It distracts attention from the illegitimate ends achieved by legitimate means and it leaves unimpaired the reputation of those whose criminal activities like fraud are rarely punished by imprisonment and even if punished are not accompanied by stigmatisation. The highly selective nature of Stigmatisation raises important theoretical problems which must be studied if Destigmatisation is to be attempted.

. . .

The data I have examined has come from the work of others or from my own observation and experience. By its nature it can only be used to question the theories of others and to present hypotheses of my own. My approach is the scientific method as presented for example by R. B. Braithwaite in his *Scientific Explanation*.[10] One essential criterion of this method is that the scientist identifies his data independently of the system he is studying by the use of operational definitions.

I have set out my thesis thus:

(1) That any behaviour that has a disapproved form also has objectively identical forms that are neutral or approved.

(2) That if behaviour is seen as goal-seeking, then the choice of the form of behaviour between objectively identical forms—approved, neutral or disapproved—may depend on chance, knowledge, learning or training.

(3) That apart from the factor of conviction there are no differences between criminals and non-criminals.

(4) That criminal behaviour is general, but the incidence of conviction is controlled in part by chance and in part by social processes which divide society into the criminal and non-criminal classes, the former corresponding to, roughly, the poor and underprivileged.

(5) That a "crime" is behaviour, defined in place and time, of a person, in some cases with another person (victim) with police, lawyers, magistrates, and/or judges and juries. All these variables are causal in the scientific sense.

(6) That all the foregoing operate to select individuals from a larger universe of individuals with identical behaviours, both objectively and symbolically cued, and that, therefore, no test of the familiar hypotheses about crime is possible unless the scientist selects his subjects independently of the social system.

(7) That crime is a functional part of the social system. This part of the thesis has itself several parts. This first is that the designation of certain actions as permitted, tolerated, or condemned in different circumstances is arbitrary; the second is that there is a lack of correspondence between the ideology and behaviour; and the third is that there is differential treatment of different social groups for behaviours which are objectively identical, identical in that they transgress the same traditional mores, but different in their treatment at law. The designation and social isolation of a relatively small group of victims permit the guilt of others to be symbolically discharged; the identification of the criminal class and its social ostracism permit the reduction of social-class hostility by deflecting aggression that could otherwise be directed towards those with status, power, reward and property. A special part of the ideology functions to prevent the designated criminal from escaping from his sacrificial role, and instituitional record-keeping maintains his identity.

(8) That, following this, there is a special problem of the immunity of certain members of society and certain groups. This arises mainly from the protective institutional environment in which they pass part, or all, of

their lives, or in which they spend part of their time or engage in some of their activities.

(9) That associated with this are covert social processes which extend whole or partial immunity to, or reduce the impact of, the legal system on members of certain social groups.

(10) That associated with the general thesis is a separate problem—that of the legal system as a crime-creating institution. That is, once an institution is created it develops a dynamic of its own and becomes involved in the behaviour with which it is concerned as a participant, and in special circumstances as an instigator. It may do this in response to social pressures, e.g., the demand that "criminals" shall be caught and punished.

(11) Finally, that the general preoccupation with contravention of the mores in symbolic culture—except, perhaps, some of the graphic arts—can be functionally related to the real situation expounded in items 1 to 10.[11]

It is not the place here to explore all the complicated analytical propositions which arise from these theses. They concern the plurality of the moral and legal order, the conflict between the "fundamental" belief system of society and its goal system. They deal with the conflict within society between the groups and classes which hold and control power and wealth and those who do not. . . . The techniques of symbolic conflict resolution, which replace emotionally disturbing stimuli with neutral or even favourable ones, control conflict within the system. The designation or stigmatisation of certain classes of persons as evil permits conflict to be resolved by their isolation, ostracism or expulsion. The scapegoat performs a function for individuals, groups and society.

Once the group is identified and accepted, the police or military are justified in behaving in a way which might otherwise be emotionally disturbing. The torture of internees by the police and the army in Ulster is valuable data and the redefinition of torture as "interrogation in depth" and the conclusion that there was "physical ill treatment" but not "physical brutality" by a committee of inquiry is an illustration of conflict resolution by redefinition.[12]

Two other analyses are involved. First, that of the penal system which, like the legal system, is accepted as given by traditional criminologists and second, that of the role of the social scientist in the system of providing "scientific" explanations (justification) of the categories of crime, deviance and delinquency and his function of providing the rationale for movements of reform which allow a penal system, whose methods have no basis in science, to survive by protecting it from the challenge which comes from the knowledge of learning theory, the growth of a secular morality and a transformation in the standard of living.

At this point it is reasonable to ask in what critical way does this analysis differ from the theories of Stigmatisation and does it offer any prospect for the solution of social problems?

To take the second point first, I must admit to being a pessimist. We have seen genocide on a gigantic scale facilitated by the exploitation of the stereotype of the aboriginal inhabitants of North America and Australia and Tasmania, of Armenians in Turkey and of Jews and Gipsies in Western Europe to mention only the most dramatic examples. We observe gross exploitation in South Africa and Rhodesia made possible by the same processes. . . . The use of the stereotype as an instrument of policy is too valuable to be lightly abandoned. The theory of the Stereotype begins with the moral order and the law. It does not begin with the person and his characteristics and behaviours. It asks why a legislature decides that an action must be punished. It is obvious that much law and morality is in the general interest. The prohibition of spitting in public places has had important benefits in reducing tuberculosis. On the other hand such legislation reflects the distribution of power in society and much legislation (and the absence of it) serves the interest of particular classes, groups, organisations, industries or even companies. Moral systems as proclaimed by churches, trade unions and organisations are likewise mixed in their intentions and effects.

. . .

It follows therefore that law and morality select persons for disapprobation and punishment and that some laws and some morals select from certain groups and not others. It must be noticed also that law and morality confer advantages and again select from some groups and not from others.

. . .

The theory of the Stereotype has two features: the wide diffusion of a hostile description of certain persons or classes of people to whom evil intentions and disastrous events are attributed and the selection through the administrative system, of persons, mainly poor and weak, to whom the description is attached. Once the person has been identified and labelled further discrimination is justified and so on—round and round. In the process the person is in some cases changed in the direction of the Stereotype. A full study would involve a complete analysis of law to see the extent to which different groups or classes of persons were treated differently for the same offence or for offences different in law but identical if defined operationally.

This would be difficult but rewarding because it would illuminate many of the underlying factors with which we are concerned. Thus the variety of crimes concerned with property would be subsumed under a general definition "The transfer of property or the rights in property from one person to another without the former's full knowledge and consent." This definition might need further elements to take account of the varieties of transfer found. If this is done then it may be discovered that "real" transfers like robbery are treated differently from "symbolic" transfers like fraud. Frauds of hundreds of thousands of pounds in England tend to attract fines and of millions relatively short prison sentences. This has an important effect, the magnitude of an offence in the belief system may be determined by the penalty that it attracts. Thus the "crimes" of the uneducated lead to the attribution of stereotype whilst those of the educated are less likely to do so.

An operational definition would also lead to the recognition and questioning of behaviour of identical consequences which is not punished, some forms of business for example.

The full development of operational definitions would indicate all the factors in the situation including the role of the victim or victims. What, for example, is the significance for criminology of the belief amongst Supermarket owners that unless goods are so accessible that thefts run at 4% of the total, the loss of sales more than outweighs the losses through thefts?

Finally, such definitions would show that not only is behaviour defined in terms of time and place by law but also by categories of person by age, by sex and in one case that of the Queen by status. (The Queen cannot do wrong.)

Personal inquiries have shown that motorists who have killed others through dangerous driving or industrialists who have had fatal accidents in their works through neglect of legal requirements to fence machinery, although suffering from shock and emotional disturbance, are not subject to stigma or hostility.

It follows therefore that the system of law selects certain categories of person who behave in certain ways for punishment and of these some are more disapproved (or stigmatised) than others. Broadly these will be men, the weak, the poor and badly educated. . . .

The next stage in the discussion is to consider the administration of the law through the police and the courts. The degree to which a person is immune or vulnerable to observation and arrest differs along class lines. The landed proprietor—in spite of the occasional spectacular case involving sexual offences—is substantially immune since most of his behaviour is in private. The differential distribution of privacy is a crucial variable. The differential pattern of policy reinforces this, the poor areas of a town are heavily policed, the rich areas lightly, and then primarily to protect the middle classes and not to control them. The fact that the more heavily policed areas produce higher rates of arrest is an example of the self-fulfilling prophecy. There are protective institutional environments often involved in the moral order or assumed to conform to the value system. Universities have in them individuals whose behaviour in other circumstances would be an offence. The same is true of religious institutions, administrative bureaucracies and the bureaucracies of business and industry. There are of course sanctions, usually enforced by informal and/or secret processes which in extreme circumstances expel the person but in such a way that he is not "stigmatised" and has an opportunity to adopt a role in the society outside.

. . .

The theory of institutional behaviour points to the importance of the concept of the "Displaced Goal." This is particularly important since the function of the police in maintaining law and order may give way to the displaced goal of obtaining successful prosecutions. To refer further to this theory the Manifest-Overt function of maintaining law and order—prescribed in statutes—may also develop into the Latent-Covert function of maintaining an order which is not so prescribed. For example a shop-steward who had been dismissed after an unsuccessful strike, and who was unemployed, was kept under surveillance and was reported to the authorities when he worked for his mother without pay. He was accused of obtaining unemployment pay by fraud. He had, by this time, obtained another job in another place. Although on appeal he was acquitted the publicity could have rendered him permanently unemployable. The keeping of records of "reds," subversives, homosexuals and suspected persons and the communication of such information through informal channels is a feature not only of the police and all those parts of the administrative system which keep records—including employment agencies, but is a form of discrimination operated in all institutions. Thus it is that a general pattern of role deprivation of the poor and uneducated is amplified and extended to other groups in society. The Nonconformist is identified as deviant!

If the situation is now considered where an action has taken place which would be criminal then a series of processes must occur before the person thus behaving can be convicted of a crime and if convicted, sentenced to go to prison. Incarceration in prison is the most important factor in stigmatisation or in conforming to the stereotype.

The action of a poorer person is more likely to be observed and if observed more likely to lead to arrest than that of a middle-class person; other stereotyped persons, youths with long hair and dark skinned persons, are also vulnerable.

. . .

A high proportion of all "crimes" are solved by confession—that is by pleas of guilty. The likelihood of a person confessing is very closely related to his education, status and access to professional advice. Since this discussion is not primarily concerned with guilt but with stereotyping the question of whether the "guilty" escape is irrelevant. Senior police officers . . . have stated that unless a person pleads guilty he stands some chance of acquittal, and if he is tried by a jury (as he may elect to do in certain cases) he stands a better chance of acquittal than if he is tried by a magistrate. Under pressure from the police unanimous findings of guilt by juries have been replaced by majority verdicts thus increasing the proportion of findings of guilt (the number of criminals and the amount of crime)! On the other hand, there is a probability that a plea of guilt in a lower court, with suitable police intervention, may attract a lower sentence than an unsuccessful plea of not guilty in a higher court. The weakness of the poor makes them susceptible to bargaining justice! Another aspect of bargaining is the mechanism whereby a person accused who has agreed to plead guilty may elect to have other offences taken into consideration thus becoming immune from future prosecution in connection with these offences. This provides the police with a means of "clearing up" offences known to the police.

Following a conviction the discriminatory process proceeds along class lines. For the same offence the middle-class person is more likely to be punished by a fine than by imprisonment (although few first offenders now receive prison sentences) and is more likely to have mitigating circumstances considered. There is an assumption that the higher in the social scale, the greater the punishment of imprisonment so that justice may require differential treatment. Nevertheless the discriminatory process is effective. The rich man is more likely to appeal, both against the conviction and the sentence, than the poorer person.

To summarise all this, the offences of the poor are those associated with the stereotype or the stigma but the offences of the middle and upper classes of equal gravity judged by their social and economic effects are not. Many actions of these groups of equal gravity are not offences.

Following this, the system of policy and the administration of justice are more likely to identify poor and uneducated persons and they are more likely to be sent to prison.

Experience in prison is the crucial factor in identifying the person as the Criminal of the Stereotype and in being agent of his desocialisation and disconnection from normal society. In contrast to the Stigma theory and the Sub-Culture theory he may become, not a member of a group, but an outcast who is not identifiable with any system of values and without any patterned social relationships.

The existence of prisons is the most baffling of all social phenomena. Their origin is largely accidental and except that they protect society from a tiny number of dangerous persons (who could find socially approved roles if vocational guidance was effective) the beliefs on which the prison is maintained are demonstrably false. Only three arguments are advanced to defend the prison. The first is that the majority of persons sent to prison do not offend a second time (or are not apprehended and/or convicted). The second is that if serious offences are not punished by imprisonment how can we punish offenders? Which, put briefly, says it is better to do something demonstrably futile than to do nothing. The third is that the "Public" demands the punishment of the "Criminal."

We can, without looking at all the well documented effects of imprisonment, be liberated from our prejudices by considering the effects of imprisonment on heroes—not villains—the prisoners of war and of concentration camps. These display the problems of social disconnection in spite of the approval of society, the affection with which they are received and the positive attempts to place them in work and in society. The effects are independent of stigmatisation. It could be argued that there may be an element of self-definition amongst prisoners of war—some of my colleagues claimed to find differences between prisoners of war who attempted to escape and those who did not and claimed to have identified "non-combatant guilt" amongst prisoners of war.

There appears, thus, to be a number of different assumptions made about the Criminal of the Stereotype and the labelled or the Stigmatised person. These are not necessarily mutually exclusive or contradictory. The first sees him largely as the victim of a society with internal contradictions, with moral plurality and class differences. The second theory sees him as initially different and the stigmatisation amplifying his differences and through self-definition directing him into a criminal or deviant subgroup or culture. The first theory sees society as the problem area, the second whilst recognising the social problem concentrates interest on criminals and the criminal sub-culture.

It may be complained that it has taken a long time to reach the topic with which the paper is concerned, Destigmatisation. This is perhaps because a consciousness of the magnitude of the task is daunting.

To begin at the beginning, the first task is to rid our minds of all we have been led to believe in this subject. Then we must ask the question, what evidence is there that human behaviour is able to be directed by legislation? If this were done we should discover that there are large areas where legislation is futile and where additional legislation to reinforce it merely compounds futility. A second stage would be to identify behaviour that has adverse social consequences by operational definition rather than traditional religious or legal definition. This is not to ask for a rational morality at once, but to begin to examine some of the contradictions between "crime" and "white collar offences." It could lead to a more effective understanding of the vast range of behaviour we designate as criminal. It would also lead to a reconsideration of the relative importance of different offences. For example, murder is a relatively unimportant form of homicide quantitatively. In most types of murder it is rare for the offence to be repeated, yet it is one of the most heavily punished offences and one which excites most public interest and police activity. Since punishment does not deter and since the offence is rarely repeated the effort seems pointless.

This suggests a major research subject—the nature of social control and the role of law in social control. A working hypothesis would be that the law is relatively unimportant for persons but important for organisations and that the role of education has been undervalued and neglected. The moral content of further and higher education is small.

This in turn might lead to a re-examination of social goals. The value system of western society abounds with contradiction and even to elucidate this would be an advance.

The difficulty is that the traditional institutions which have the task of inculcating the moral order—the churches, are themselves involved in the Establishment, are compromised and their teaching has become directed towards the latent function of the growth and survival of their bureaucracies. Robespierre's attempt to declare a rational religion based on the concept of a supreme being by law, was not a success.

The value system is now largely diffused through the press and perhaps the easiest task would be first to examine the content of newspapers and journals. It will be found that stereotypes abound as does selective reporting. For example, a variety of anti-social behaviours are attributed to vandals. It is possible that stereotyping or stigmatising in the reporting of the courts might be controlled by legislation or voluntary action. . . .

The belief, largely undemonstrated, in the effectiveness of deterrents and punishments makes it difficult to change the main forces in stereotyping, police methods and imprisonment. The confession—the plea of guilty—is the most frequent method of obtaining conviction. It assumes punishment and involves, as does the Stigma theory, self-definition. It might be possible to reconsider confession and punishment by reference to the function of confession in some Christian churches. Confession, repentance and atonement are major instruments of social control. In confession it is the sin which excludes, not the self-definition following confession. Confession brings absolution, redefinition and readmittance into the society of the church—it is the means of removing all stigma. This is partly understood in such procedures as probation, although this is stigmatising and is effective in many forms of counselling including "Marriage Guidance."

Imprisonment is the major force in stereotyping and in the processes described in the Stigma theory but not sufficient attention has been given to the dynamic social processes in prison, the interaction between the prison officers and the prisoners. Goffman has directed attention to this, arguing that prison officers are as much the product of prison as the prisoners. . . .[13]

It follows that any changes in the penal system which reduce the number of persons who suffer any form of detention will reduce the processes of stigmatisation and the consequences of stereotyping.

Prison in itself is crucial, but record-keeping reinforces the effects of imprisonment. It could be argued that the ex-prisoner will accept the hostile picture of himself because he knows that it is written permanently in records accessible to every police officer for all time. He may suspect that these records may be more widely diffused. In addition press reporting leaves a permanent record. The widespread development of agencies which keep records of a person's financial status may have an influence. The convicted person will have been noticed, his offense recorded. When he applies for credit to purchase an item, say of furniture, or to obtain a mortgage to buy a house he may fail because he receives an adverse report—the existence of which he may not know. . . .

The argument of the police for maintaining criminal records is that some criminal behaviour is patterned and repeated, and that records establish the probability that a particular action was that of a particular person.

It would be Utopian to hope that all police and other administrative records would be destroyed immediately a person had completed his punishment, although it should be argued that he is entitled to consider himself fully restored to normal citizenship. The acceptance of this as a legal fact would be an important step forward. Nevertheless there is a strong case for limiting the time that records are kept to a relatively short period. This would be justified on cost-benefit analysis anyhow.[14]

Following the theory that legislation is more effective for institutions than the individuals, it could be made law that any reporting of criminal cases in the court and any disclosure of information about sentencing or any derogatory reporting by credit agencies, employment agencies, political and industrial agencies or administrative bodies could not escape an action for defamation by arguing that the statement was true. Such a proposal would still give an advantage to the educated and the prosperous and would have to be accompanied by the provision of legal aid for the poor and weak.

The discussion so far has given little attention to the social function of the scapegoat in societies with endemic moral or social conflicts. All societies go from crisis to crisis solving each in turn by expedients. The major crises can be contained by the direction of hostility on to large classes of people—Kulaks, Jews, Reds, etc., the continuing crisis of values by stigmatising a sacrificial group of the weak, poor and uneducated. If we begin to solve the problem of Stigmatisation this must be a step towards an examination of the conflict of values that the process helps to contain. If we fail to resolve the conflict of values we may find the criminal scapegoat merely replaced by another.

NOTES

1. E. Goffman, *Stigma* (Englewood Cliffs, 1960); S. Shoham, *The Mark of Cain: The Stigma Theory of Crime and Deviation* (Chicago, 1968).

2. *Ibid.*

3. *Ibid.*

4. E. Goffman, *Stigma* (Englewood Cliffs, 1960); E. Lemmert, *Human Resources Social Problems and Social Control* (Englewood Cliffs, 1960).

5. R. A. Cloward and L. E. Ohlin, *Delinquency and Opportunity* (Glencoe, 1960).

6. G. E. Lenski and J. C. Leggett, "Cast, class and deference in the research interview," *Amer. Jour. of Sociology* 65, 463 (1959–60).

7. D. R. Cressey, *Organized Crime and Criminal Organization* (Cambridge, 1971).

8. E. H. Sutherland and D. R. Cressey, *Principles of Criminology* (New York, 1960).

9. L. T. Wilkins, *Social Deviance* (London, 1964).

10. R. B. Braithwaite, *Scientific Explanation* (Cambridge, 1953).

11. D. Chapman, *Sociology and Stereotype of the Criminal* (London, 1968).

12. Report of the inquiry into allegations against the security forces of physical brutality in N. Ireland arising out of events on 9th August, 1971. H.M. S.O. London Comm. 4823 (1971).

13. E. Goffman, *Asylums* (N.Y. 1961).

14. The Rt. Hon. Lord Gardiner, *Living It Down* (London, 1972).

Chapter Nineteen

Offenders as Employees

J. P. Martin

. . . The findings of this study are based on the experiences of employers in Reading but their implications may be of wider significance. No doubt the extent and intensity of such experiences will vary from place to place, but it is difficult to think that they will be concerned with problems that are different in kind. Furthermore, there is reason to believe that many of our results stem from fundamental attitudes towards criminals and the law, and from the general nature of industrial organisations. In so far as this is true, results stated in terms of these factors may be of general application. . . .

Our first general finding was that at least two-thirds of firms in Reading had employed offenders at one time or another. This figure was based on a solid majority of firms who could quote details of actual cases, to which were added those who were sure they had employed ex-offenders but who made a practice of not enquiring about the past records of potential employees. . . .

. . .

There was some difference between the larger and the smaller firms, the overall figures being somewhat higher for the larger firms. This was not surprising in view of the much greater number of men

---

Reprinted by permission of MacMillan: London and Basingstoke, 1962.

employed. When, however, the figures were related to the number of men recruited over a given period it became clear that the smaller firms took on relatively more known ex-offenders than did the larger. Owing to the offenders' concealment of their records some were taken on unknowingly but were discovered later; in the larger firms about a third of the ex-offenders came into this category, in the smaller the proportion was just over a half. Taking the sample as a whole, firms which had consciously taken on ex-offenders were in a minority. The larger firms were noticeably more thorough in discovering whether men had criminal records; to a greater extent, in fact, they 'knew' what they were doing. . . .

It was important to discover how many firms had some jobs for which men were recruited without being asked questions on their past; to the man faced with difficulties in getting a job these represent the last resort, and it is vital that such jobs should exist. In this respect it was encouraging that nearly two-thirds of the larger firms, and just over 40 per cent of the smaller, had some sections where recruitment was on a 'No questions' basis. The practice was most common in construction firms, but was fairly widespread for labouring jobs generally. At the opposite extreme were firms where this was never done, particularly in insurance, banking and finance, and in professional and scientific employment. Although in some ways the policy of asking no questions is socially desirable, one of its consequences was that it was impossible to discover the true proportion of ex-offenders among the men recruited by our firms. . . .

This evidence allows several comments. First, it would not seem difficult for an offender to get a job of a kind, without questions being asked. Second, even where questions are asked there is a chance of being employed; in the past the majority of firms have at some time taken on ex-offenders. A number of these, however, did so unwittingly, and it has to be said that only a minority of firms in the area was prepared knowingly to engage ex-offenders. It would, therefore, be foolish to minimise the difficulties, particularly where a man wants something better than an unskilled job, and where he has been convicted of certain types of offence. We do not, in any case, know how many ex-offenders were unsuccessful in obtaining jobs. Furthermore, our evidence related to a decade of full-employment and there is no means of knowing how offenders would fare if faced with fiercer competition.

There is no doubt, in fact, that our informants regarded ex-offenders as particularly difficult to place; our hypothetical questions showed that in this respect they were second only to men who had been mentally ill. Two findings slightly redeem this situation: first, the fact that many employers expressed their views in qualified terms, which might imply a willingness to consider men who were suitably presented to them. Second, the fact that a fairly large proportion of offenders concealed their records, got jobs, and were kept on when their pasts were discovered. Our impression was that in spite of the deception the offender who had worked well would stand quite a good chance of being kept on. Certainly there was no evidence that offenders who concealed their records were worse employees than those who did not.

. . .

How satisfactory were the ex-offenders as employees? In the larger firms 29 per cent were rated as good workers, most of whom were still in their firm's employment. Exactly the same proportion were definitely unsatisfactory, in that they were dismissed or left under suspicion, or were still with their firm but regarded as bad workers. A further eight per cent left on reconviction, so that the total who were unsatisfactory from the employer's point of view reached 37 per cent.

On the other hand, judged in terms of the duration of employment, the ex-offenders had a reasonably good record of job stability. In round figures the firm taking on a known ex-offender could expect that there was a fifty-fifty chance that he would stay with them for the best part of a year. At the semi-skilled and unskilled level this is not a bad record. Indeed some of the men still with the firms in the sample were clearly regarded as well above the average: some verbatim comments included 'one of the best men we've got,' 'very good lad,' 'first-class craftsman,' 'a damn good worker.'

The experience of the smaller firms was rather less encouraging. Only 17 per cent were ranked as good workers, while 27 per cent were dismissed or left under suspicion; 7 per cent were actually reconvicted, so that the over-all proportion of those in the unsatisfactory categories was 34 per cent.

It is not easy to compare these figures with other studies of labour turnover, etc., because of the range of firms, jobs, and the period of time covered. The picture is fairly encouraging, but the experience of larger firms suggests that careful selection and supervision produce somewhat better results.

. . . Our tentative conclusions were that the building industry and retail distribution seemed to be rather unfortunate in their experience—possibly owing to the temptations presented and the difficulties of supervision involved. The most successful firms were in certain sections of manufacturing industry; it may be that this was a result of careful placing and supervision together with a relative absence of temptation.

An interesting negative conclusion is that some suspicions, fairly widespread among employers and social workers appear, at the least, not to be supported by our evidence. In particular, men previously convicted of embezzlement, fraud, and sex offences seem to have been among the more successful employees in our sample. There may, therefore, be grounds for re-examining some of the conventional judgements about the risks involved in employing the various types of offender in different kinds of job. The gain in understanding might be particularly fruitful in dispelling some of the fears which now make it difficult for certain offenders to obtain suitable employment.

. . .

When asked a direct question, the great majority of firms said they did not, in practice, regard dishonesty by employees as a serious problem. Only some 16 per cent of the larger and 8 per cent of the smaller were seriously troubled by it. This was not to say, however, that our firms were unacquainted with the problem; 82 per cent of the larger, and 56 per cent of the smaller could recall at least one case. On an average basis the larger firms had roughly one case a year; the smaller averaged one approximately every five years. Being based on small numbers, the latter figure should probably be interpreted as meaning that a substantial proportion never have any cases, whereas a few will have them fairly often. When these rates were related to the numbers of men employed, the rate for the smaller firms was shown to be over three times as high as that for the larger.

But what is dishonesty? Are these numbers absurdly small? The answer seems to be that they are low mainly because many employers (and workers) treat the taking of goods by the firm's employees as 'pilfering'; hence much that is technically stealing is not described as such, and therefore cannot be a 'problem.' A minority of employers, perhaps about one in six, take a strictly legal view and condemn any unauthorized taking, but the majority seem to exist in a rather vague state where a blind eye is turned on 'pilfering' which, however, merges at an ill-defined point into theft.

The point at which this distinction was drawn varied from industry to industry and from firm to firm. It was often defined by description and the judgements tended to be made in the following broad terms:

'Pilfering' (when 'legitimate') involves one or more of the following features—the items are of 'small' value, they are taken for the worker's own use, the quantities involved are small, and the act is unpremeditated.

'Stealing' is any taking of cash (the only definition with which no one disagreed), or one or more of the following—taking of stamps, items from 'stock' goods in large quantities (by the box, bag, sack or crate), items over a given value, small items taken repeatedly, taking for re-sale, taking with premeditation and unauthorised taking when it is known the items would be given away on request.

The criterion mentioned most frequently when giving examples of stealing was the value of the goods taken.

. . .

We did not of course enquire into employees' attitudes to such matters, but on another occasion it might be fruitful to investigate the rationale involved. One suspects that the existence of small 'perks' of this kind is seen as the worker's equivalent to the boss's expense account. It may be a rationalisation, but one can understand the point of view which argues that if the boss drives a car costing, say, fifteen hundred pounds (assumed to be run at the firm's expense), then the rank and file are entitled to their 'cut' too. This is probably felt to be even more justified when the goods have already been paid for, e.g., in the overall cost of a building, and the amounts left over are of no use to a contractor who works on a large scale, whereas to the man who wants some paint to re-decorate his wife's kitchen a quart or so is both useful and valuable.

Beyond the pilfering which is at least tacitly acceptable lie those actions definitely regarded as criminal. Here, the employers' reactions were much more clear cut. . . . Considering only offences connected with the firm's activities it is clear that when possible firms neither call the police nor prosecute. Sixty-one cases occurred in the larger firms; 41 per cent resulted in prosecution, while in only 31 per cent (19) were the police asked to investigate. The smaller firms were even more disposed to keep such matters private, the corresponding figures being 24 per cent (prosecuted) and 21 per cent (police investigations). Taking all the evidence together it seemed fairly clear that the employer's definite opinion about whether a man should be prosecuted is likely to correspond very closely to what actually happens.

The fact that firms preferred to deal with offenders privately did not mean that the matter was treated lightly. In cases where the men concerned did not leave of their own accord the majority were dismissed, mainly on the grounds that they were untrustworthy, but sometimes because it was the rule of the firm, or because to have kept a man on would be to risk bad feeling among the rest of the staff. When men were kept on they did tolerably well, particularly in the larger firms.

In their actions the firms appear to have been motivated by three main considerations: first the nature of the offence (if it was a serious one); second, and perhaps most important, the expected repercussions on the working of the firm; and third, the personal qualities and attitude of the man concerned.

. . . Most reactions to offences were dominated by concern for the welfare of the firm. Thus most of the men prosecuted were used as examples, while those who escaped prosecution did so most commonly on such grounds as 'Not worth publicity/unpleasantness,' 'waste of time,' 'case not serious enough' (by implication = not worth publicity, time involved, etc.). The only other reasons frequently given were that the man was a good worker or a 'decent chap.' Where men were dismissed the commonest ground was that they were felt to be untrustworthy, or that it was a rule of the firm (which probably took into account both untrustworthiness and the need to set an example). Almost all men kept on were regarded as 'good workers/highly thought of.'

It is not easy to decide how far the policy of dismissing men without prosecuting them results from a genuine wish to be lenient. Several different views may be held. Some larger firms have a comparatively sophisticated policy of prosecuting men but keeping them on afterwards, presumably on the grounds that this is both maintaining correct standards of honesty and affording constructive assistance as well. It was much more common, however, simply to dismiss the offender. As in the great majority of cases it was thought that the man could easily get another job, while the fact of his offence was kept out of the papers (and perhaps even from his family) and, above all, he did not become 'known' to the police as a man with a criminal record, this practice was probably one of leniency. By following it the employer managed both to dispose of the whole business as quickly as possible, and to gain a justified reputation for being sympathetic to men in difficulty.

It does not appear that concern for the enforcement of the criminal law as such was prominent in more than a small proportion of cases.

. . .

The Foundations of Employers' Attitudes

. . . We have concluded that in large measure the attitudes displayed are basically pragmatic. Crime and criminals are mostly too rare to be the subject of a policy; decisions tend to be *ad hoc*. This being so, we must ask what is their fundamental rationale: what are the assumptions involved?

One answer which suggests itself is that in this context employers conceive their workers as comprising an organic body, and this group, like any other organism, can stand a certain amount of irritation or injury, but beyond that point its efficiency is endangered. It is the employer's function to protect this body from external and internal damage, and his reaction to crime and criminals is very largely determined by what he thinks will be their effects on the organism as a whole.

In estimating these effects a number of factors have to be taken into account. In general terms some organisms are more flexible than others; the more flexible they are the more risks can be taken in such matters as recruiting men with criminal records. If, for example, a man is placed in an unsuitable department, there still exist others to which he may be transferred. This flexibility is very largely a function of size and variety of working situations; in a large firm it should be quite easy to see that embezzlers do not handle money, or that the man who has assaulted a woman works in an exclusively male shop. In a word, careful placing and supervision may go far to give a man a suitable job in a situation where his known weaknesses are subjected to a minimum of temptation.

In a small firm, however, such arrangements may be quite impossible, so that once a man behaves in a way which makes him a threat to the cohesion of the group it must seem to the employer that the only remedy is to get rid of him. Furthermore, in the small firm relationships between the employer and his workers are inevitably more personal, and it is more likely that a breach of trust will be taken as a personal affront. In a larger firm, however, the personnel officer may be less deeply involved and even perhaps not so shocked by the fact that human beings have weaknesses. It may quite frequently be that, both by training and circumstances, he has sufficient room for manoeuvre to allow him to treat the placing of an offender as a problem to be solved; to the man without such room the proposition must seem impossible.

. . .

In law a man who assists a criminal by not reporting to the police a crime of which he has knowledge may himself commit a criminal offence. It would appear that, outside the ranks of professional criminals, few people are more likely to commit these offenses than are employers. They do so on the principle that, to adapt a famous phrase, 'every employer's factory is his castle.'

But how does this very understandable attitude stand in relation to the maintenance of respect not only for the law, but also for the principles of honesty which the law seeks to uphold? Our answer is bound to be incomplete, but a few consequences should be mentioned: first, that any process by which a citizen takes the law into his own hands runs the risk that injustice may be done because standards of judicial proof may not be satisfied. Second, there is the danger that what might be relatively harmless leniency in some cases, may in others mean that quite serious crime is covered up in order to preserve a firm's reputation for having a staff of complete integrity. Such a practice may have consequences beyond those immediately sought—the 'offender' may go on to commit further crimes, he may find it difficult to get another job, or, perhaps more likely, he will get even deeper into the difficulties which led him to commit the offence in the first place. In fact we know very little of what happens under these circumstances. The only certainty is that the firm's reputation is protected.

Fourth, although the importance of honesty is partly affirmed, much of what is done involves an implicit criticism of the machinery of justice. Fifth, there are bound to be considerable differences from firm to firm in this respect, so that for similar acts one man may be imprisoned while another may go virtually unscathed. Hence some men become 'criminals' not so much for what they have done, but by the chance of where they have been employed.

The employer's responsibility is great. He, more than most people, often has the power to put his fellow-citizens into the hands of the law; once that is done a man is a decisive step nearer to being someone on whom, sensibly enough, the police keep an eye as a man who might offend another time. Such a power should not be exercised lightly, but each time an employer refrains from using it he is, in effect, making a decision that his action is in the public interest.

. . .

It has been made abundantly clear to us that many offenders get jobs, and perhaps can only get them, in firms where no questions are asked about their previous lives. This practice is common in the building industry and it undoubtedly means that ex-offenders flock to such jobs.

. . .

The facts are not very surprising, but should they be regarded as shocking? Two points must be made: first, that ex-offenders must be allowed to get jobs somewhere. No court has sentenced them to perpetual unemployment; indeed, to do so would deny them the right to show that they can make good by dint of their own efforts. Second, if the right to attempt to redeem oneself as a citizen is not to be denied, then a different question must be asked; namely, where can men get jobs where they will be least danger to their fellow-citizens while trying to re-establish themselves as honest men? This is a difficult question to answer, but it does not seem surprising, or so very unreasonable, that many men have found temporary work as unskilled labourers, both on building sites and elsewhere.

. . .

In many ways this study can be seen as a rather large 'pilot' enquiry which, although it has provided answers to some questions, has revealed others which are clearly important.

The first main need is for comparative information from other areas, or obtained on an industrial basis. There is reason to suppose that the practice of a particular industry has a substantial influence on its crime rate; for example, offences against employers in the building industry may be relatively rare because of the extent to which the taking of moderate quantities of goods is a custom of the industry.

Second, what is the relationship between an ex-offender's previous crime, the job he undertakes, and his success as an employee? Are there, for example, jobs in which embezzlers, or sex offenders, can make good?

Third, how far do ex-offenders need special care in placing in employment, and is it possible to make a significant improvement in their chances by careful guidance and supervision? What, in fact, is the real nature of the difference between larger and smaller firms?

Fourth, what happens to men who are dismissed but not prosecuted? How many take the warning and keep out of trouble in the future, and how many go on committing offences until they end in court?

In making this study we did not set out to prove a case. What we have done is to show that some, at least, of the fears and suspicions towards men labelled criminals are unfounded. We have shown, too, that the process of labelling, the impact of the law, is erratic in its operation. The time surely has come for some of the now accepted views of offenders as employees to be re-examined.

Chapter Twenty

The Proper Role of a Victim-Compensation System

Stephen Schafer

If it were realized that a kind of spiritual satisfaction is implicit in any system of punishment, a new concept of the purpose of punishment might arise, strengthening the restitutive character of punishment on the one hand and, on the other, infusing compensation with a punitive quality.

Most modern criminological literature urges that more attention be given to compensating victims of crime. If the state sets a norm of conduct it should, besides punishing breaches of this norm, see that where it is transgressed any injury caused is repaired. That restitution deserves a place in criminal procedure should be evident if only because, without the crime which is being tried, the victim would not have suffered the damage for which he seeks restitution. Another reason for allowing claims for restitution to victims of crime a place in criminal procedure is that it would save time, expense, and repetition of evidence. It would also avoid the possibility that a criminal court, a civil court, and the specially established victim compensation boards might reach different decisions on the same facts. It has been argued that a criminal court judge may not be versed in the niceties

Reprinted, with permission of the National Council on Crime and Delinquency, from *Crime and Delinquency*, Vol. 21, No. 1, 1975, pp. 45–49.

of the law of civil compensation, but the criminal law is already the most complex of all legal sciences.

Voices raised against the consideration of compensation in criminal procedure would be less effective if compensation were given a punitive or corrective character. To require the offender to pay money as a punishment is not novel. The origin of the present-day fine is restitution. The only difference between compensation and the fine is that the former (originally called "composition") reimburses the victim while the latter serves as a source of income for the state. If punitive compensation or restitution were part of a criminal court sentence, it would make no difference to the offender's resources, similarly affected whether the punishment is called a fine, court costs, or compensation, but it would make a great deal of difference to his understanding of the nature of justice.[1]

The idea of a central state fund, amassed through fines, out of which the state pays restitution to victims of crime, first took concrete form in Cuba. It is in harmony with modern sociology: the state acknowledges responsibility for the welfare of its citizens, without admitting blame for the commission of crime and without assuming responsibility for damages caused by a malefactor.[2]

State compensation by itself guarantees only restitution; it does not utilize the further possibility of reform of the criminal implicit in restitution and may indeed exclude him beforehand and at state expense from an obligation that he ought to discharge. The offender should understand that he injured not only the state and law and order but also the victim—primarily the victim and through this injury the abstract values of society. The institutions of compensation and restitution can not only make good the injury or loss of the victim but also, at the same time, help the task of punishment. This is where victim compensation should fit into the criminal justice system.

Compensation and restitution cannot undo the wrong but they may soften its effects and may have a real educative value for the offender. What is required is an evaluation of their deterrent and reformative requirements and potentialities. In many cases payment or service to the injured party will have a stronger inner punishment value than the payment of a sum or labor for the neutral state.[3]

Although penal methods have changed and are changing, the concept of the purpose of punishment—the reform of the offender to ways of social conformity—has not changed for a long time. Whatever might be thought of the differing methods for achieving this purpose, they hardly differ in their central aims: to make the criminal aware that he has done wrong and to produce this awareness with the least possible suffering. However, without the assistance of compensation and restitution, punishment can impress upon the criminal only the awareness that he has done wrong to the state and to law and order; recognition that he has also wronged an individual victim becomes dull and disappears.

Few systems of reforming the criminal do not include among their aims the arousal of his understanding and expiation of guilt. While this sort of psychological process can be initiated and assisted by others, it cannot be performed *for* him; it must be carried out by the criminal himself. The proposed restitution in the form of compensation is something *he* does, not something done by others *for* him or *to* him, and, since it requires him to make an effort, it may be especially useful in strengthening his feelings of responsibility. Being related to the offense, "creative restitution" may constructively redirect the same conscious or unconscious thoughts, emotions, or conflicts that motivated the offense.[4]

Just as we know that "rectification" or "making good" is an effective disciplinary technique with children, preventing repetition of misbehavior and creating little resentment, so we have reason to believe that the relationship between the adult offender and restitution to his victim may, in addition to recompensing the victim, be reformative as well.

Some may hold the view that punitive restitution should, in certain cases, completely replace punishment as we understand it today. One reason for this is that it would relieve the state of the great burden of supporting in penal institutions those guilty of minor offenses and would reduce the number of inmates so that individual methods could be used to better advantage for those committed to these institutions.

However, substituting punitive restitution for punishment to relieve prison overcrowding may evade the problem of criminality. While using punitive restitution as *one* method of dealing with criminals is reasonable, using it as the *only* sentence available for a crime would weaken the sense of wrongdoing attached to that crime and would foster social injustice: the affluent, possibly professional, criminal could purchase his liberty, while the indigent casual criminal might eventually serve a longer punishment for a minor crime. Substituting restitution for punishment might well have an effect opposite the one intended. A man ought not to be permitted to "buy his way out" of criminal liability.

How is punitive restitution distinguished from civil damage remedy? The latter is subject to compromise and is not in every case enforced; the former, like punishment, must always be the subject of judicial consideration; it must, without exception be performed personally by the wrongdoer; and it should be equally burdensome and just for all criminals, irrespective of their means, whether they be millionaires or laborers.

Should the offender compensate, by his own work, for the damage he has caused? Should prison work and the prisoner's income be the means of making restitution? Should the offender be kept in prison until the damage has been repaired? If the offender is solvent, should his property be confiscated and restitution made therefrom by order of the court? If he is insolvent, should he be made a state workman? According to one proposal to balance the burden of fines and restitution between the rich and the poor, a poor man would pay in days of work; a rich man, by his income or salary for the same number of days.

The "noble way" [5] to care for the victim is to make it possible for the offender to fulfill his obligation by way of the income or service of his free work—provided that the punitive aspect of restitution, its criminal reform quality, is not neglected. Compensation or restitution unconnected with the offender's personal work may help the victim but would minimize restitution's punitive-reformative character. However, if it is made through the offender's personal work, it retains its punitive-reformative character, while at the same time, relieving the state to a certain extent of the need to solve the problem of restitution to victims of crime.

The movement for the satisfaction of claims of victims of crime seemed to slow down by 1970; it might gather force if more public and official attention were given to the social, moral, and political reasons offered for state compensation to, at least, victims of violent crimes. Almost all proponents of state compensation—actually a crippled and inefficient form of restitution based on shifting responsibility from the offender to society or the state—have relied on one or more of the six arguments: [6]

1. *"Legal Obligation."*—This, perhaps the most popular and forceful argument, bases compensation on the state's "failure to protect" its individual members: since the state forbids a victim to take the law into his own hands, it is obligated to recover damages for him after failing to protect him. This idea is not new and not a radical departure from prevailing political and legal norms. [7]

2. *"Social Welfare."*—Just as modern democracy dictates public assistance for the disabled veteran, the sick, the unemployed, and the aged, so should public assistance be afforded the suffering victim of crime. The argument rests not on any inherent obligation of the

state but rather on the modern conscience, which cannot stomach the misery of the helpless.

3. *"Grace of the Government."*—This plan mirrors the merciful intervention of the state in individual cases, in contrast to the "Social Welfare" view, which reflects whole classes or categories of people.

4. *"Crime Prevention."*—This point of view emphasizes compensation for "Good Samaritans" injured in attempting to aid victims or the police. According to this argument, a compensation plan for those injured while attempting to help enforce the law might encourage citizen assistance and prevent certain crimes.

5. *"Political" Reasons.*—The articulators of political opinion enthusiastically endorse the concept of compensation. "This," they say, "is what the people want."

6. *"Anti-alienation."*—This compensation argument points to the disillusionment of victimized individuals who have suffered not only criminal injury but also, as a consequence of their desire to cooperate with the prosecution, the insult of losses of time and income.

None of these arguments present the case for restitution by the offender, a correctional principle employing his personal obligation. All victim compensation systems of the last decade have one characteristic in common: they are governed by the spirit of damages and do not aim at any restitutive correctional goal. Even in this narrow context the eventual inclusion of any compensation program in the *criminal* law code would be an achievement. Current proposals usually suggest that compensation (not restitution) be placed under the jurisdiction of a state commission totally outside the criminal justice system, thus making compensation proceedings parallel with civil law practice. Such suggestions are little more than sophisticated tort or insurance-law propositions.

The present popular view is that the compensation claim, even though it is the result of a crime, is a civil matter and should be divorced from the disposition of the criminal case and correctional action against the offender. Most legal provisions now in force and almost all planning for future law distinguish between criminal and civil wrong. A proper consideration of the place of compensation or restitution in our norm-system calls for more than speculation about the elusive boundary between criminal and civil law: it demands an understanding of how the functional relationship between the offender and the restitution to his victim may activate reformative, corrective, and rehabilitative goals in penal law.

The proposal that the offender should, by his own work, compensate for the damage he has caused—the essential idea of correctional restitution—has a long history. It appeared as early as 1516, in Book I of Sir Thomas More's *Utopia:* "Whoever . . . is found guilty of theft must make restitution to the owner, and not . . . to the prince . . . [because] the prince has no more right to the stolen goods than the thief." Correctional restitution is something the offender must perform himself and not something done for or to him. In this respect it goes a significant step further than compensation, for it requires him to maintain a relationship with the victim until the victim's pre-injury condition has been restored to the fullest extent possible. Correctional restitution compensates the victim, relieves the state of some burden of responsibility, and permits the offender to pay his debt to society and to his victim. As such it makes a contribution to the reformative and corrective goals of criminal law and finds its proper place in the criminal justice system.

NOTES

1. Margery Fry, "Justice for Victims," *The Observer* (London), July 7, 1957.

2. Stephen Schafer, *Compensation and Restitution to Victims of Crime,* 2nd ed. (Montclair, N.J., 1970), pp. 123–35.

3. Hans von Hentig, *The Criminal and His Victim* (New Hanve, 1948), p. 217.

4. Albert Eglash, "Creative Restitution—Some Suggestions for Prison Rehabilitation Programs," *American Journal of Correction* (November-December 1958), pp. 20–34; similarly August Aichorn, *Wayward Youth* (New York, 1948), ch. 10.

5. Carlo Waeckerling, Die Sorge für den Verletzten im Strafrecht (Zurich, 1946), p. 130.

6. Report to the Special Commission on the Compensation of Victims of Violent Crimes, Commonwealth of Massachusetts, House No. 5151 (Boston, 1967), pp. 10–14.

7. Marvin E. Wolfgang, "Victim Compensation in Crimes of Personal Violence," in Walter C. Reckless, ed., *Interdisciplinary Problems in Criminology* (Columbus, Ohio, 1965), p. 169.

Index